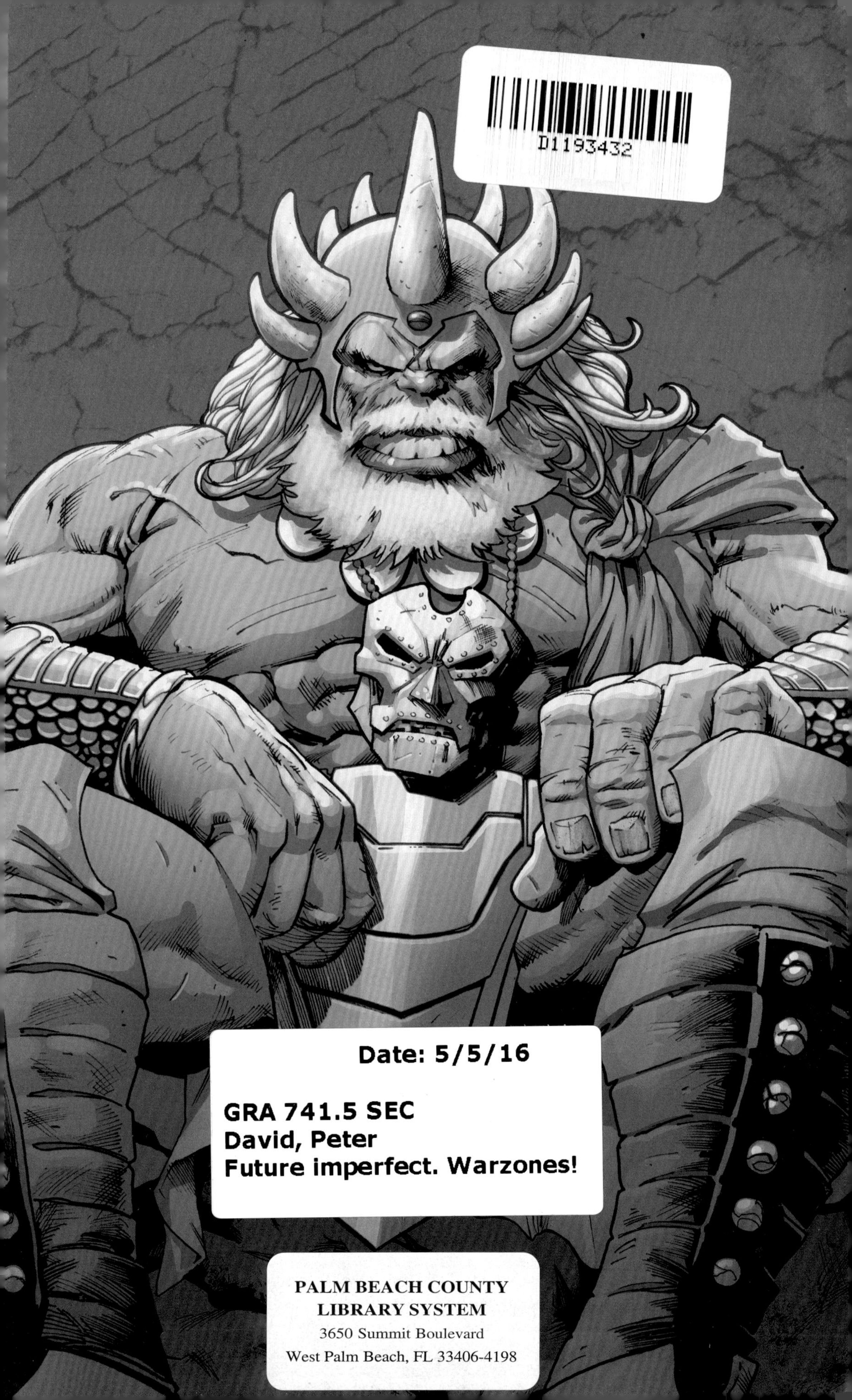

future imperfect
WARZONES!

WRITER	peter david
PENCILER	greg land
INKER	jay leisten
COLORIST	nolan woodard
COVER ART	greg land & nolan woodard

"silver surfer vs. maestro"

WRITER	peter david
ARTIST	daniel valadez
COLOR ARTIST	david curiel
COVER ART	francesco francavilla

ASSISTANT EDITOR	chris robinson
EDITOR	mark paniccia

COLLECTION EDITOR	jennifer grünwald		
ASSISTANT EDITOR	sarah brunstad		
ASSOCIATE MANAGING EDITOR	alex starbuck	EDITOR IN CHIEF	axel alonso
EDITOR, SPECIAL PROJECTS	mark d. beazley	CHIEF CREATIVE OFFICER	joe quesada
SENIOR EDITOR, SPECIAL PROJECTS	jeff youngquist	PUBLISHER	dan buckley
SVP PRINT, SALES & MARKETING	david gabriel	EXECUTIVE PRODUCER	alan fine

FUTURE IMPERFECT: WARZONES! Contains material originally published in magazine form as FUTURE IMPERFECT #1-5 and SECRET WARS: BATTLEWORLD #4. First printing 2015. ISBN# 978-0-7851-9869-7. Published by MARVEL WORLDWIDE, INC., a subsidiary of MARVEL ENTERTAINMENT, LLC. OFFICE OF PUBLICATION: 135 West 50th Street, New York, NY 10020. Copyright © 2015 MARVEL No similarity between any of the names, characters, persons, and/or institutions in this magazine with those of any living or dead person or institution is intended, and any such similarity which may exist is purely coincidental. **Printed in Canada.** ALAN FINE, President, Marvel Entertainment; DAN BUCKLEY, President, TV, Publishing and Brand Management; JOE QUESADA, Chief Creative Officer; TOM BREVOORT, SVP of Publishing; DAVID BOGART, SVP of Operations & Procurement, Publishing; C.B. CEBULSKI, VP of International Development & Brand Management; DAVID GABRIEL, SVP Print, Sales & Marketing; JIM O'KEEFE, VP of Operations & Logistics; DAN CARR, Executive Director of Publishing Technology; SUSAN CRESPI, Editorial Operations Manager; ALEX MORALES, Publishing Operations Manager; STAN LEE, Chairman Emeritus. For information regarding advertising in Marvel Comics or on Marvel.com, please contact Jonathan Rheingold, VP of Custom Solutions & Ad Sales, at jrheingold@marvel.com. For Marvel subscription inquiries, please call 800-217-9158. **Manufactured between 10/30/2015 and 12/7/2015** by SOLISCO PRINTERS, SCOTT, QC, CANADA.

10 9 8 7 6 5 4 3 2 1

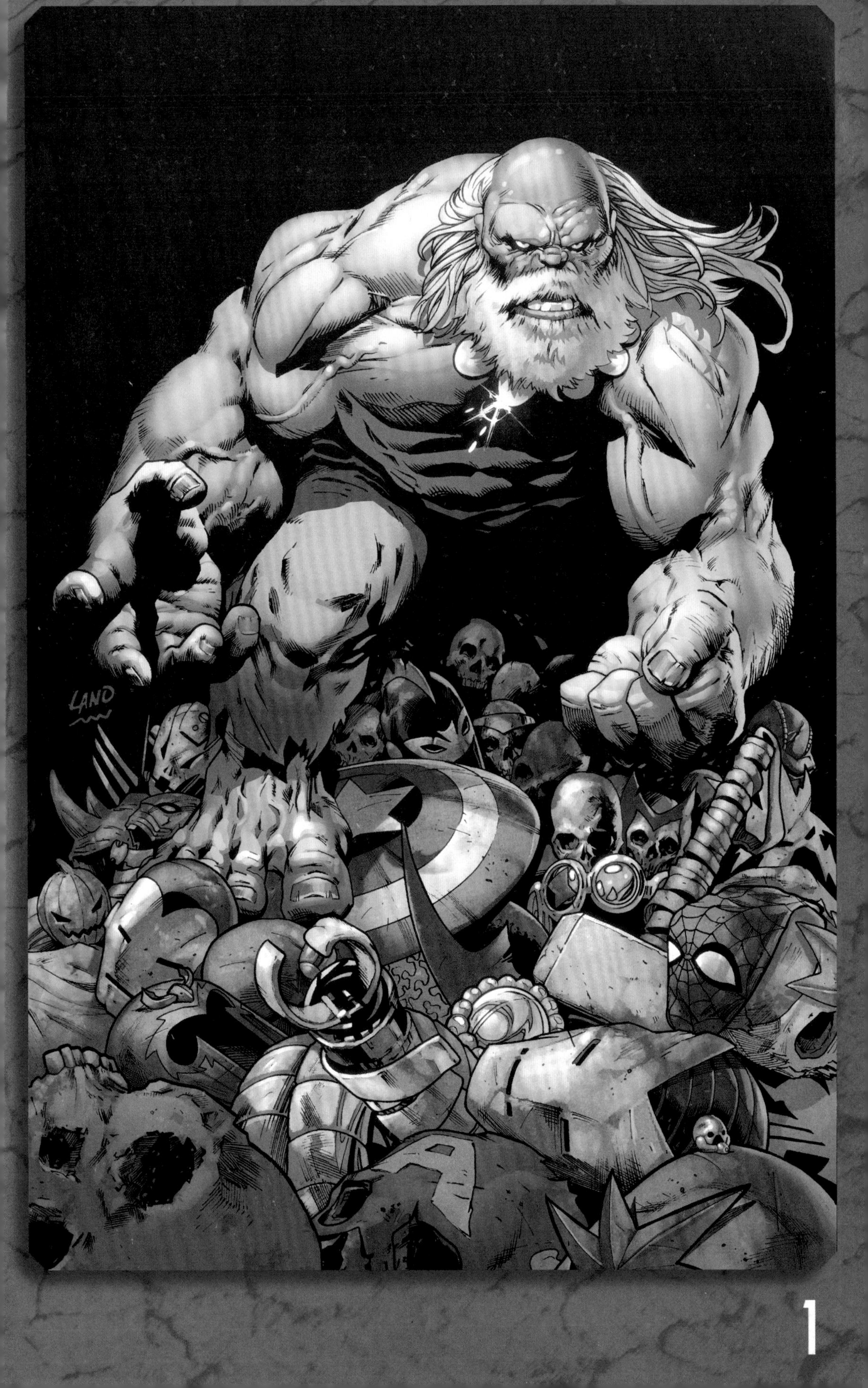
LAND

1

THE MULTIVERSE WAS DESTROYED!

THE HEROES OF EARTH-616 AND EARTH-1610 WERE POWERLESS TO SAVE IT!

NOW, ALL THAT REMAINS...IS BATTLEWORLD!

A MASSIVE, PATCHWORK PLANET COMPOSED OF THE FRAGMENTS OF WORLDS THAT NO LONGER EXIST, MAINTAINED BY THE IRON WILL OF ITS GOD AND MASTER, VICTOR VON DOOM!

EACH DOMAIN RULED BY POWERFUL BARONS, BUT NONE MORE TIGHTLY CONDUCTED THAN...

DYSTOPIA

SECRET WARS

OUR EXALTED BARON, THE MAESTRO, WELCOMES YOU TO HIS TROPHY ROOM OF CONQUERED OPPONENTS.

*PLEASE REMAIN QUIET AND RESPECTFUL

EXHIBITING THIS SEASON:

- BABY GROOT POTTED PLANT
- CAPTAIN AMERICA'S SHIELD
- HELL CHARGER TIRE
- IRON MAN REPULSOR GLOVE
- MAGNETO HELMET
- MS MARVEL'S SCARF
- NOVA HELMET
- SILVER SURFER BOARD
- SPIDER-MAN MASK
- THOR HAMMER

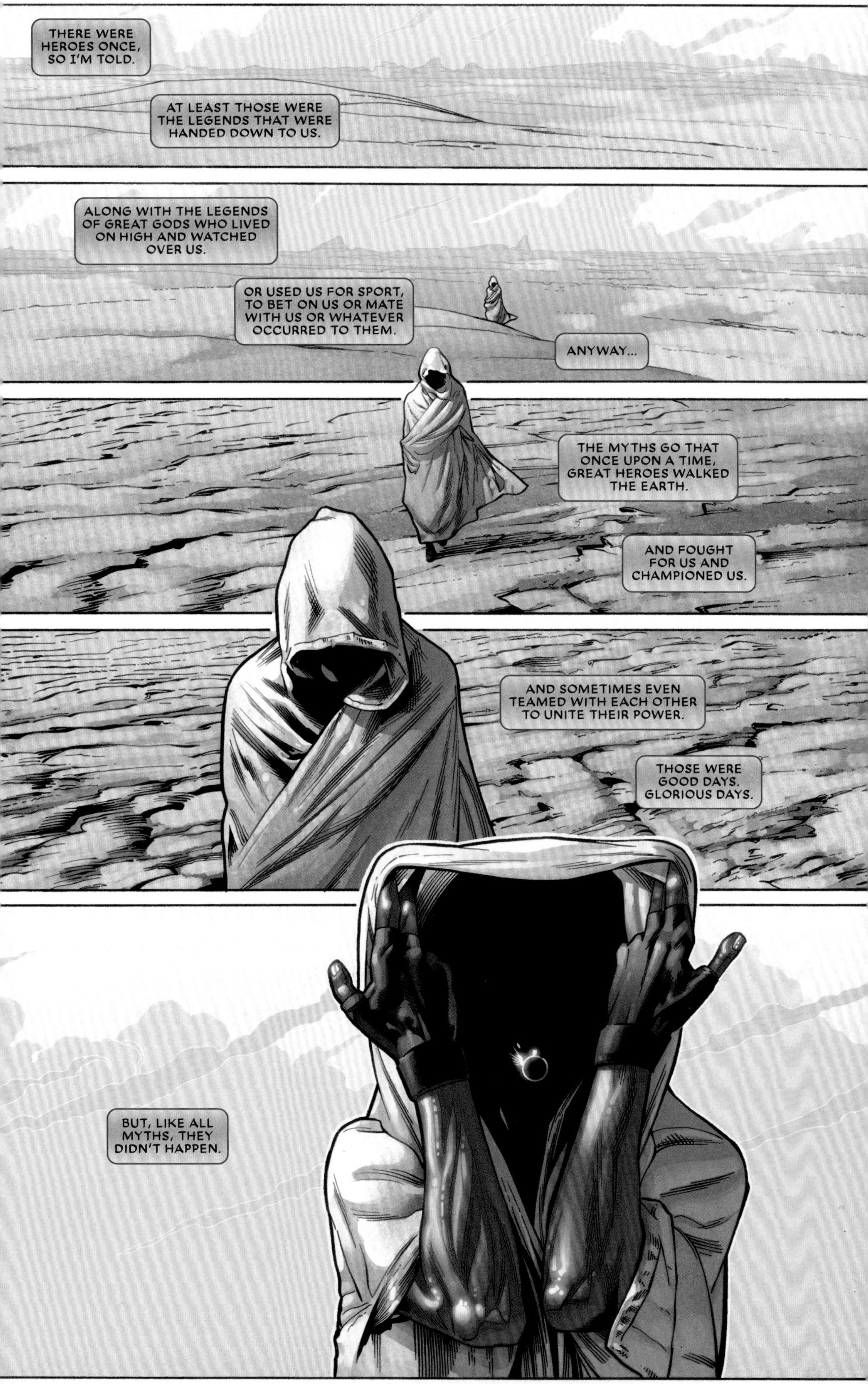
THERE WERE HEROES ONCE, SO I'M TOLD.
AT LEAST THOSE WERE THE LEGENDS THAT WERE HANDED DOWN TO US.
ALONG WITH THE LEGENDS OF GREAT GODS WHO LIVED ON HIGH AND WATCHED OVER US.
OR USED US FOR SPORT, TO BET ON US OR MATE WITH US OR WHATEVER OCCURRED TO THEM.
ANYWAY...
THE MYTHS GO THAT ONCE UPON A TIME, GREAT HEROES WALKED THE EARTH.
AND FOUGHT FOR US AND CHAMPIONED US.
AND SOMETIMES EVEN TEAMED WITH EACH OTHER TO UNITE THEIR POWER.
THOSE WERE GOOD DAYS. GLORIOUS DAYS.
BUT, LIKE ALL MYTHS, THEY DIDN'T HAPPEN.

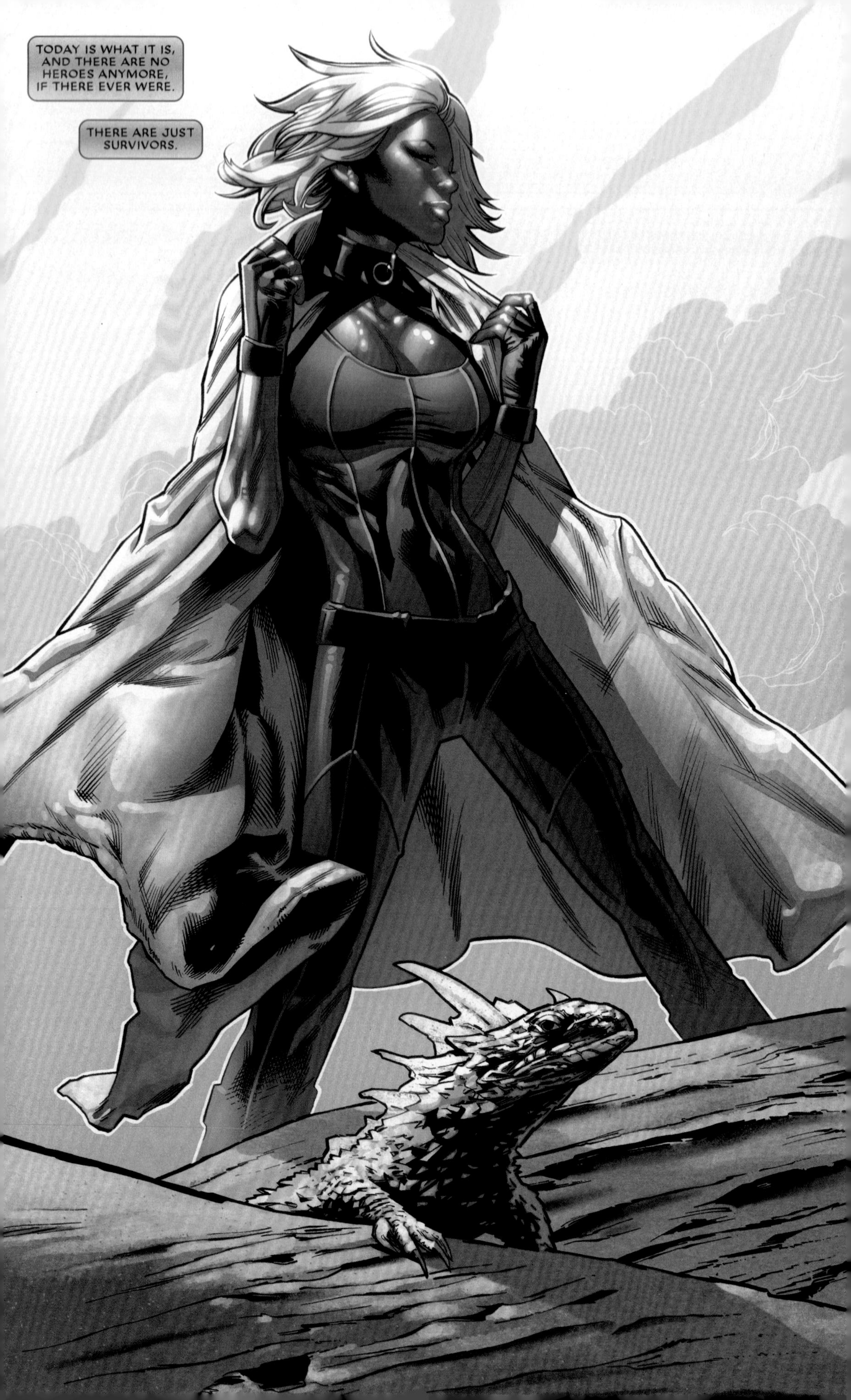
TODAY IS WHAT IT IS, AND THERE ARE NO HEROES ANYMORE, IF THERE EVER WERE.
THERE ARE JUST SURVIVORS.

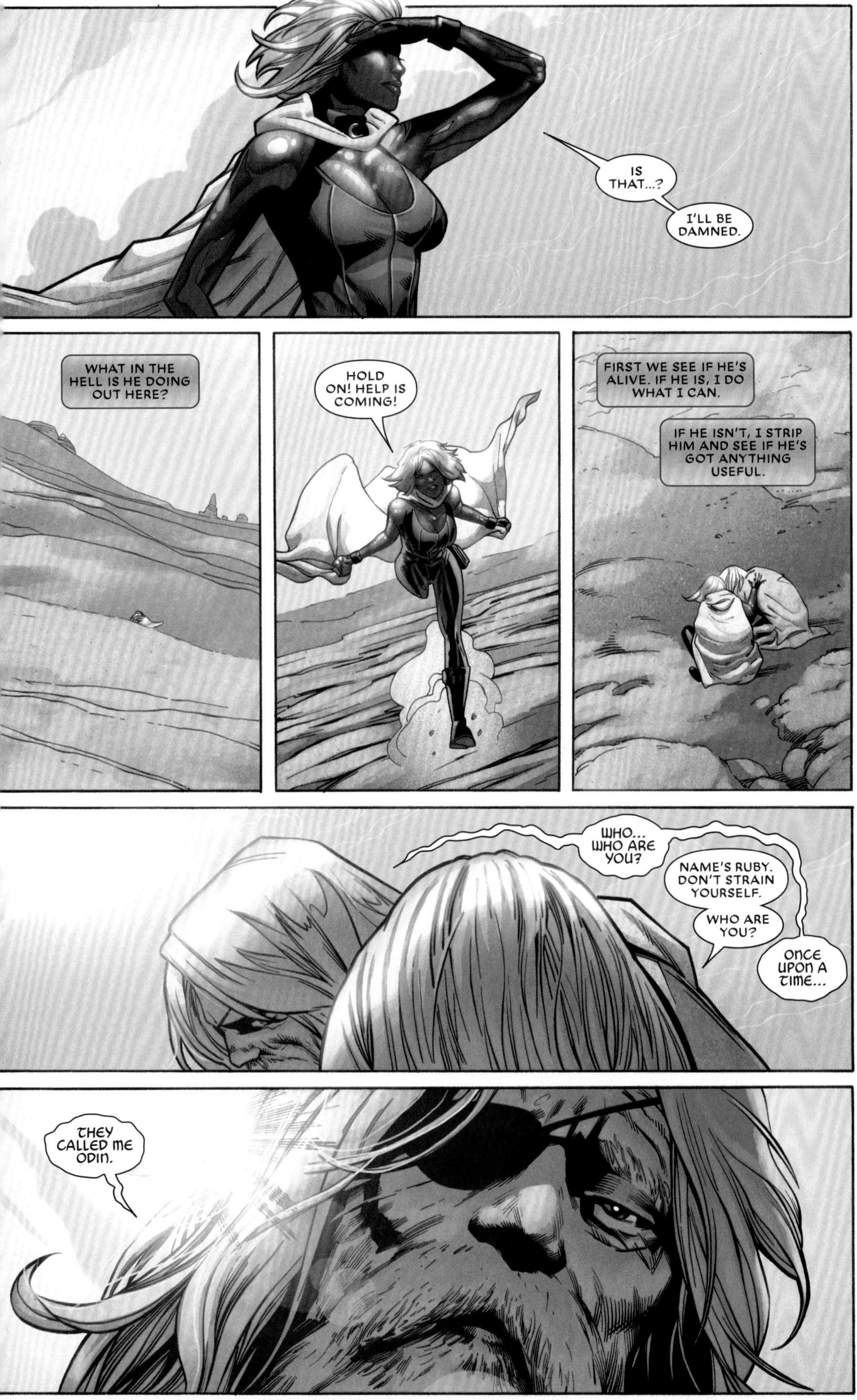
IS THAT...?
I'LL BE DAMNED.
WHAT IN THE HELL IS HE DOING OUT HERE?
HOLD ON! HELP IS COMING!
FIRST WE SEE IF HE'S ALIVE. IF HE IS, I DO WHAT I CAN.
IF HE ISN'T, I STRIP HIM AND SEE IF HE'S GOT ANYTHING USEFUL.
WHO... WHO ARE YOU?
NAME'S RUBY. DON'T STRAIN YOURSELF.
WHO ARE YOU?
ONCE UPON A TIME...
THEY CALLED ME ODIN.

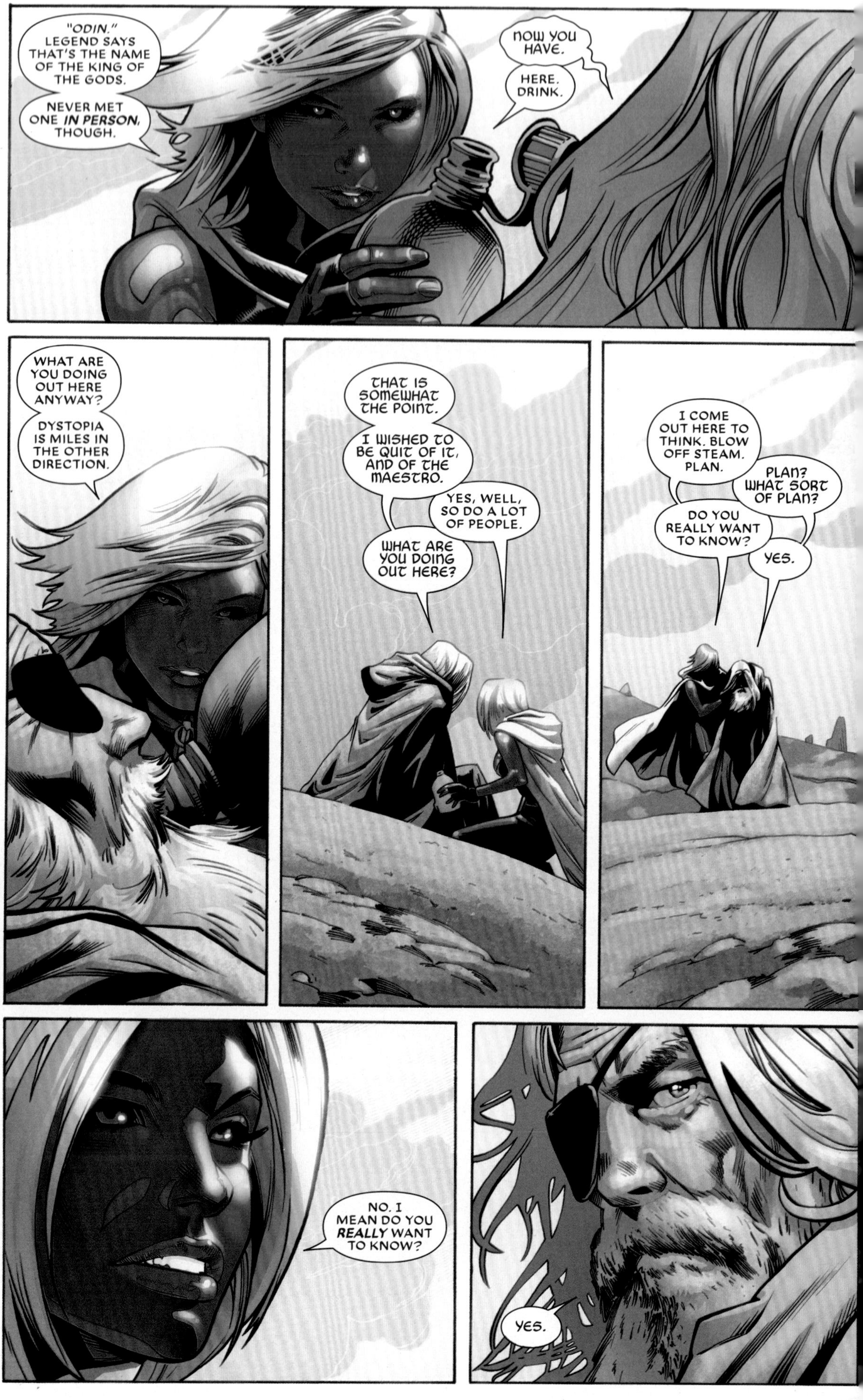
"ODIN." LEGEND SAYS THAT'S THE NAME OF THE KING OF THE GODS.
NEVER MET ONE IN PERSON, THOUGH.
NOW YOU HAVE.
HERE. DRINK.
WHAT ARE YOU DOING OUT HERE ANYWAY?
DYSTOPIA IS MILES IN THE OTHER DIRECTION.
THAT IS SOMEWHAT THE POINT.
I WISHED TO BE QUIT OF IT, AND OF THE MAESTRO.
YES, WELL, SO DO A LOT OF PEOPLE.
WHAT ARE YOU DOING OUT HERE?
I COME OUT HERE TO THINK. BLOW OFF STEAM. PLAN.
PLAN? WHAT SORT OF PLAN?
DO YOU REALLY WANT TO KNOW?
YES.
NO. I MEAN DO YOU REALLY WANT TO KNOW?
YES.

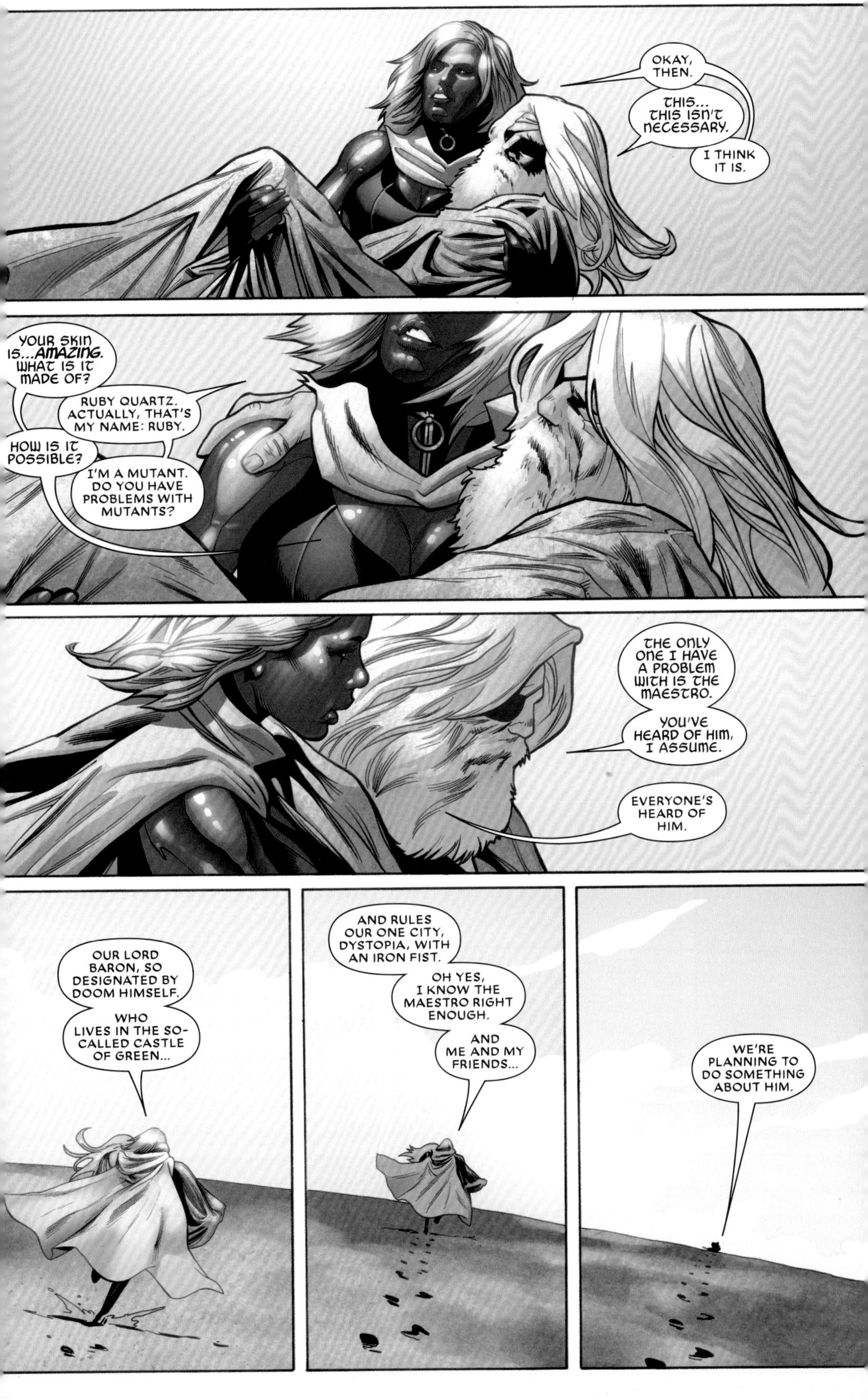
OKAY, THEN.
THIS... THIS ISN'T NECESSARY.
I THINK IT IS.
YOUR SKIN IS...AMAZING. WHAT IS IT MADE OF?
RUBY QUARTZ. ACTUALLY, THAT'S MY NAME: RUBY.
HOW IS IT POSSIBLE?
I'M A MUTANT. DO YOU HAVE PROBLEMS WITH MUTANTS?
THE ONLY ONE I HAVE A PROBLEM WITH IS THE MAESTRO.
YOU'VE HEARD OF HIM, I ASSUME.
EVERYONE'S HEARD OF HIM.
OUR LORD BARON, SO DESIGNATED BY DOOM HIMSELF.
WHO LIVES IN THE SO-CALLED CASTLE OF GREEN...
AND RULES OUR ONE CITY, DYSTOPIA, WITH AN IRON FIST.
OH YES, I KNOW THE MAESTRO RIGHT ENOUGH.
AND ME AND MY FRIENDS...
WE'RE PLANNING TO DO SOMETHING ABOUT HIM.

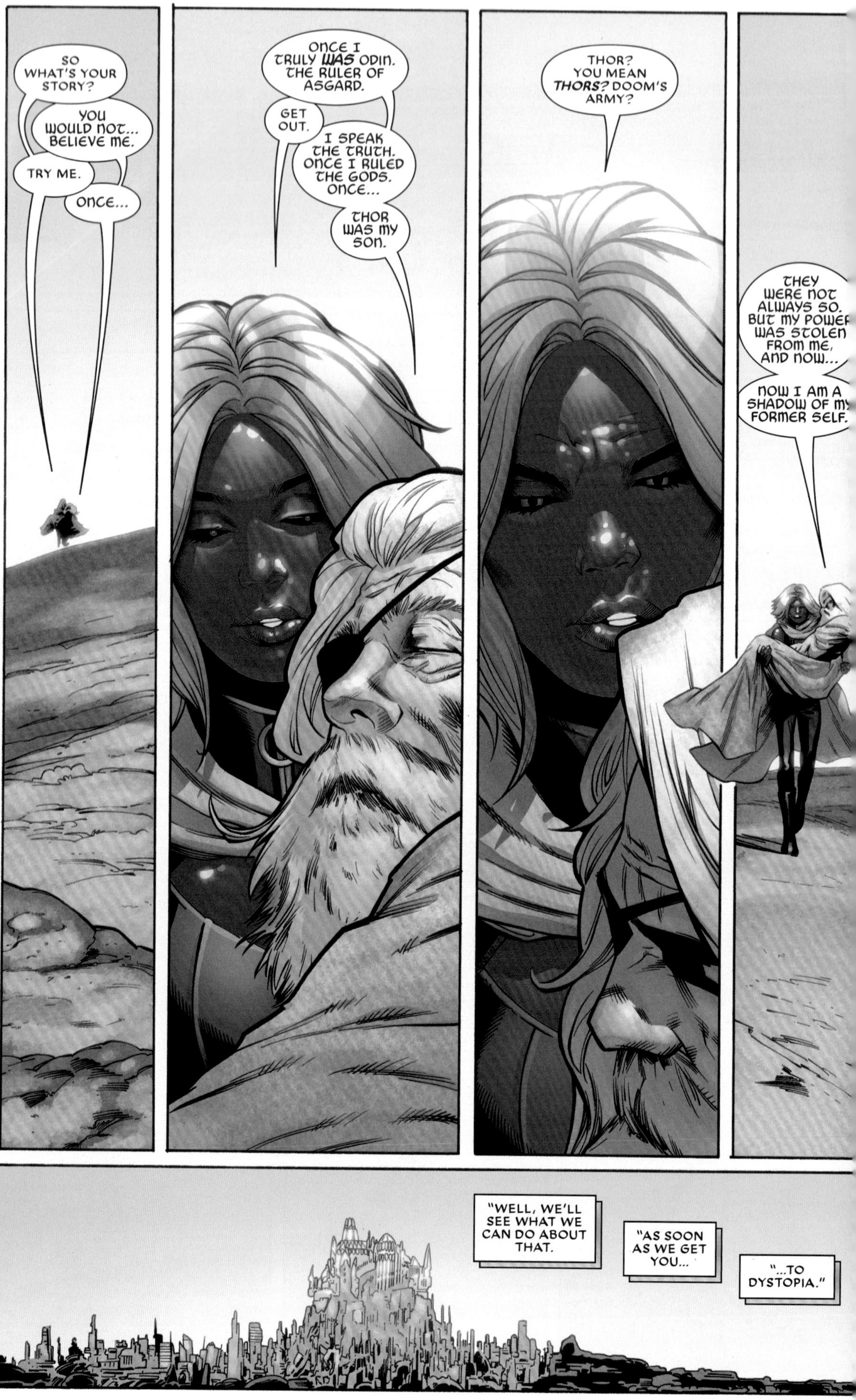
SO WHAT'S YOUR STORY?
YOU WOULD NOT... BELIEVE ME.
TRY ME.
ONCE...
ONCE I TRULY WAS ODIN. THE RULER OF ASGARD.
GET OUT.
I SPEAK THE TRUTH. ONCE I RULED THE GODS. ONCE...
THOR WAS MY SON.
THOR? YOU MEAN THORS? DOOM'S ARMY?
THEY WERE NOT ALWAYS SO. BUT MY POWER WAS STOLEN FROM ME, AND NOW...
NOW I AM A SHADOW OF MY FORMER SELF.
"WELL, WE'LL SEE WHAT WE CAN DO ABOUT THAT.
"AS SOON AS WE GET YOU...
"...TO DYSTOPIA."

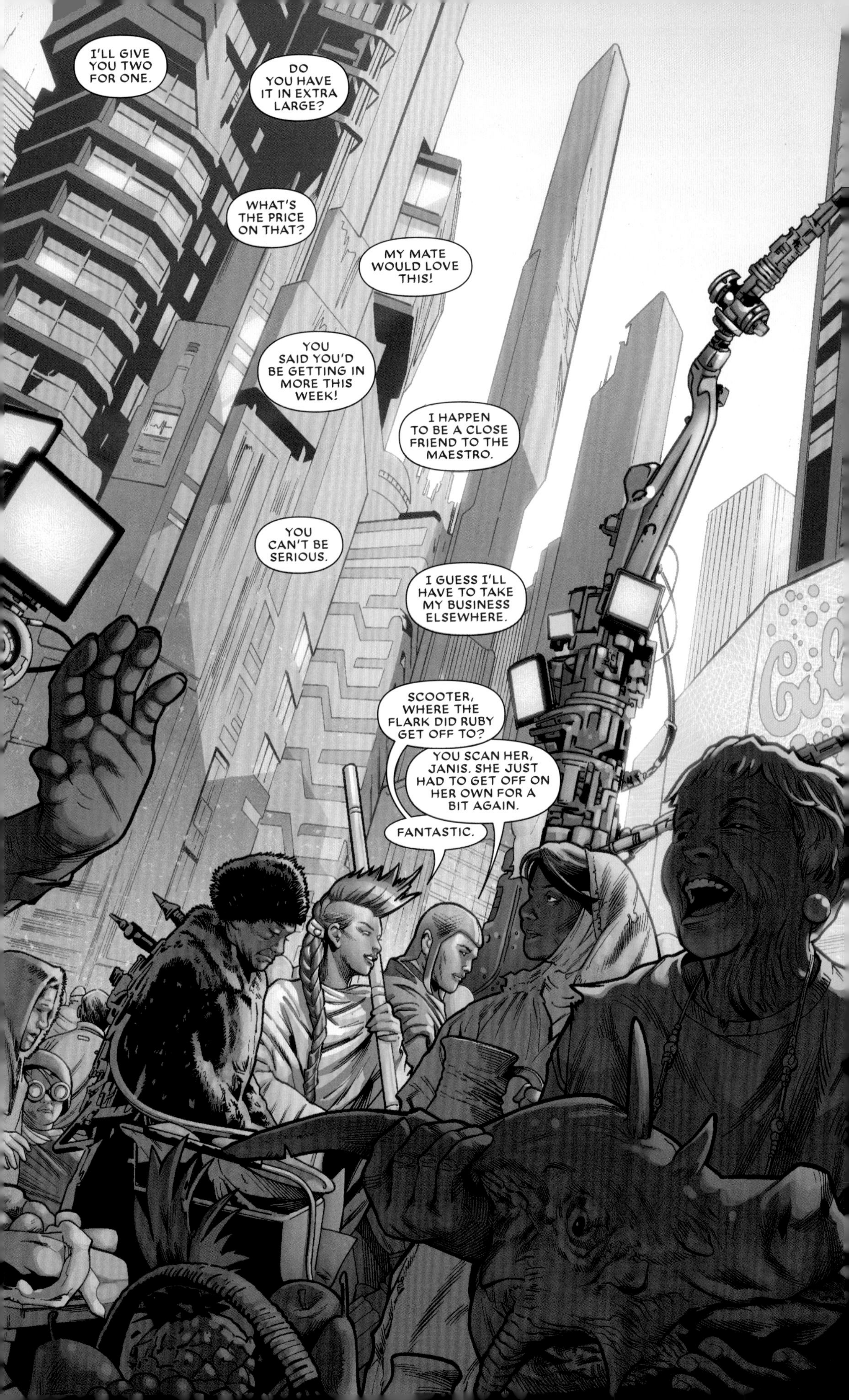
I'LL GIVE YOU TWO FOR ONE.
DO YOU HAVE IT IN EXTRA LARGE?
WHAT'S THE PRICE ON THAT?
MY MATE WOULD LOVE THIS!
YOU SAID YOU'D BE GETTING IN MORE THIS WEEK!
I HAPPEN TO BE A CLOSE FRIEND TO THE MAESTRO.
YOU CAN'T BE SERIOUS.
I GUESS I'LL HAVE TO TAKE MY BUSINESS ELSEWHERE.
SCOOTER, WHERE THE FLARK DID RUBY GET OFF TO?
YOU SCAN HER, JANIS. SHE JUST HAD TO GET OFF ON HER OWN FOR A BIT AGAIN.
FANTASTIC.

WE'RE BUSY TRYING TO TAKE CARE OF A WHOLE COMMUNITY OF ESCAPEES FROM THE MAESTRO'S *"ATTENTIONS"*...

AND SHE'S OFF WANDERING BY HERSELF. THAT'S PERFECT. THAT'S...

÷PSSSSTT÷

WANT TO KEEP COMPLAINING ABOUT ME OR DO YOU WANT TO HELP?

GOT SOMEONE MAJOR HERE.

MAJOR?

THIS GUY IS ODIN.

ODIN? LIKE THE NORSE GOD?

NOT LIKE. *THE.*

ARE YOU RIFFING ME? YOU'RE RIFFING ME, AREN'T YOU?

THIS GUY IS THE FATHER OF THOR? THE THORS?

THAT'S WHAT HE TOLD ME ON THE WAY HERE.

IT IS A...LONG STORY.

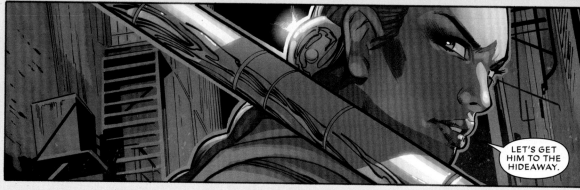

LET'S GET HIM TO THE HIDEAWAY.

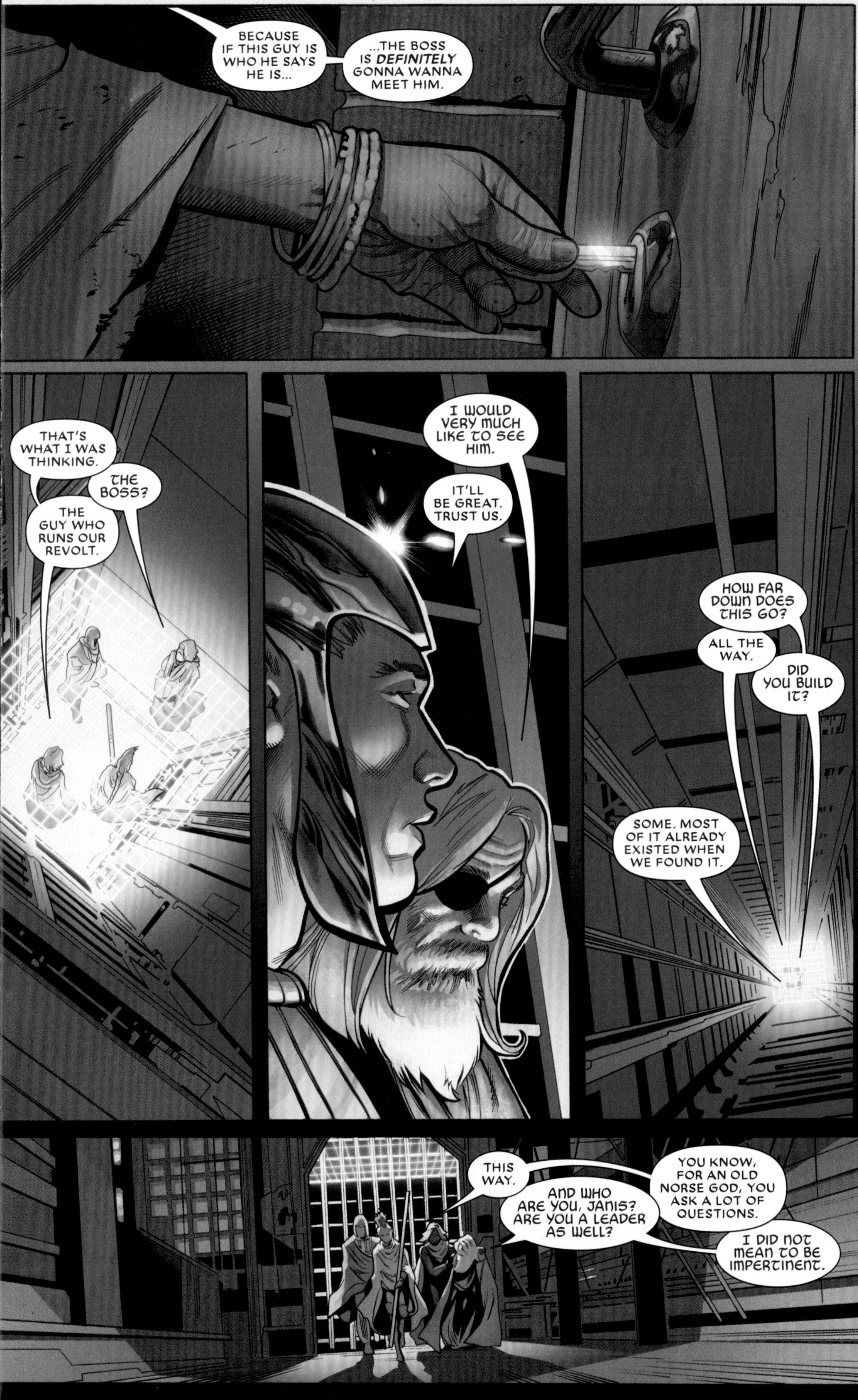
BECAUSE IF THIS GUY IS WHO HE SAYS HE IS...
...THE BOSS IS **DEFINITELY** GONNA WANNA MEET HIM.
THAT'S WHAT I WAS THINKING.
THE BOSS?
THE GUY WHO RUNS OUR REVOLT.
I WOULD VERY MUCH LIKE TO SEE HIM.
IT'LL BE GREAT. TRUST US.
HOW FAR DOWN DOES THIS GO?
ALL THE WAY.
DID YOU BUILD IT?
SOME. MOST OF IT ALREADY EXISTED WHEN WE FOUND IT.
THIS WAY.
AND WHO ARE YOU, JANIS? ARE YOU A LEADER AS WELL?
YOU KNOW, FOR AN OLD NORSE GOD, YOU ASK A LOT OF QUESTIONS.
I DID NOT MEAN TO BE IMPERTINENT.

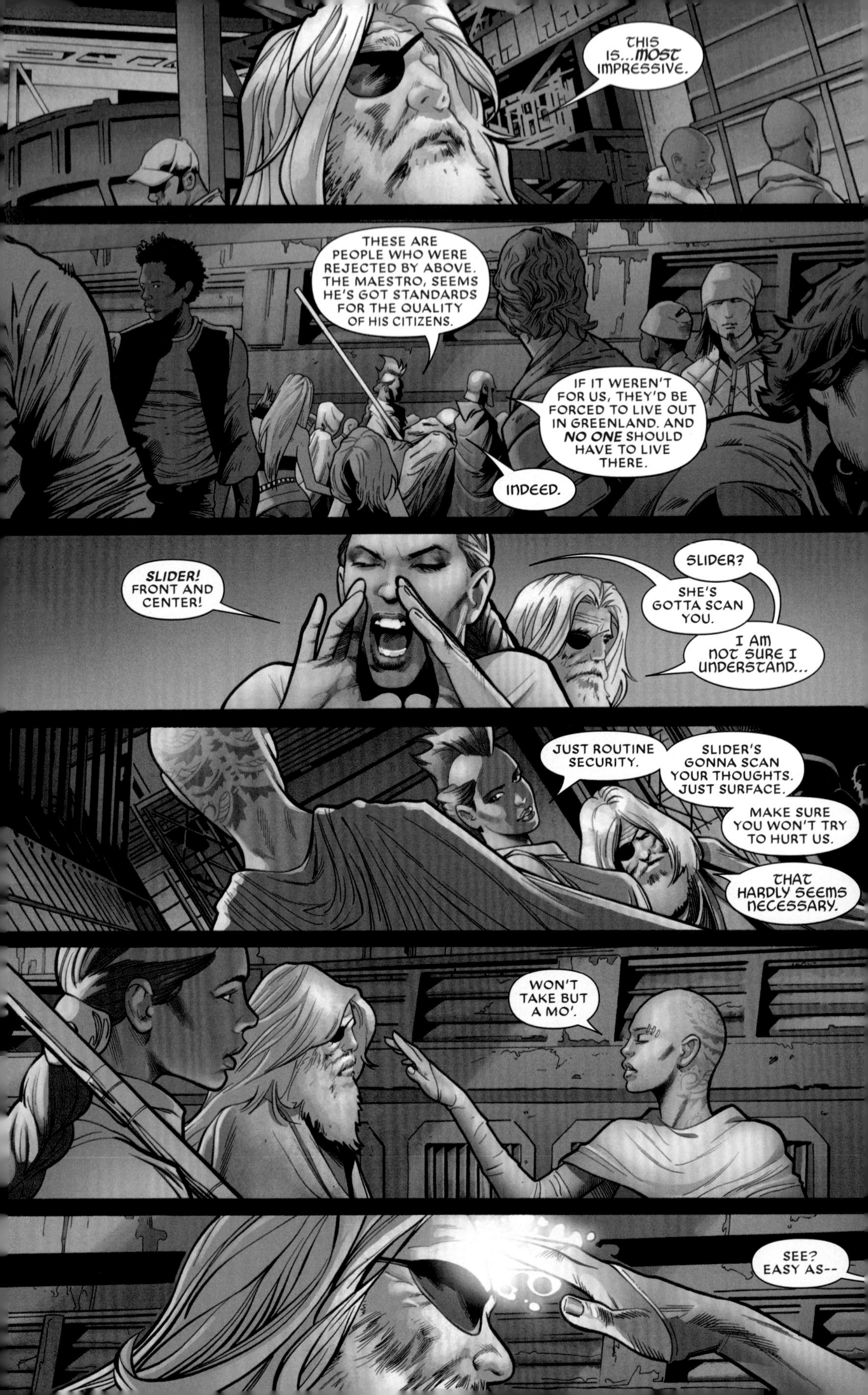
THIS IS...MOST IMPRESSIVE.
THESE ARE PEOPLE WHO WERE REJECTED BY ABOVE. THE MAESTRO, SEEMS HE'S GOT STANDARDS FOR THE QUALITY OF HIS CITIZENS.
IF IT WEREN'T FOR US, THEY'D BE FORCED TO LIVE OUT IN GREENLAND. AND NO ONE SHOULD HAVE TO LIVE THERE.
INDEED.
SLIDER! FRONT AND CENTER!
SLIDER?
SHE'S GOTTA SCAN YOU.
I AM NOT SURE I UNDERSTAND...
JUST ROUTINE SECURITY.
SLIDER'S GONNA SCAN YOUR THOUGHTS. JUST SURFACE.
MAKE SURE YOU WON'T TRY TO HURT US.
THAT HARDLY SEEMS NECESSARY.
WON'T TAKE BUT A MO'.
SEE? EASY AS--

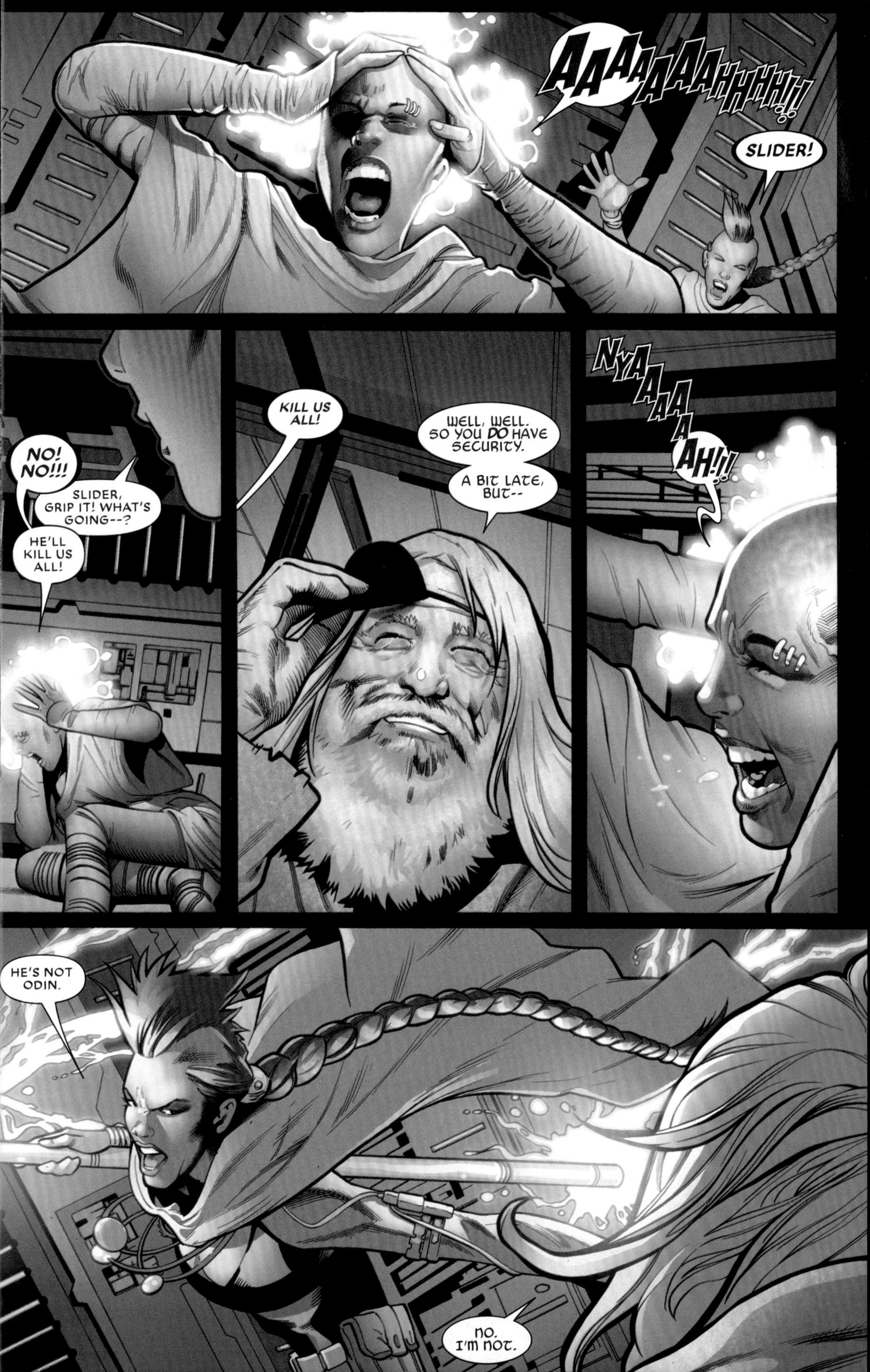
AAAAAAAHHHH!!!
SLIDER!
NO! NO!!!
SLIDER, GRIP IT! WHAT'S GOING--?
HE'LL KILL US ALL!
KILL US ALL!
WELL, WELL. SO YOU DO HAVE SECURITY.
A BIT LATE, BUT--
NYAAAAAAH!!!
HE'S NOT ODIN.
NO. I'M NOT.

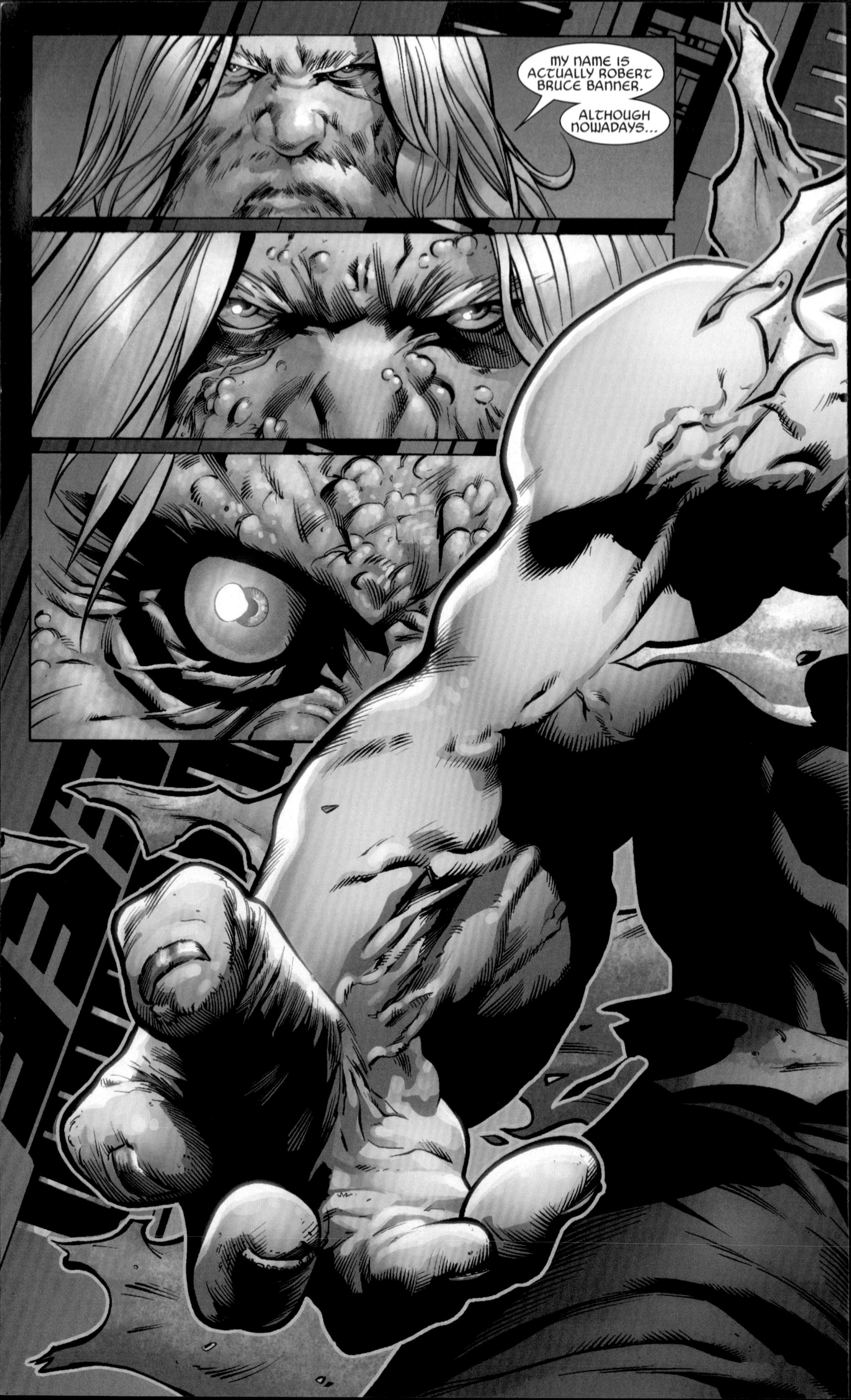
MY NAME IS ACTUALLY ROBERT BRUCE BANNER.
ALTHOUGH NOWADAYS...

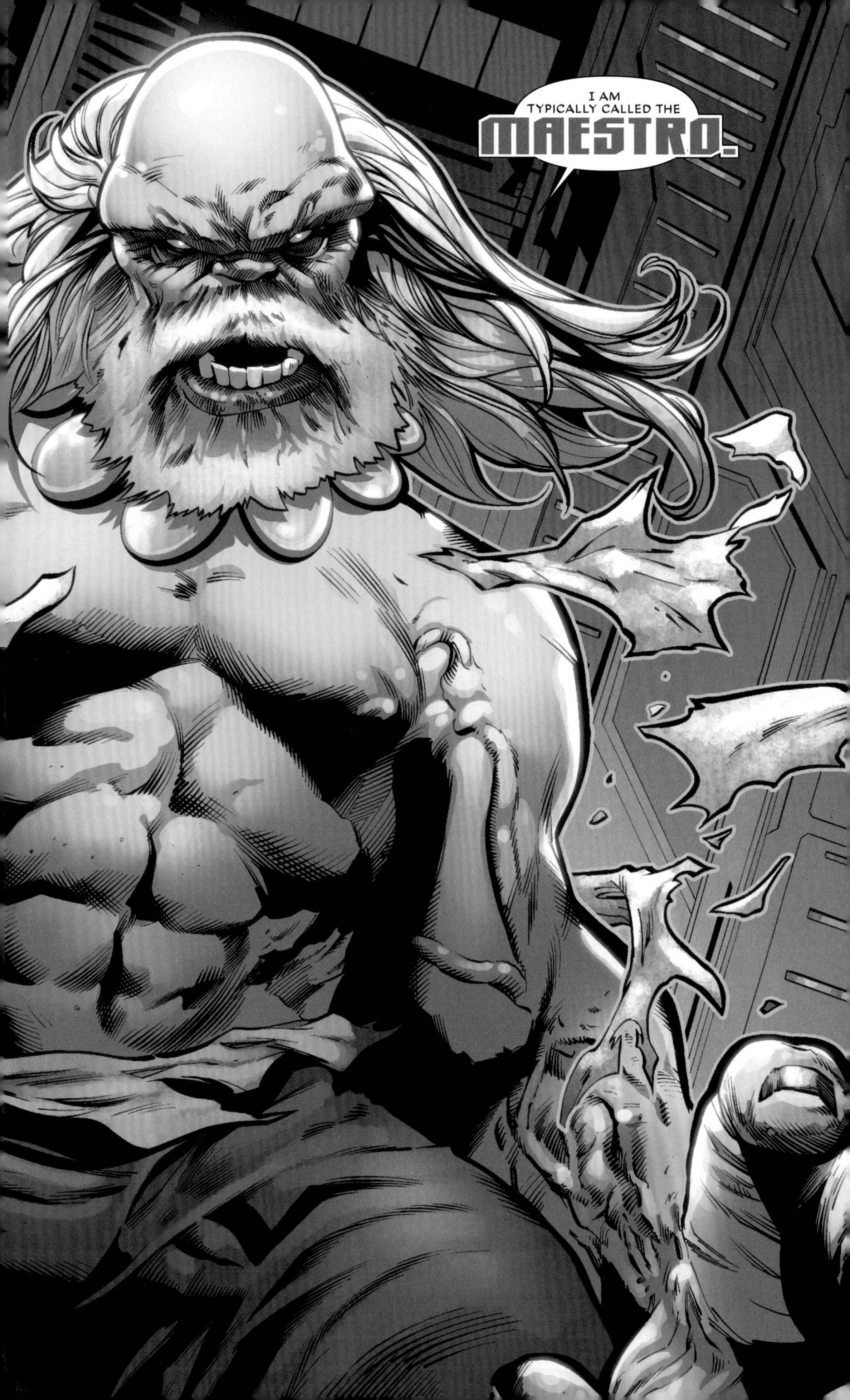
I AM TYPICALLY CALLED THE MAESTRO.

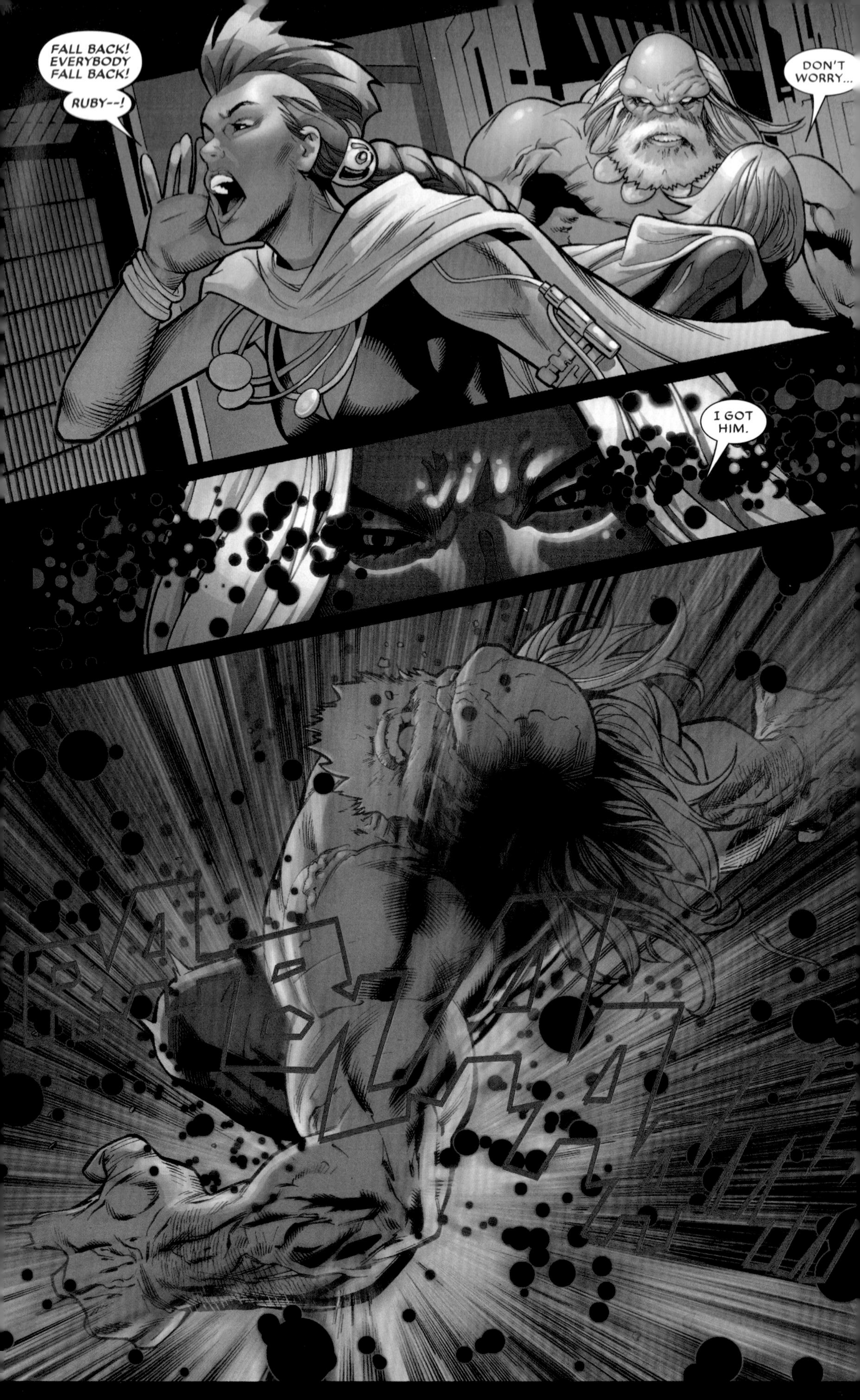
FALL BACK! EVERYBODY FALL BACK!
RUBY--!
DON'T WORRY...
I GOT HIM.

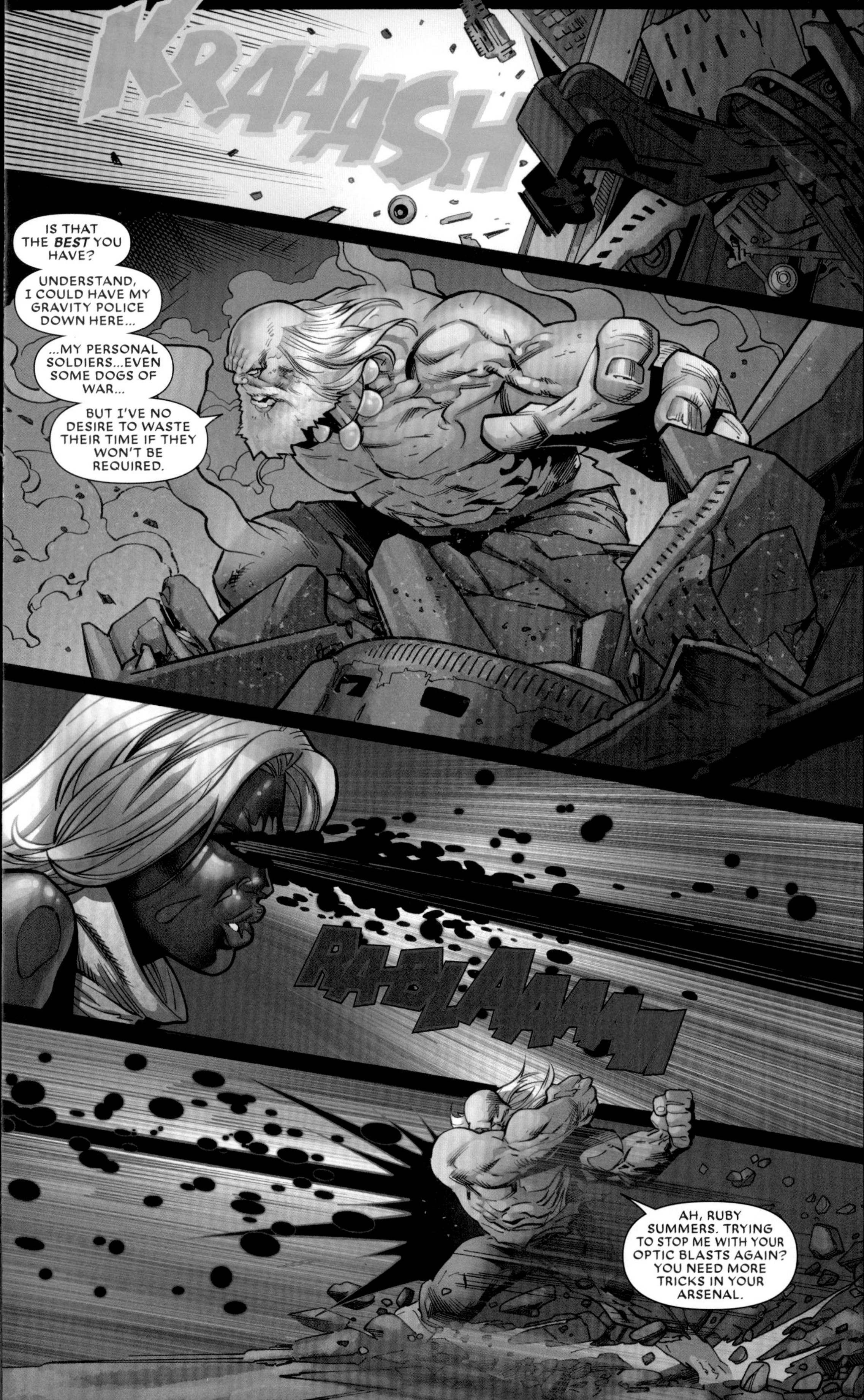
KRAAAASH
IS THAT THE BEST YOU HAVE?
UNDERSTAND, I COULD HAVE MY GRAVITY POLICE DOWN HERE...
...MY PERSONAL SOLDIERS...EVEN SOME DOGS OF WAR...
BUT I'VE NO DESIRE TO WASTE THEIR TIME IF THEY WON'T BE REQUIRED.
RAHBLAAAM
AH, RUBY SUMMERS. TRYING TO STOP ME WITH YOUR OPTIC BLASTS AGAIN? YOU NEED MORE TRICKS IN YOUR ARSENAL.

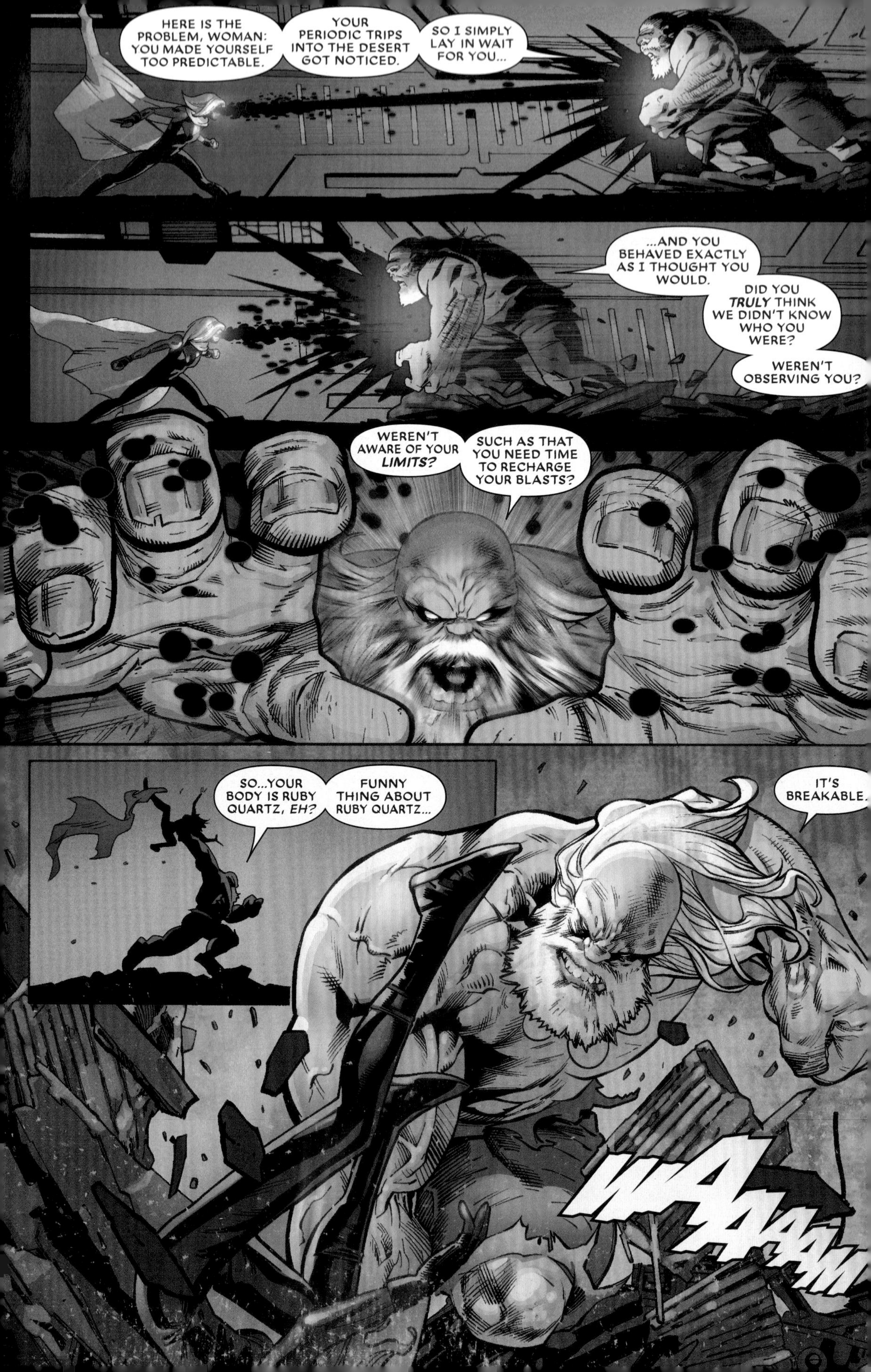
HERE IS THE PROBLEM, WOMAN: YOU MADE YOURSELF TOO PREDICTABLE.
YOUR PERIODIC TRIPS INTO THE DESERT GOT NOTICED.
SO I SIMPLY LAY IN WAIT FOR YOU...
...AND YOU BEHAVED EXACTLY AS I THOUGHT YOU WOULD.
DID YOU *TRULY* THINK WE DIDN'T KNOW WHO YOU WERE?
WEREN'T OBSERVING YOU?
WEREN'T AWARE OF YOUR *LIMITS?*
SUCH AS THAT YOU NEED TIME TO RECHARGE YOUR BLASTS?
SO...YOUR BODY IS RUBY QUARTZ, *EH?*
FUNNY THING ABOUT RUBY QUARTZ...
IT'S BREAKABLE.
WHAAAM

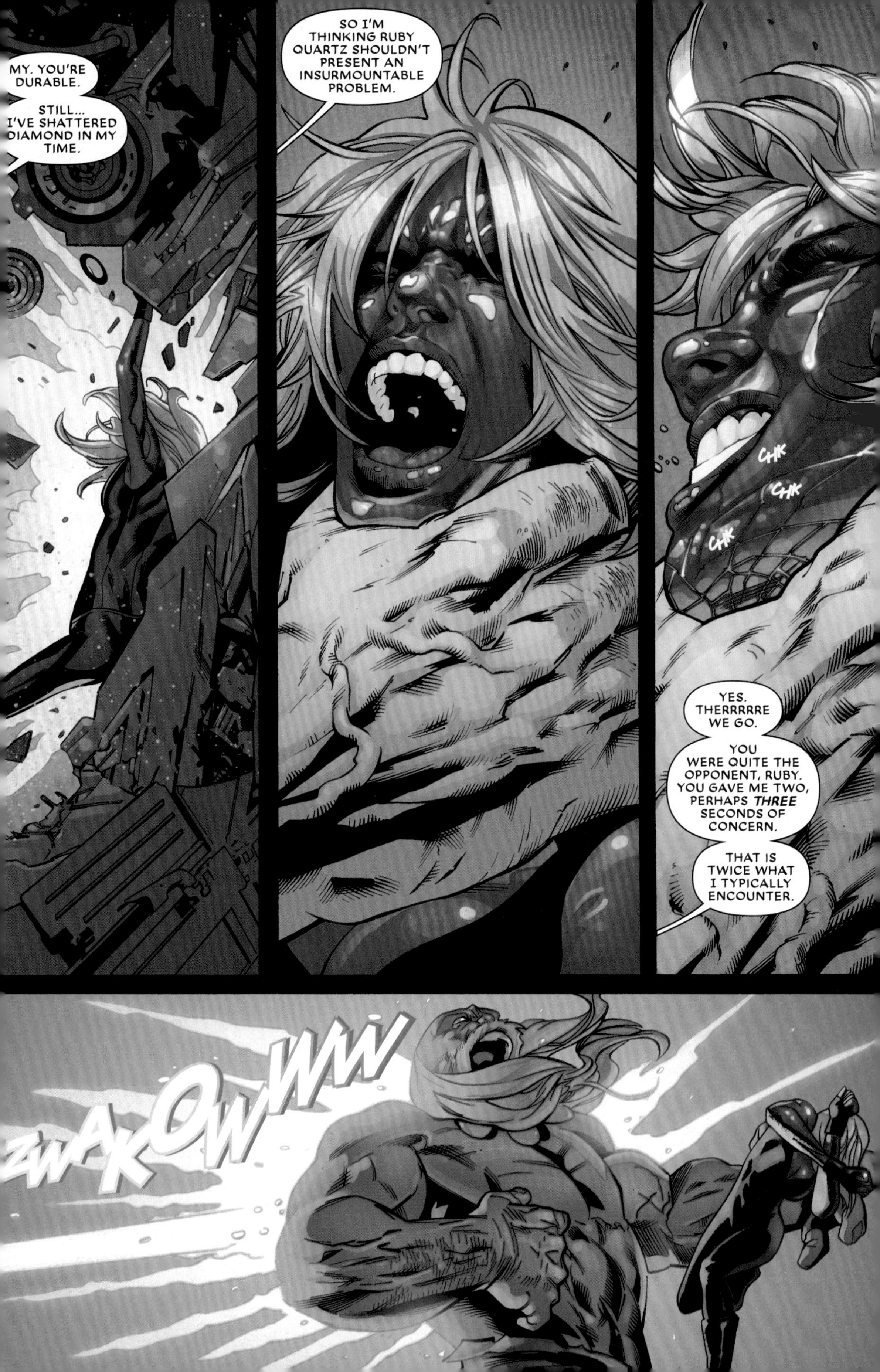
MY. YOU'RE DURABLE.
STILL... I'VE SHATTERED DIAMOND IN MY TIME.
SO I'M THINKING RUBY QUARTZ SHOULDN'T PRESENT AN INSURMOUNTABLE PROBLEM.
CHK
CHK
CHK
YES. THERRRRRE WE GO.
YOU WERE QUITE THE OPPONENT, RUBY. YOU GAVE ME TWO, PERHAPS *THREE* SECONDS OF CONCERN.
THAT IS TWICE WHAT I TYPICALLY ENCOUNTER.
ZWAKOWWW

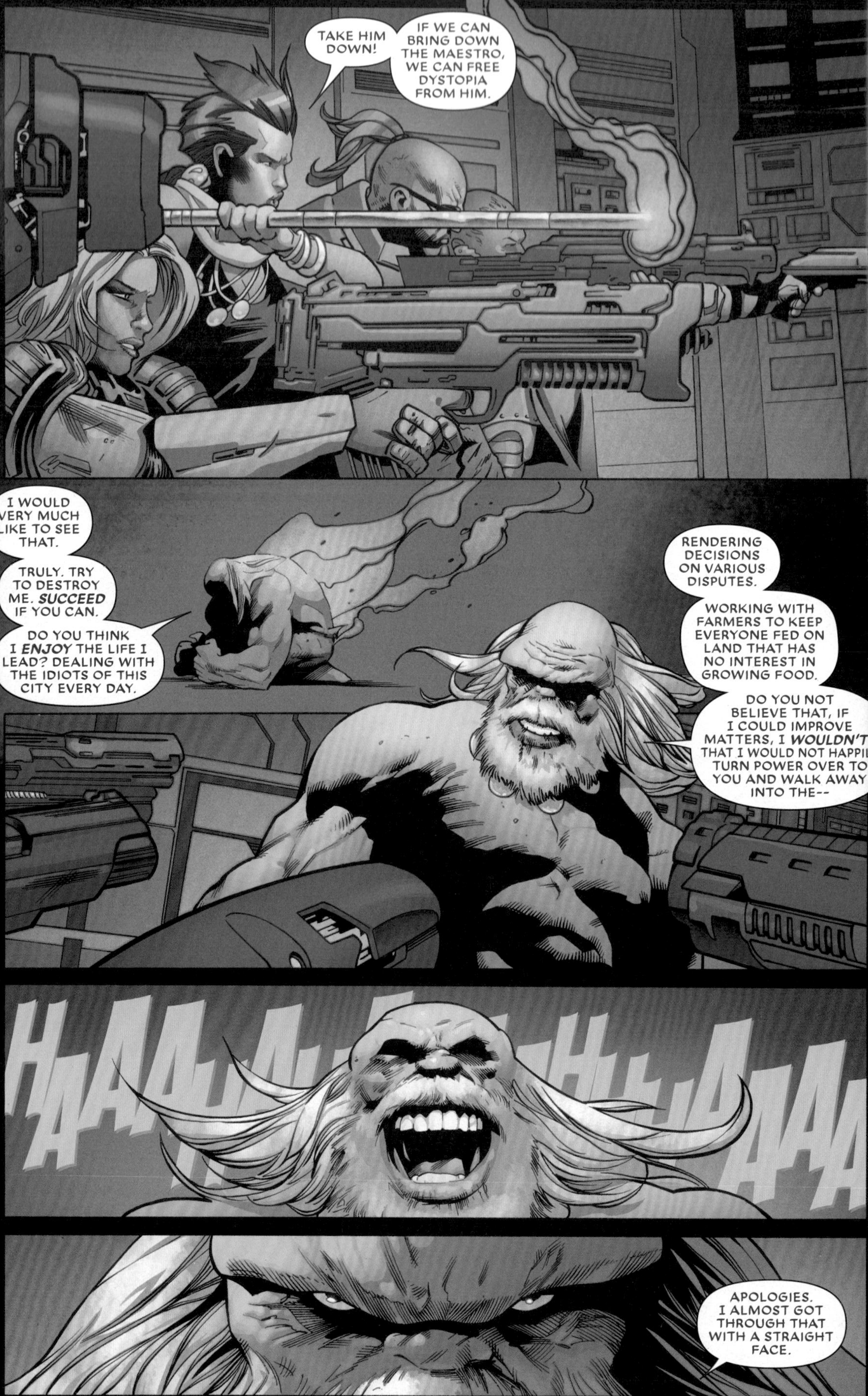

TAKE HIM DOWN!
IF WE CAN BRING DOWN THE MAESTRO, WE CAN FREE DYSTOPIA FROM HIM.
I WOULD VERY MUCH LIKE TO SEE THAT.
TRULY. TRY TO DESTROY ME. *SUCCEED* IF YOU CAN.
DO YOU THINK I *ENJOY* THE LIFE I LEAD? DEALING WITH THE IDIOTS OF THIS CITY EVERY DAY.
RENDERING DECISIONS ON VARIOUS DISPUTES.
WORKING WITH FARMERS TO KEEP EVERYONE FED ON LAND THAT HAS NO INTEREST IN GROWING FOOD.
DO YOU NOT BELIEVE THAT, IF I COULD IMPROVE MATTERS, I *WOULDN'T* THAT I WOULD NOT HAPPI TURN POWER OVER TO YOU AND WALK AWAY INTO THE--
APOLOGIES. I ALMOST GOT THROUGH THAT WITH A STRAIGHT FACE.

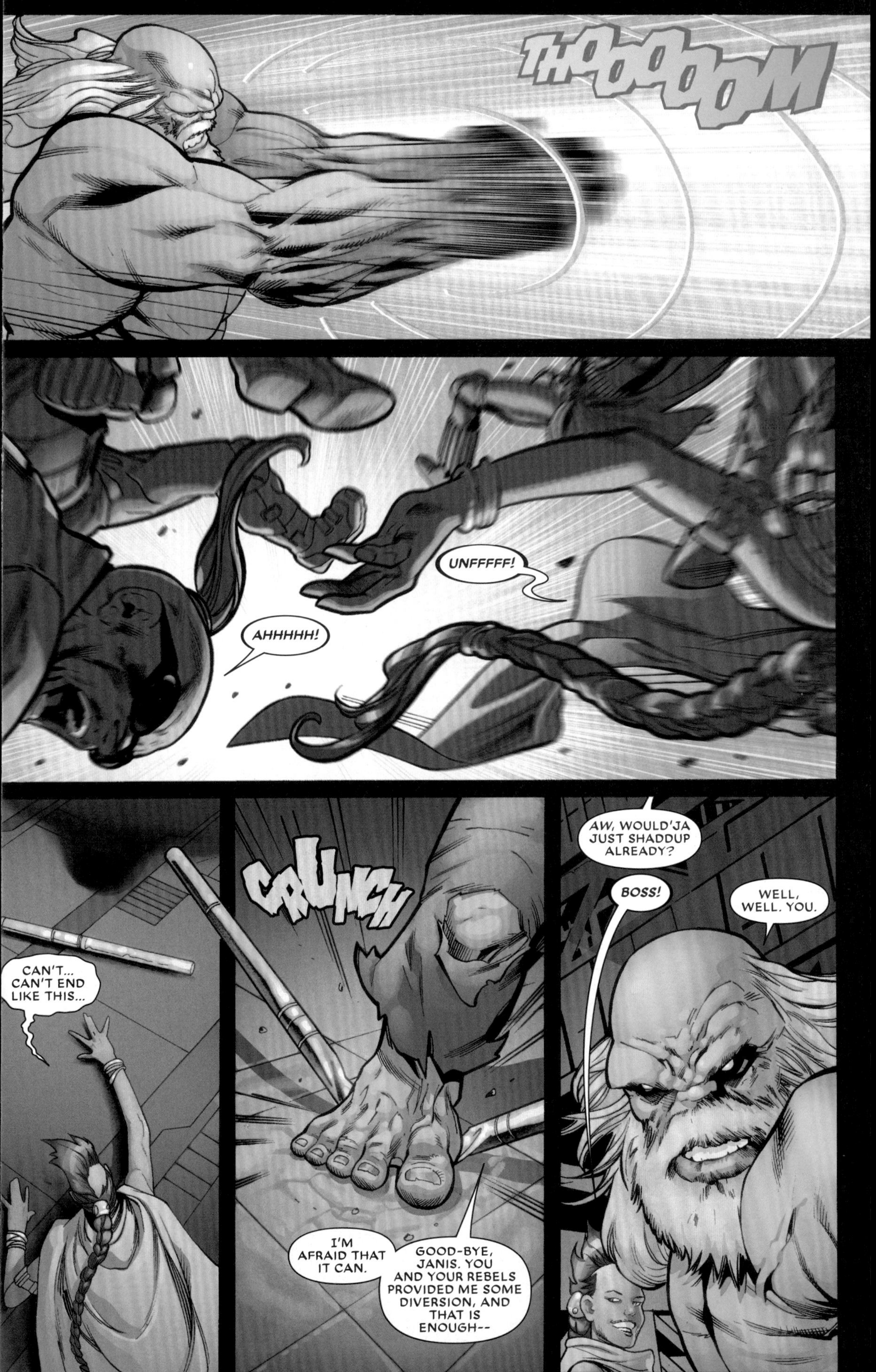
THOOOOOOM
UNFFFFF!
AHHHHH!
CAN'T... CAN'T END LIKE THIS...
CRUNCH
I'M AFRAID THAT IT CAN.
GOOD-BYE, JANIS. YOU AND YOUR REBELS PROVIDED ME SOME DIVERSION, AND THAT IS ENOUGH--
AW, WOULD'JA JUST SHADDUP ALREADY?
BOSS!
WELL, WELL. YOU.

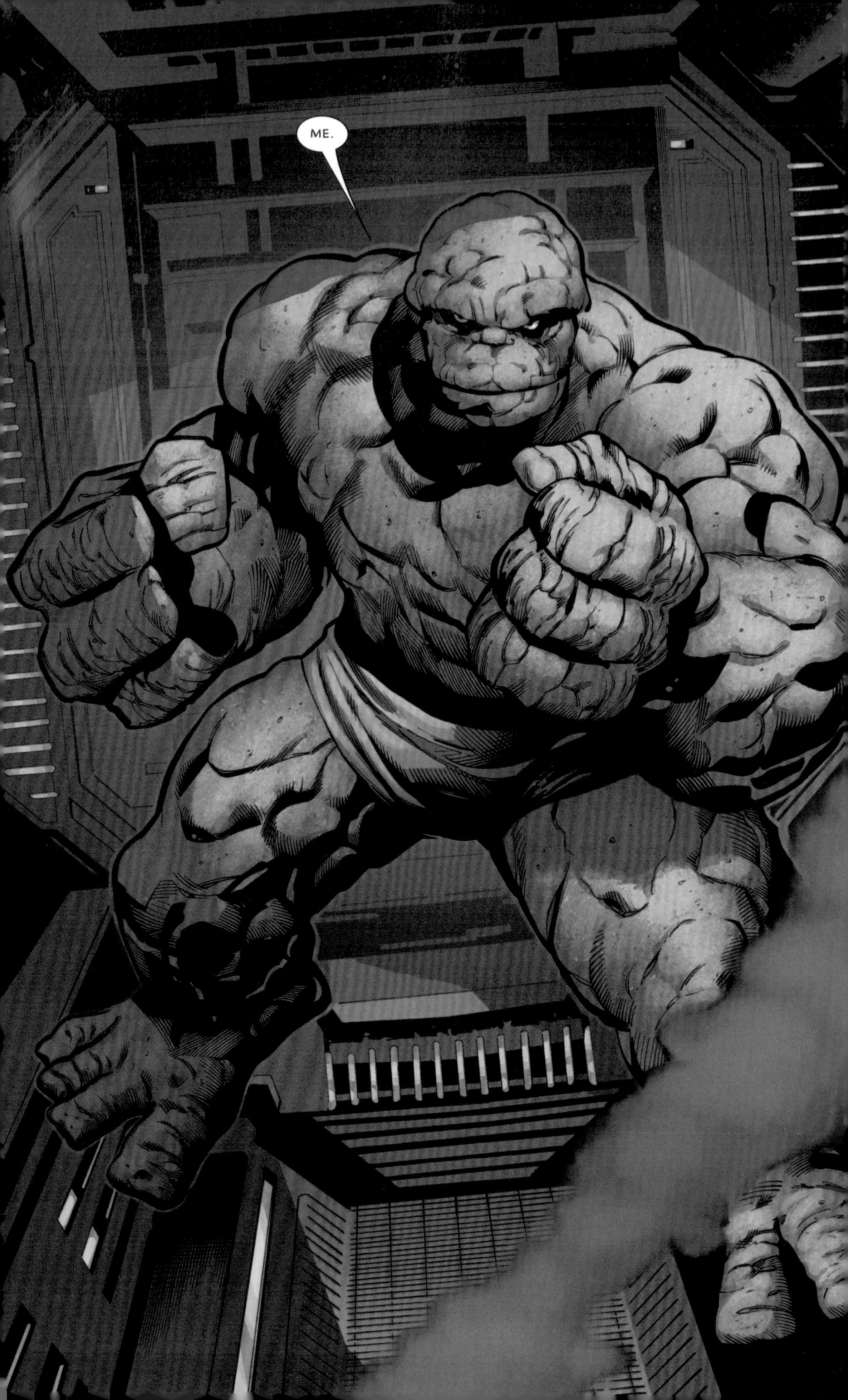
ME.

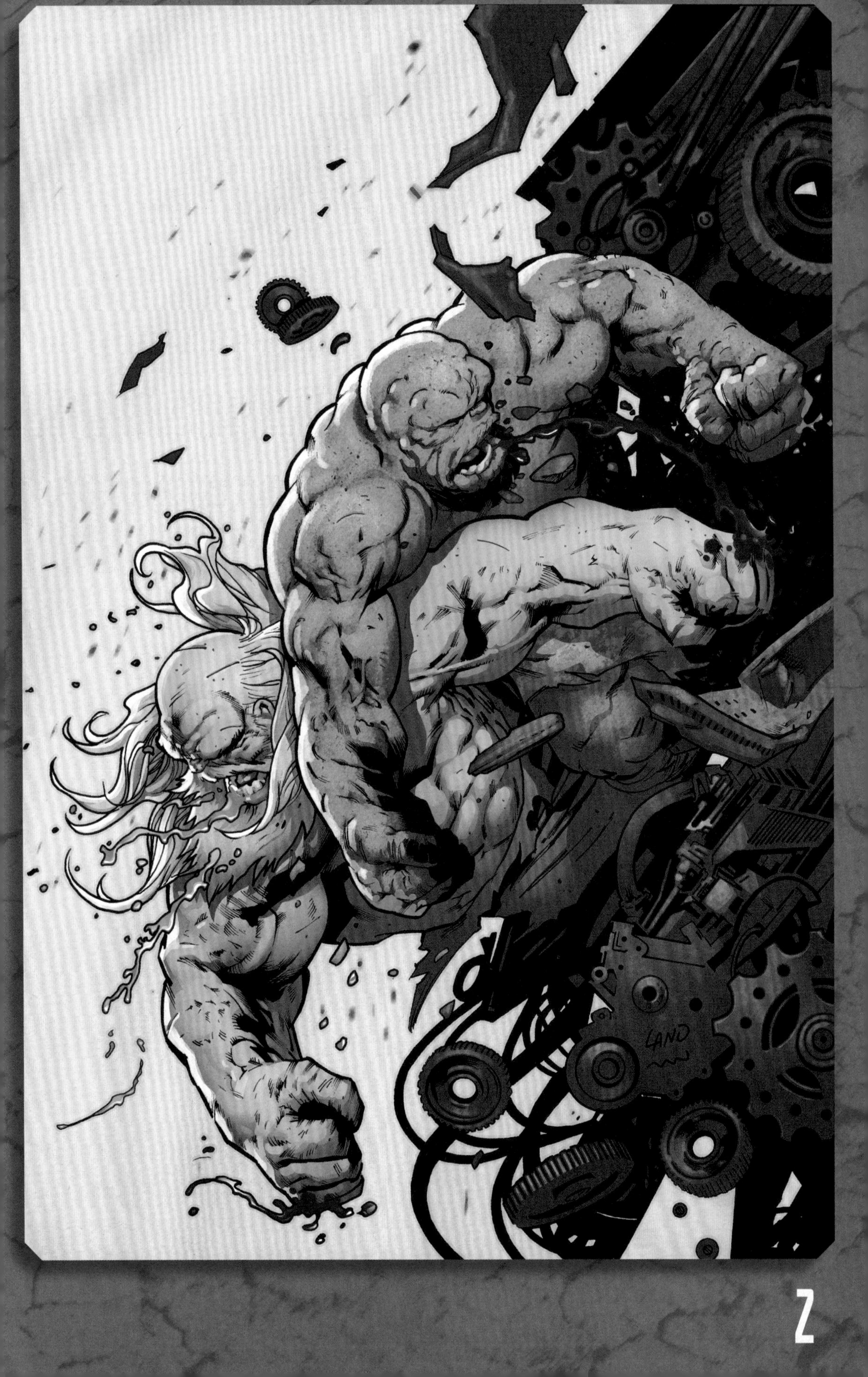
LAND

Z

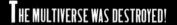

THE MULTIVERSE WAS DESTROYED!

THE HEROES OF EARTH-616 AND EARTH-1610 WERE POWERLESS TO SAVE IT!

NOW, ALL THAT REMAINS...IS **BATTLEWORLD!**

A MASSIVE, PATCHWORK PLANET COMPOSED OF THE FRAGMENTS OF WORLDS THAT NO LONGER EXIST, MAINTAINED BY THE IRON WILL OF ITS GOD AND MASTER, VICTOR VON DOOM!

EACH DOMAIN RULED BY POWERFUL BARONS, BUT NONE MORE TIGHTLY CONDUCTED THAN...

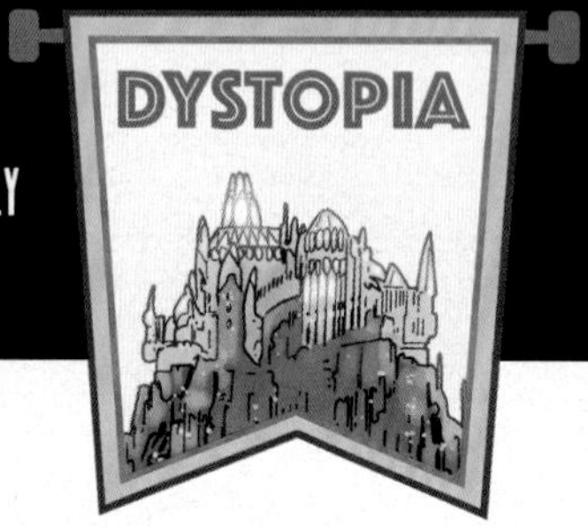
DYSTOPIA

SECRET WARS

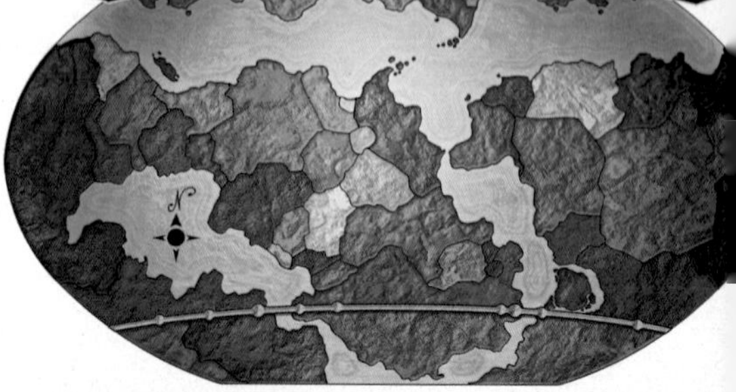

OUR EXALTED BARON, THE MAESTRO, WELCOMES YOU TO HIS TROPHY ROOM OF CONQUERED OPPONENTS.

EXHIBITING THIS SEASON:

- ELEKTRA SAI
- LOKI SCEPTER
- WINTER SOLDIER ARM
- STAR-LORD FACE MASK
- ANT-MAN HELMET
- SQUIRREL GIRL TAIL
- WOLVERINE CLAWS
- MAGIK SWORD
- DEADPOOL CHIMICHANGA
- NAMOR TRUNKS

EAST WING

*PLEASE REMAIN QUIET AND RESPECTFUL!

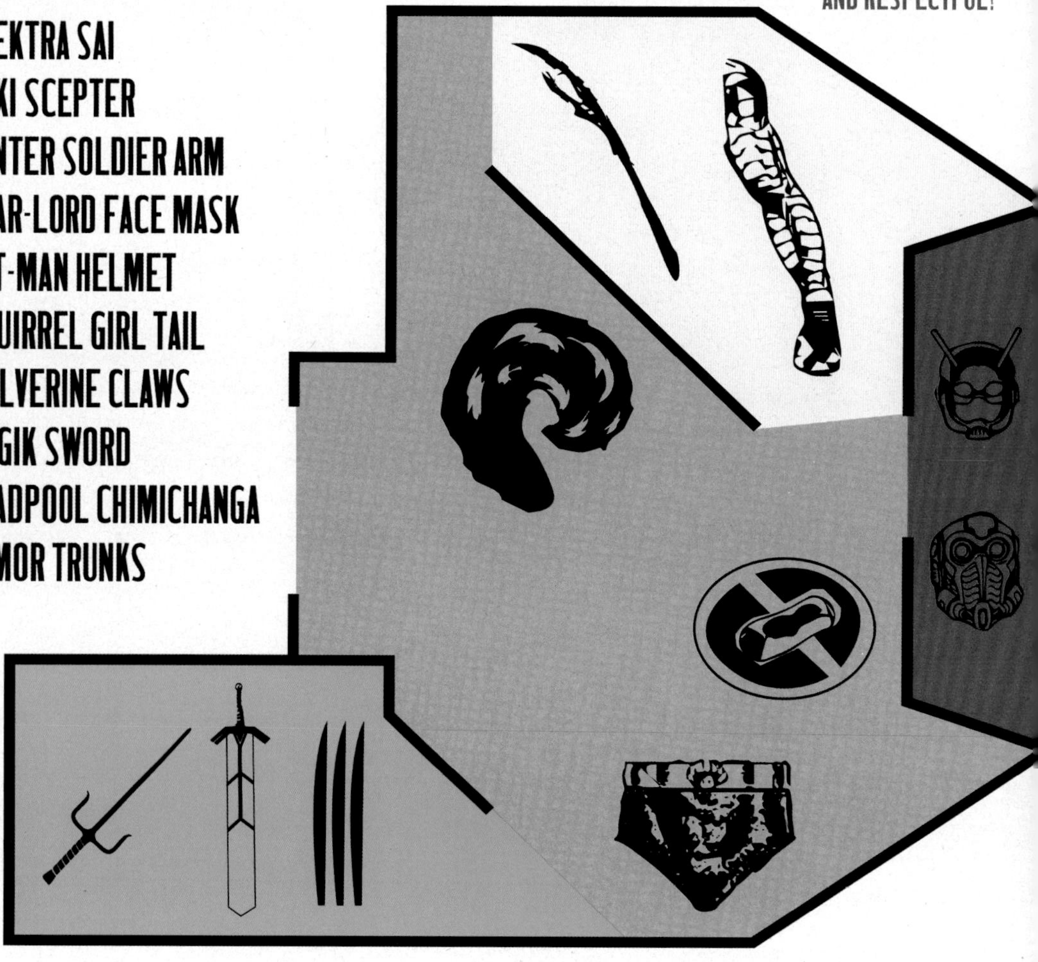

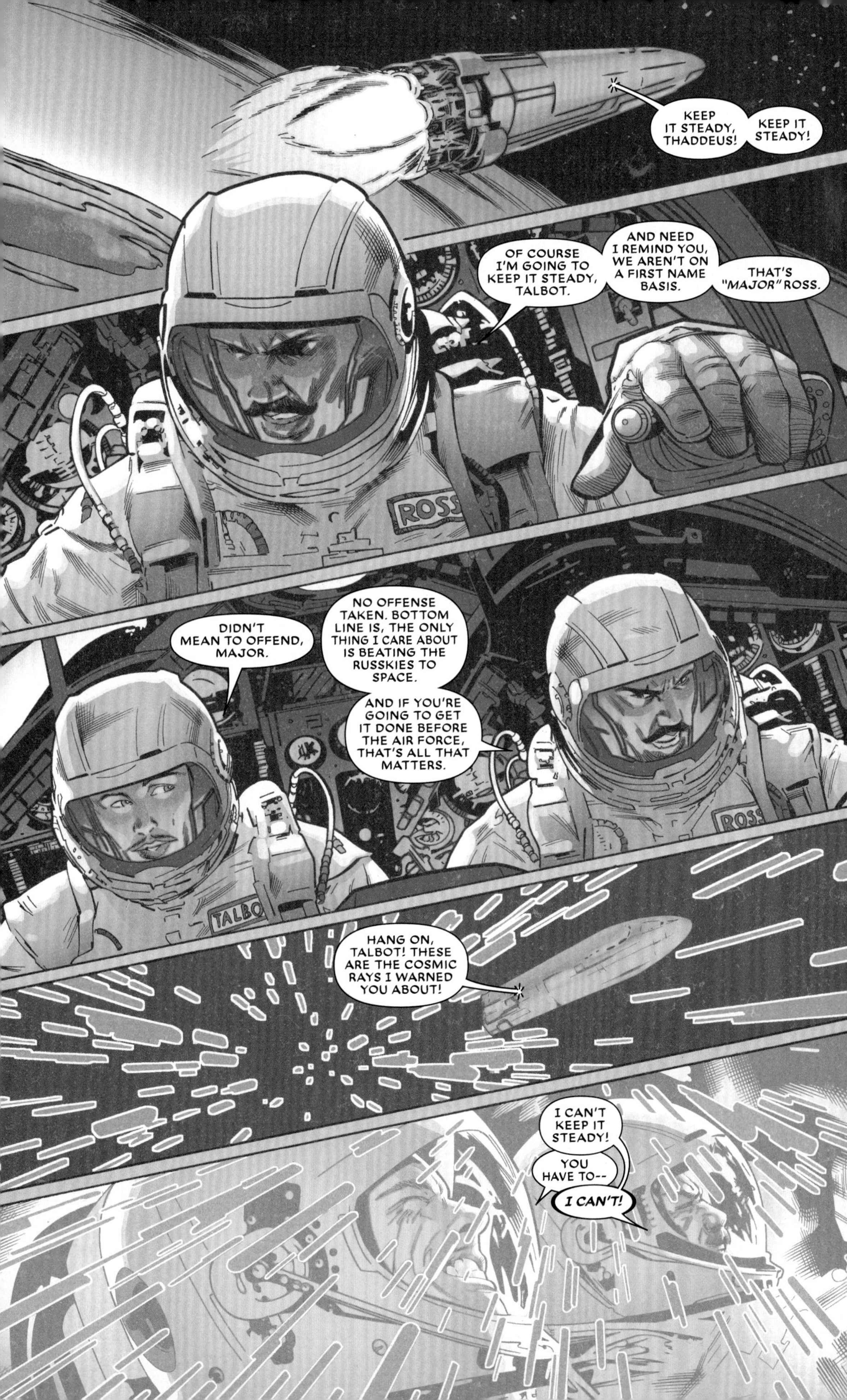
KEEP IT STEADY, THADDEUS!
KEEP IT STEADY!
OF COURSE I'M GOING TO KEEP IT STEADY, TALBOT.
AND NEED I REMIND YOU, WE AREN'T ON A FIRST NAME BASIS.
THAT'S "MAJOR" ROSS.
ROSS
DIDN'T MEAN TO OFFEND, MAJOR.
NO OFFENSE TAKEN. BOTTOM LINE IS, THE ONLY THING I CARE ABOUT IS BEATING THE RUSSKIES TO SPACE.
AND IF YOU'RE GOING TO GET IT DONE BEFORE THE AIR FORCE, THAT'S ALL THAT MATTERS.
TALBO
ROSS
HANG ON, TALBOT! THESE ARE THE COSMIC RAYS I WARNED YOU ABOUT!
I CAN'T KEEP IT STEADY!
YOU HAVE TO--
I CAN'T!

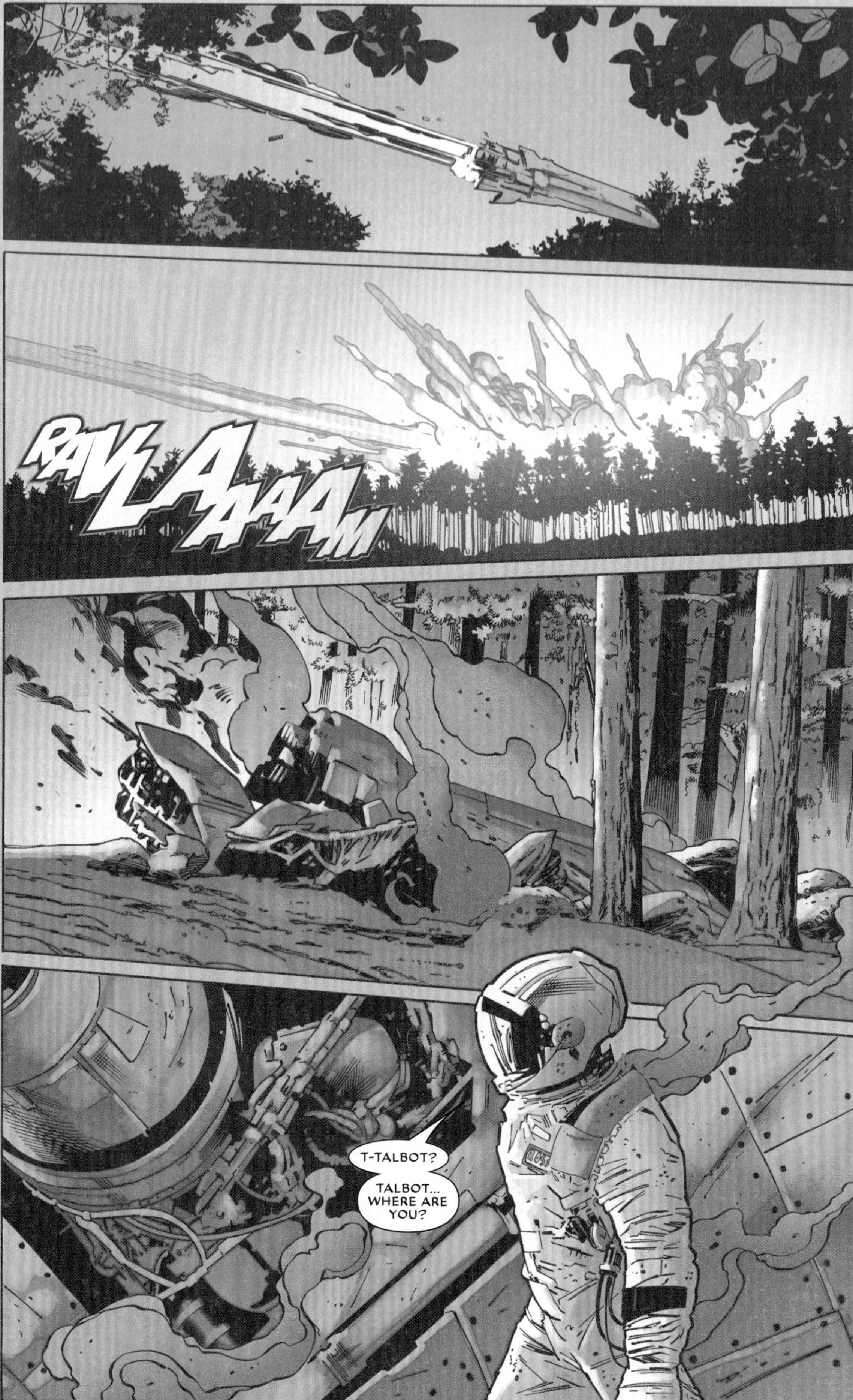
RAVLAAAAM
T-TALBOT?
TALBOT... WHERE ARE YOU?

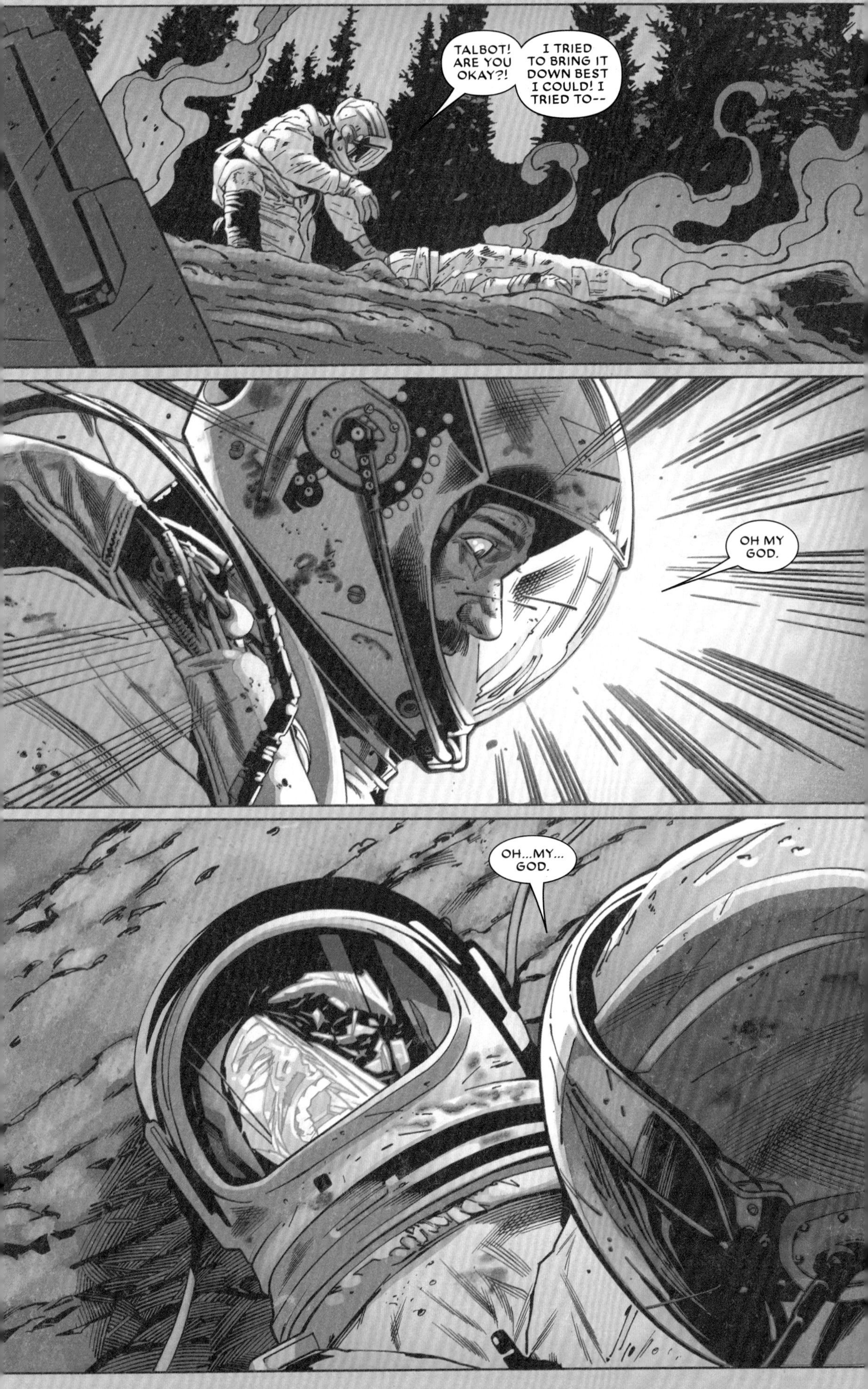
TALBOT! ARE YOU OKAY?!
I TRIED TO BRING IT DOWN BEST I COULD! I TRIED TO--
OH MY GOD.
OH...MY... GOD.

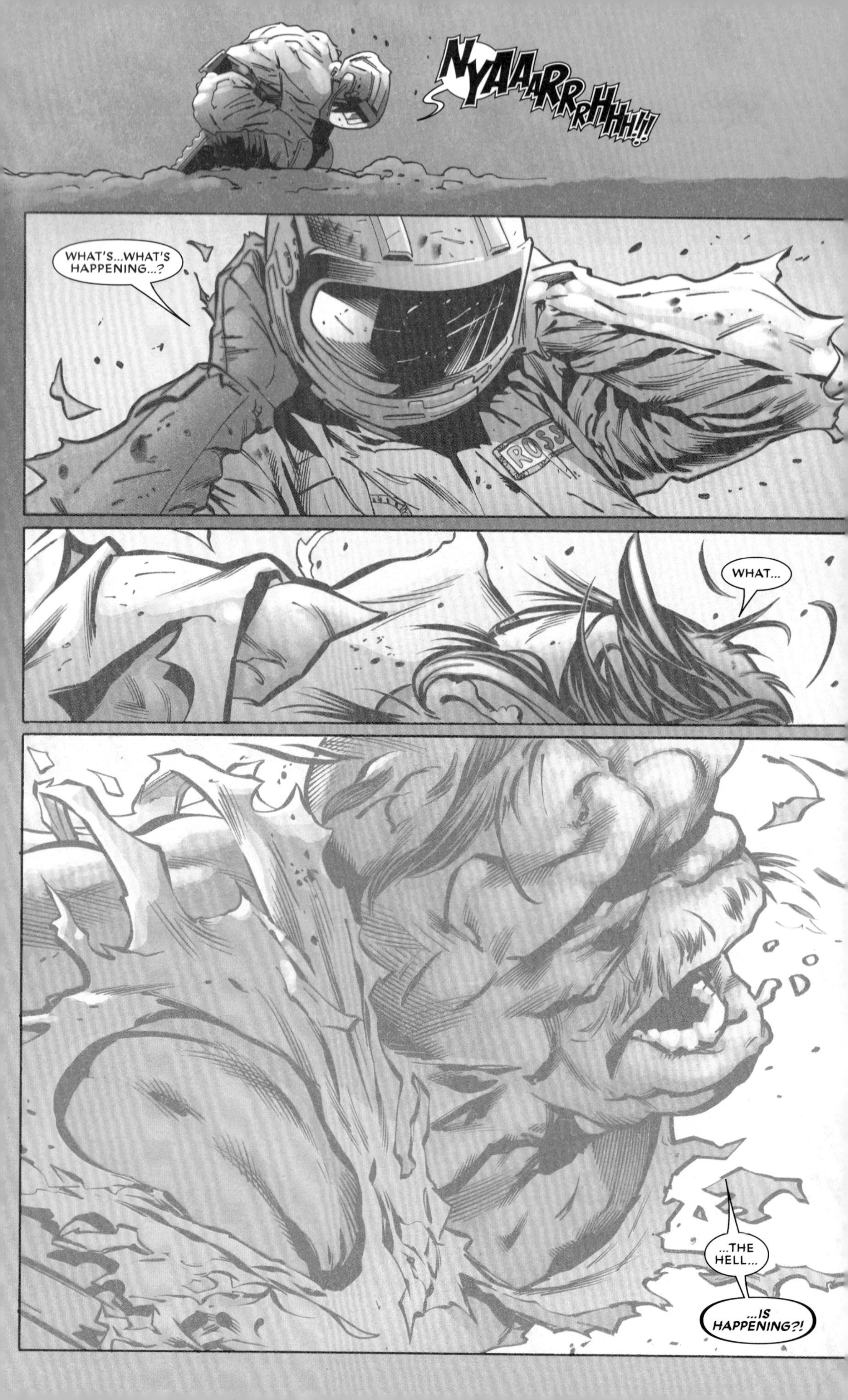
NYAAARRRHHH!!
WHAT'S...WHAT'S HAPPENING...?
ROSS
WHAT...
...THE HELL...
...IS HAPPENING?!

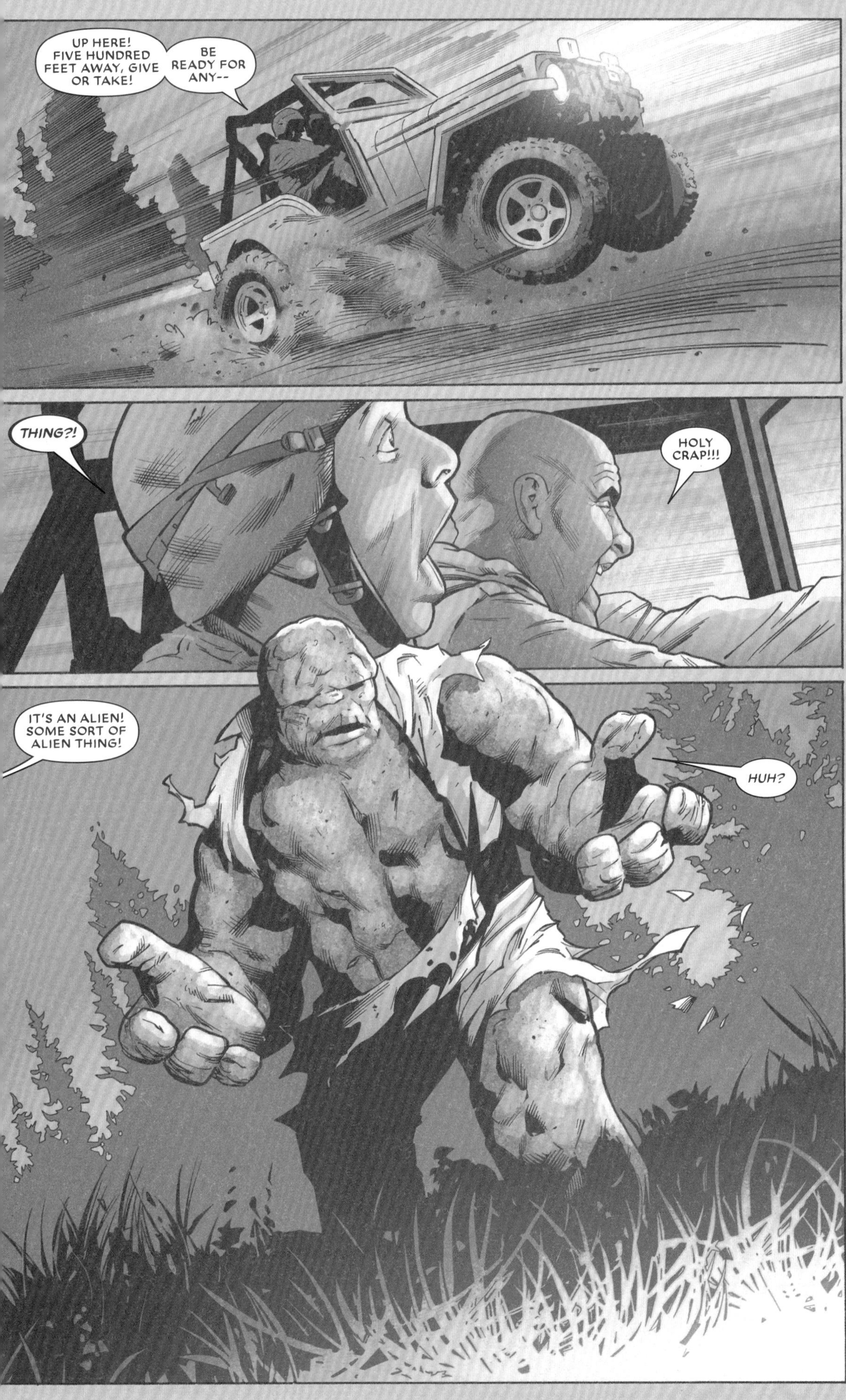
UP HERE! FIVE HUNDRED FEET AWAY, GIVE OR TAKE!
BE READY FOR ANY--
THING?!
HOLY CRAP!!!
IT'S AN ALIEN! SOME SORT OF ALIEN THING!
HUH?

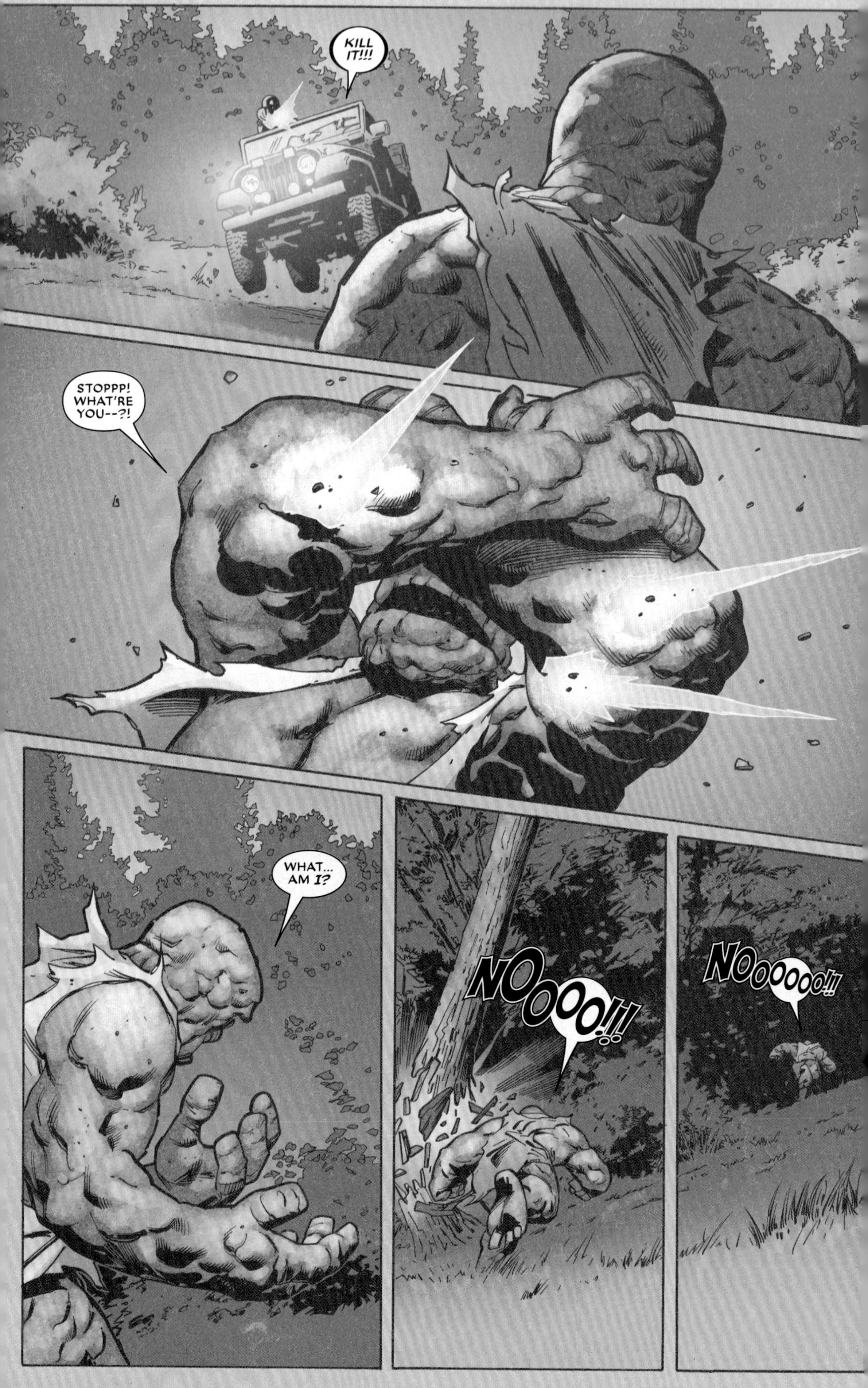
KILL IT!!!
STOPPP! WHAT'RE YOU--?!
WHAT... AM I?
NOOOO!!!
NOOOOOO!!!

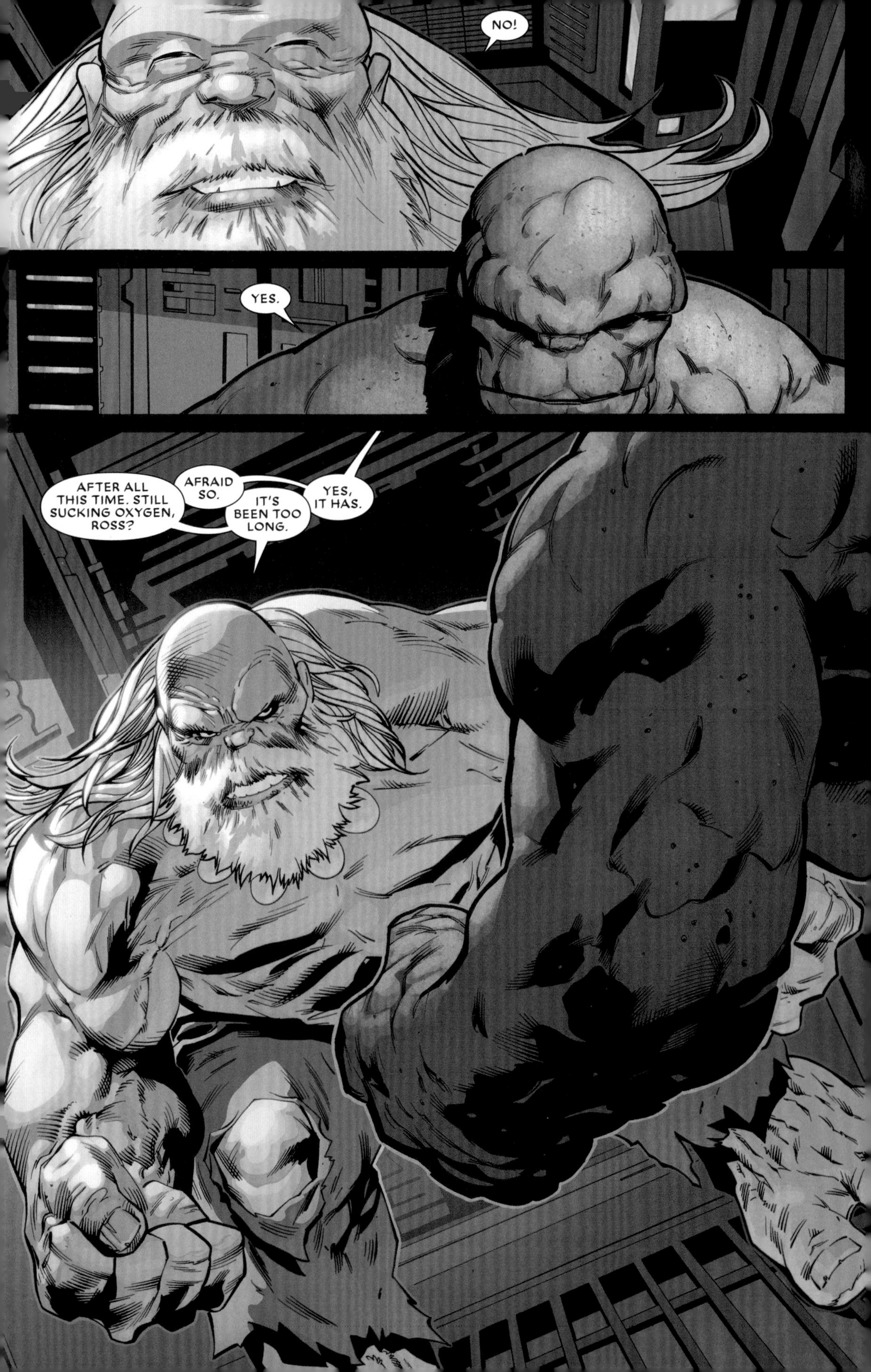
NO!
YES.
AFTER ALL THIS TIME. STILL SUCKING OXYGEN, ROSS?
AFRAID SO.
IT'S BEEN TOO LONG.
YES, IT HAS.

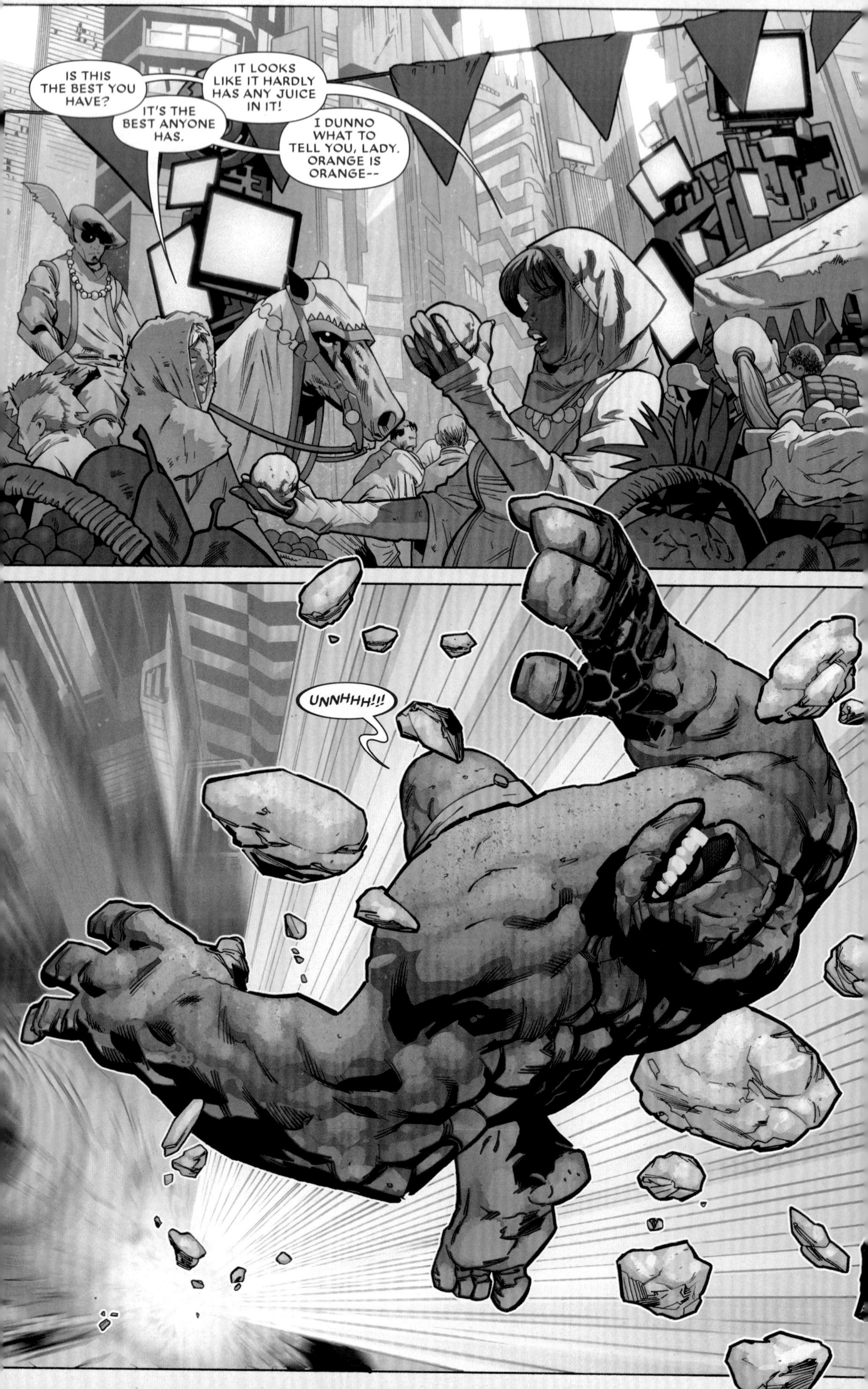
IS THIS THE BEST YOU HAVE?
IT LOOKS LIKE IT HARDLY HAS ANY JUICE IN IT!
IT'S THE BEST ANYONE HAS.
I DUNNO WHAT TO TELL YOU, LADY. ORANGE IS ORANGE--
UNNHHH!!!

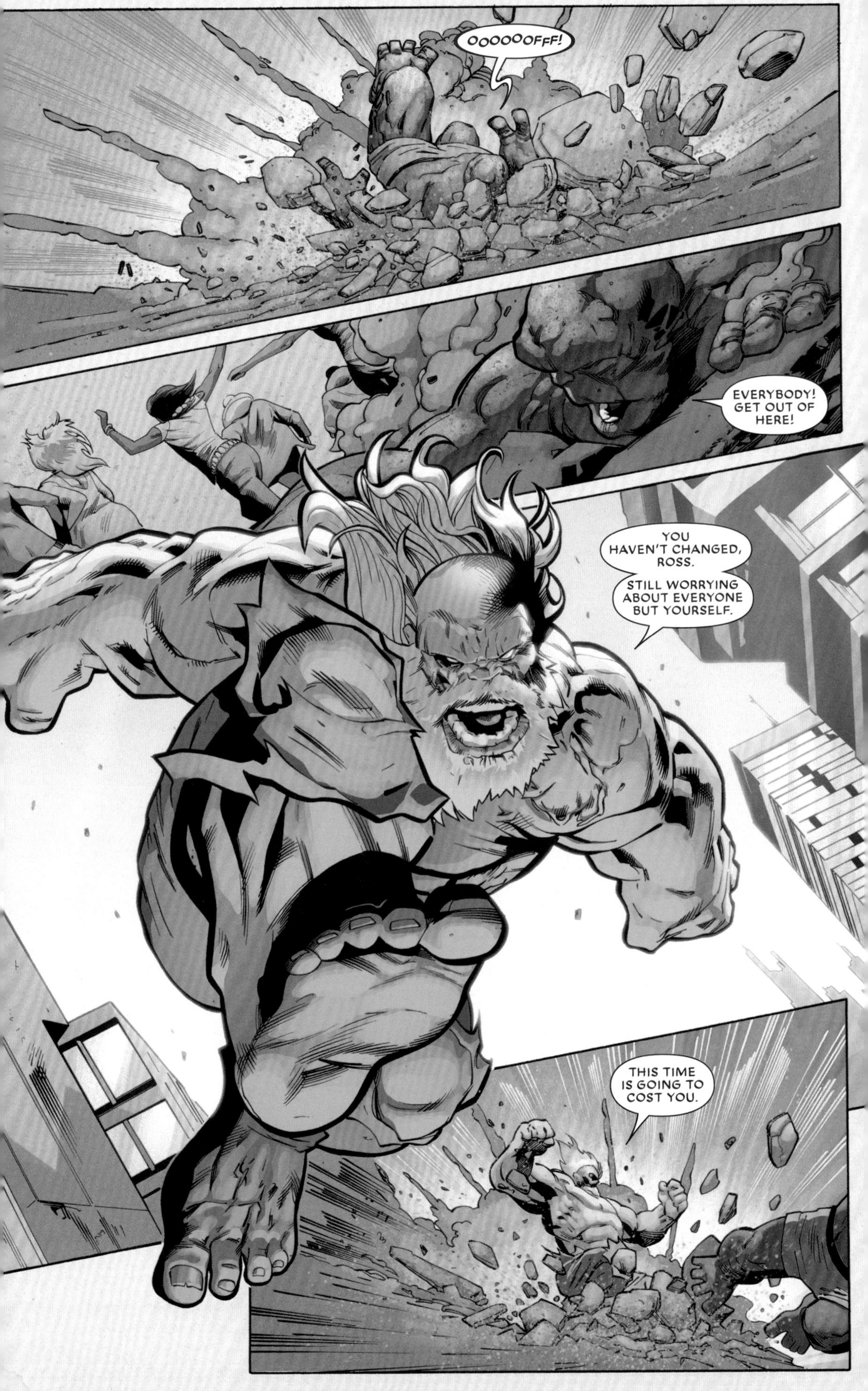
OOOOOOFFF!
EVERYBODY! GET OUT OF HERE!
YOU HAVEN'T CHANGED, ROSS.
STILL WORRYING ABOUT EVERYONE BUT YOURSELF.
THIS TIME IS GOING TO COST YOU.

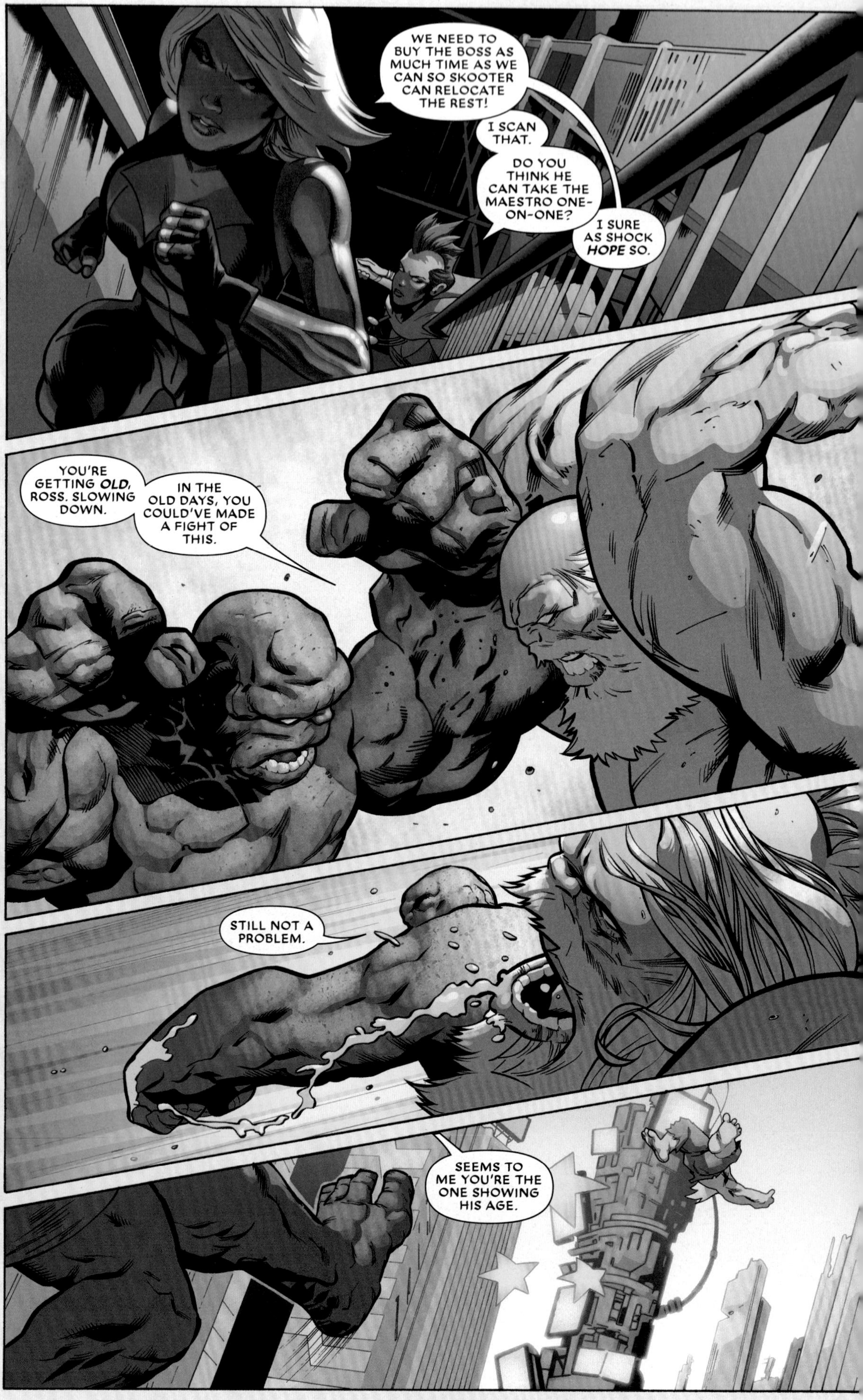
WE NEED TO BUY THE BOSS AS MUCH TIME AS WE CAN SO SKOOTER CAN RELOCATE THE REST!
I SCAN THAT.
DO YOU THINK HE CAN TAKE THE MAESTRO ONE-ON-ONE?
I SURE AS SHOCK *HOPE* SO.
YOU'RE GETTING *OLD*, ROSS. SLOWING DOWN.
IN THE OLD DAYS, YOU COULD'VE MADE A FIGHT OF THIS.
STILL NOT A PROBLEM.
SEEMS TO ME YOU'RE THE ONE SHOWING HIS AGE.

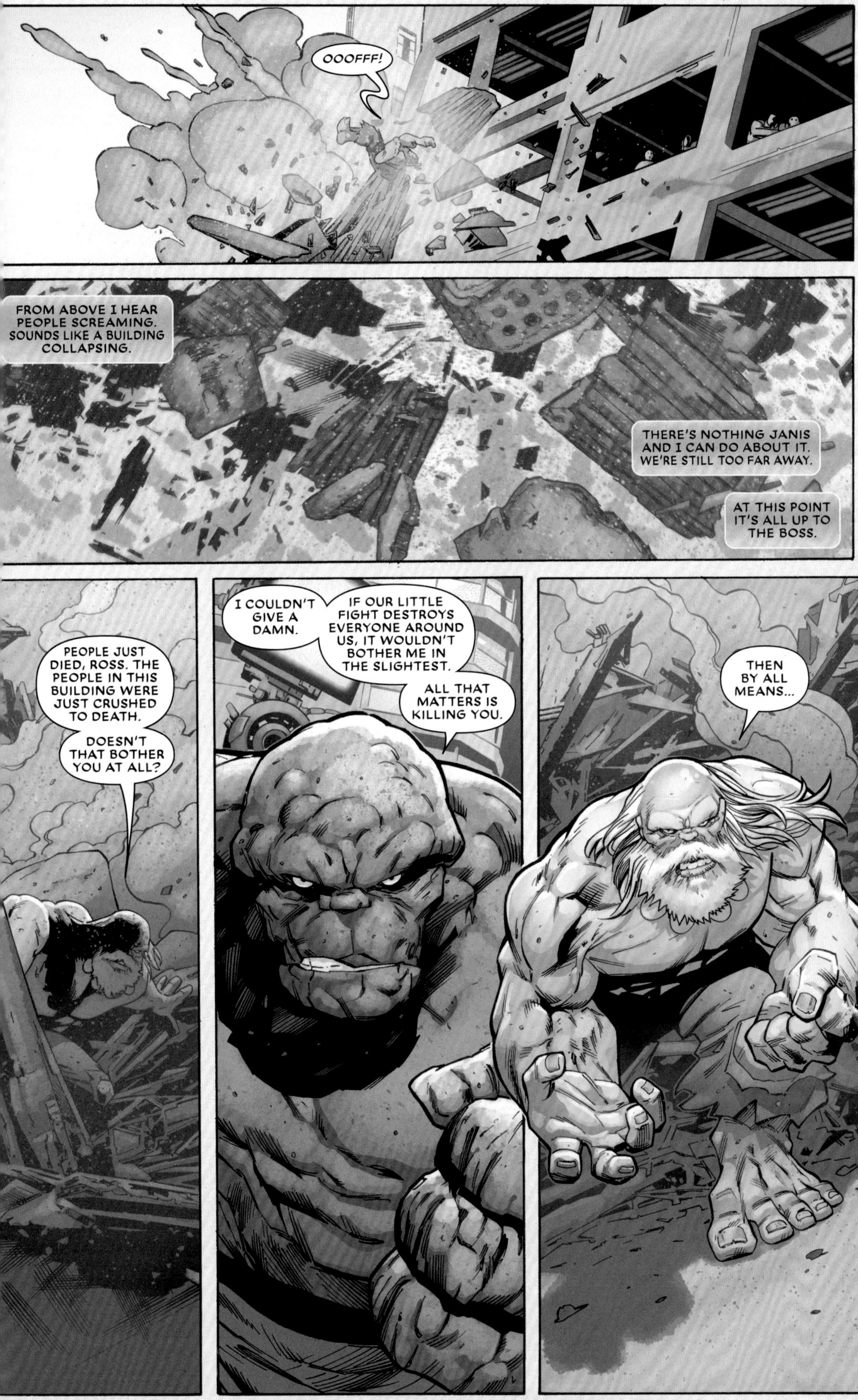
OOOFFF!
FROM ABOVE I HEAR PEOPLE SCREAMING. SOUNDS LIKE A BUILDING COLLAPSING.
THERE'S NOTHING JANIS AND I CAN DO ABOUT IT. WE'RE STILL TOO FAR AWAY.
AT THIS POINT IT'S ALL UP TO THE BOSS.
PEOPLE JUST DIED, ROSS. THE PEOPLE IN THIS BUILDING WERE JUST CRUSHED TO DEATH.
DOESN'T THAT BOTHER YOU AT ALL?
I COULDN'T GIVE A DAMN.
IF OUR LITTLE FIGHT DESTROYS EVERYONE AROUND US, IT WOULDN'T BOTHER ME IN THE SLIGHTEST.
ALL THAT MATTERS IS KILLING YOU.
THEN BY ALL MEANS...

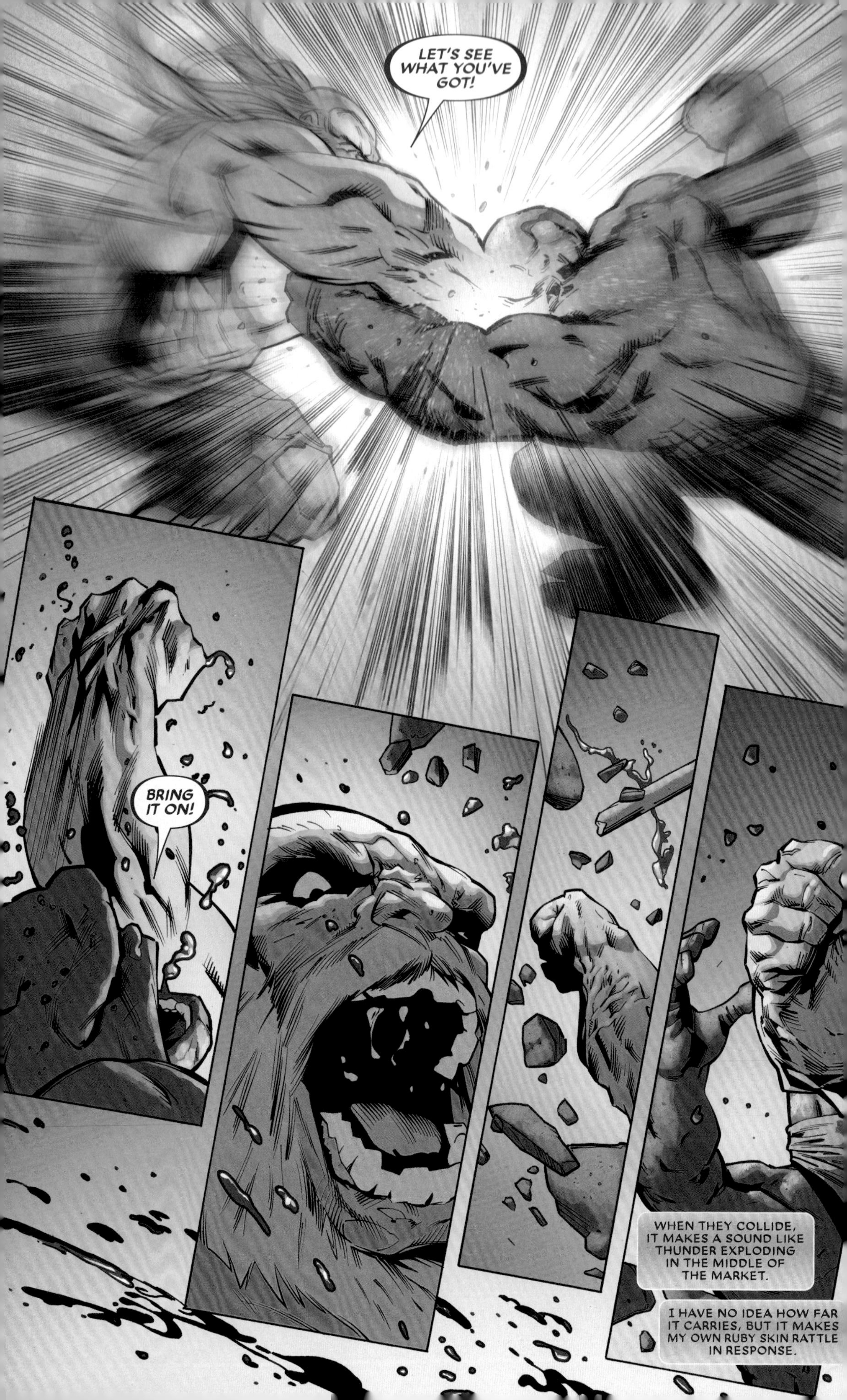

LET'S SEE WHAT YOU'VE GOT!
BRING IT ON!
WHEN THEY COLLIDE, IT MAKES A SOUND LIKE THUNDER EXPLODING IN THE MIDDLE OF THE MARKET.
I HAVE NO IDEA HOW FAR IT CARRIES, BUT IT MAKES MY OWN RUBY SKIN RATTLE IN RESPONSE.

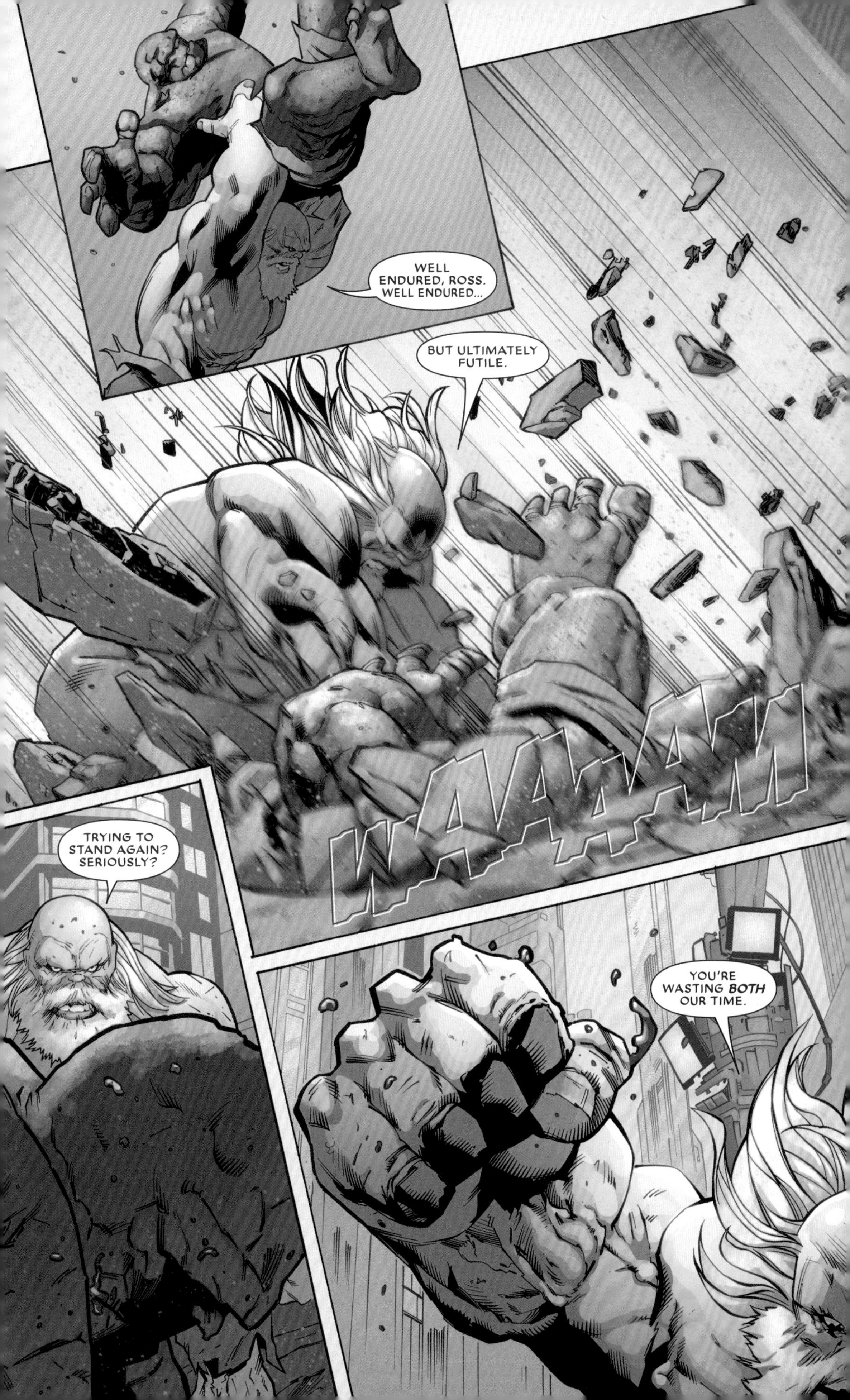
WELL ENDURED, ROSS. WELL ENDURED...
BUT ULTIMATELY FUTILE.
WAAAM
TRYING TO STAND AGAIN? SERIOUSLY?
YOU'RE WASTING *BOTH* OUR TIME.

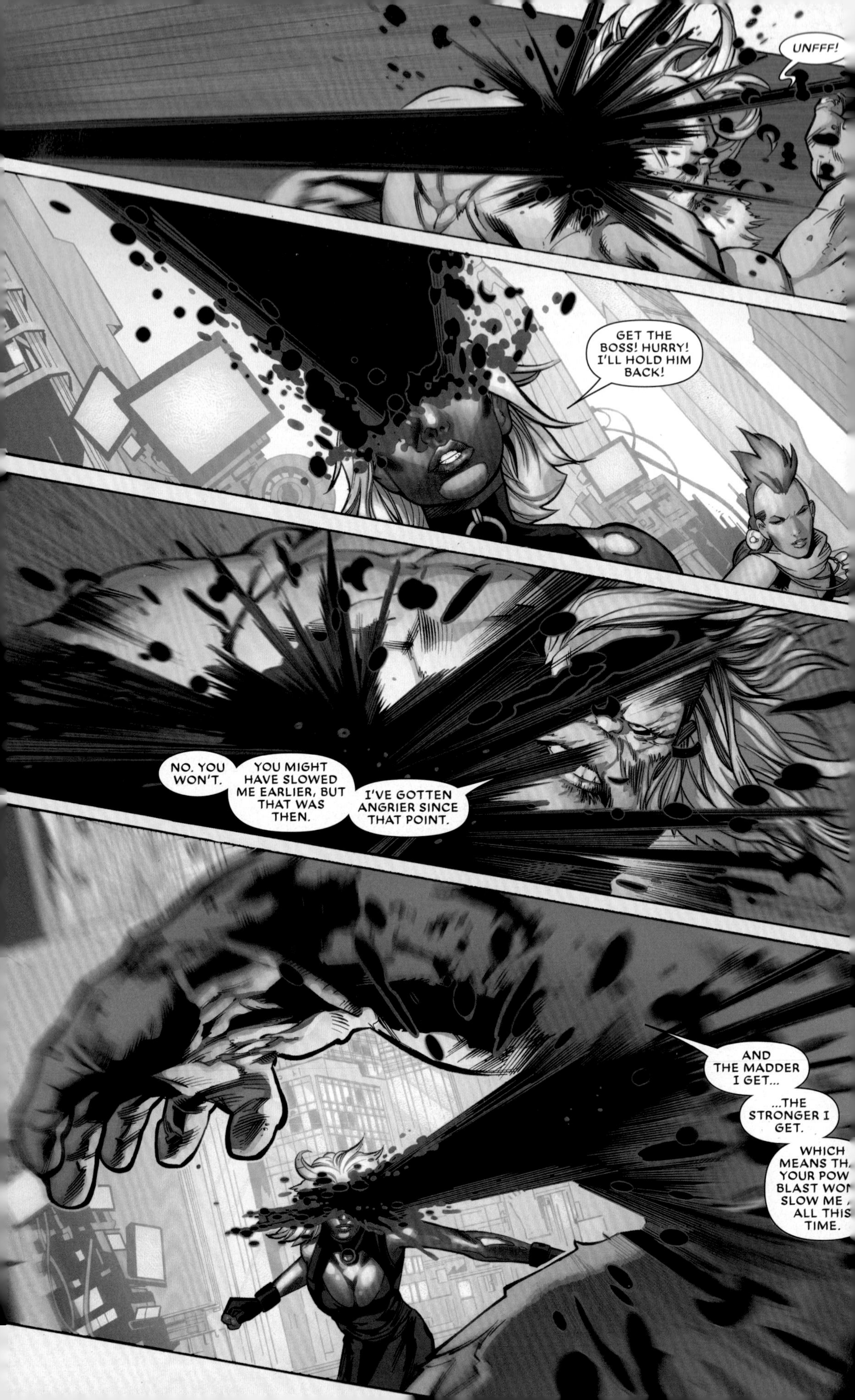
UNFFF!
GET THE BOSS! HURRY! I'LL HOLD HIM BACK!
NO. YOU WON'T.
YOU MIGHT HAVE SLOWED ME EARLIER, BUT THAT WAS THEN.
I'VE GOTTEN ANGRIER SINCE THAT POINT.
AND THE MADDER I GET...
...THE STRONGER I GET.
WHICH MEANS THA YOUR POW BLAST WON SLOW ME ALL THIS TIME.

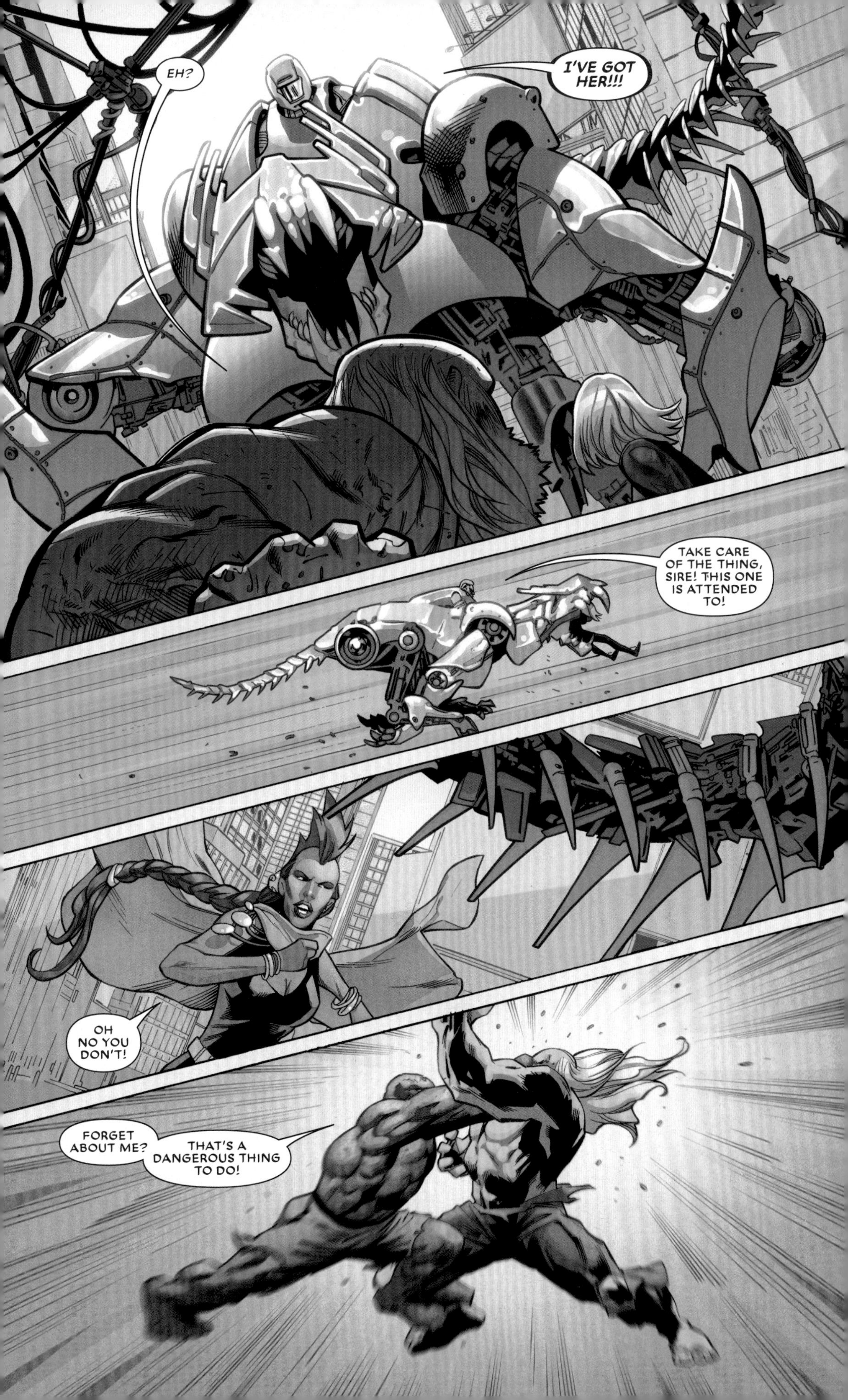
EH?
I'VE GOT HER!!!
TAKE CARE OF THE THING, SIRE! THIS ONE IS ATTENDED TO!
OH NO YOU DON'T!
FORGET ABOUT ME?
THAT'S A DANGEROUS THING TO DO!

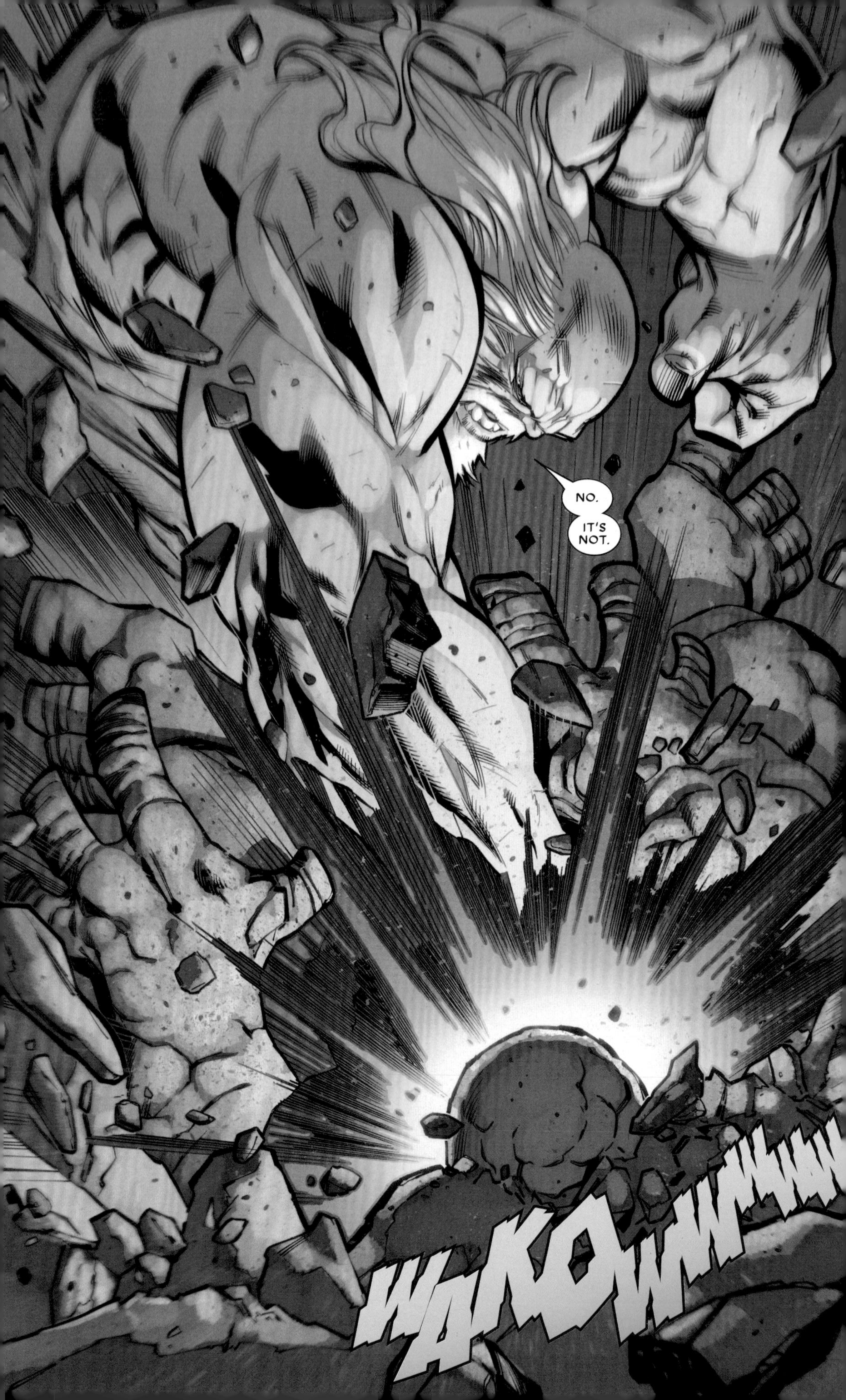
NO.
IT'S NOT.
WHAKOWWWWW

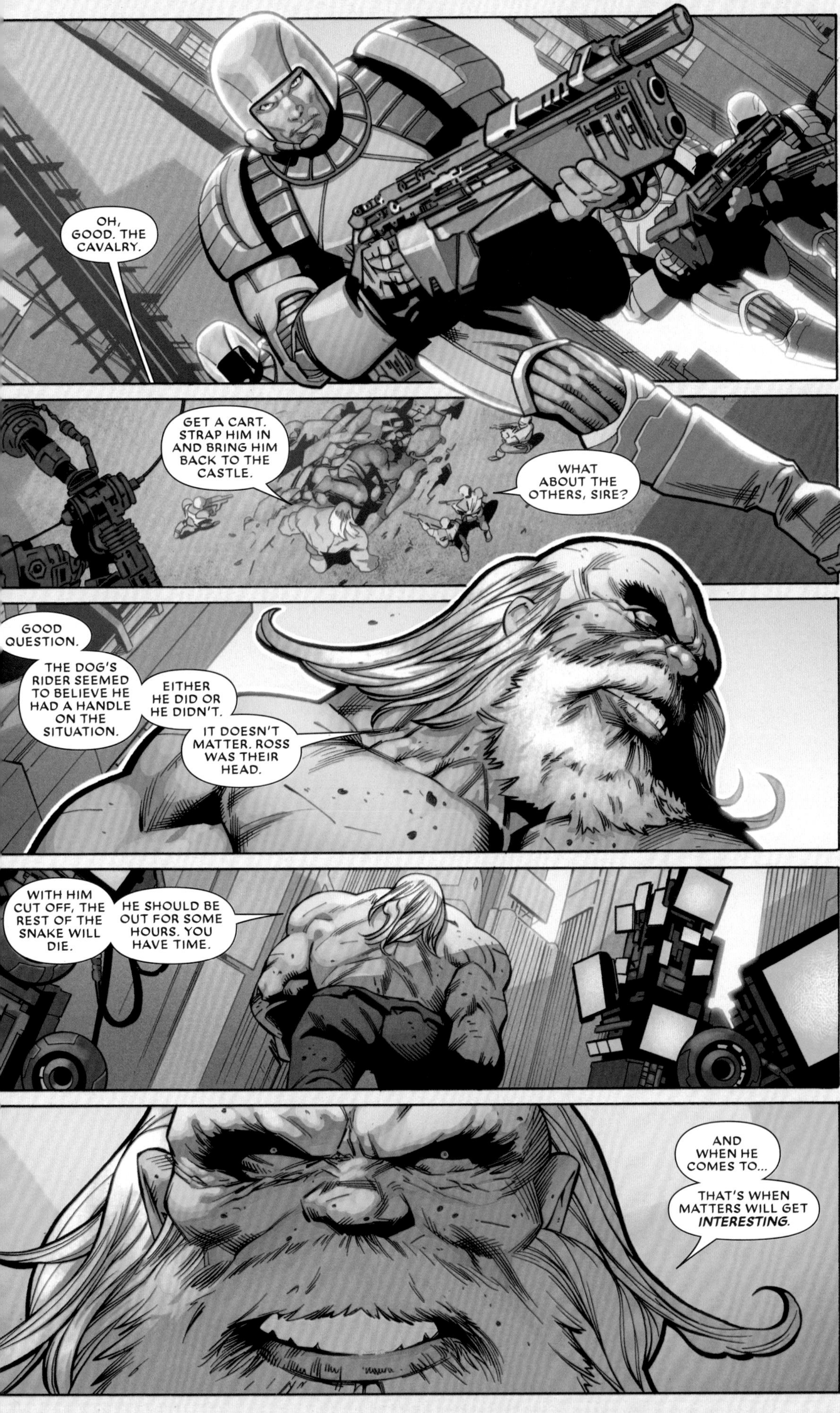
OH, GOOD. THE CAVALRY.
GET A CART. STRAP HIM IN AND BRING HIM BACK TO THE CASTLE.
WHAT ABOUT THE OTHERS, SIRE?
GOOD QUESTION.
THE DOG'S RIDER SEEMED TO BELIEVE HE HAD A HANDLE ON THE SITUATION.
EITHER HE DID OR HE DIDN'T.
IT DOESN'T MATTER. ROSS WAS THEIR HEAD.
WITH HIM CUT OFF, THE REST OF THE SNAKE WILL DIE.
HE SHOULD BE OUT FOR SOME HOURS. YOU HAVE TIME.
AND WHEN HE COMES TO...
THAT'S WHEN MATTERS WILL GET *INTERESTING*.

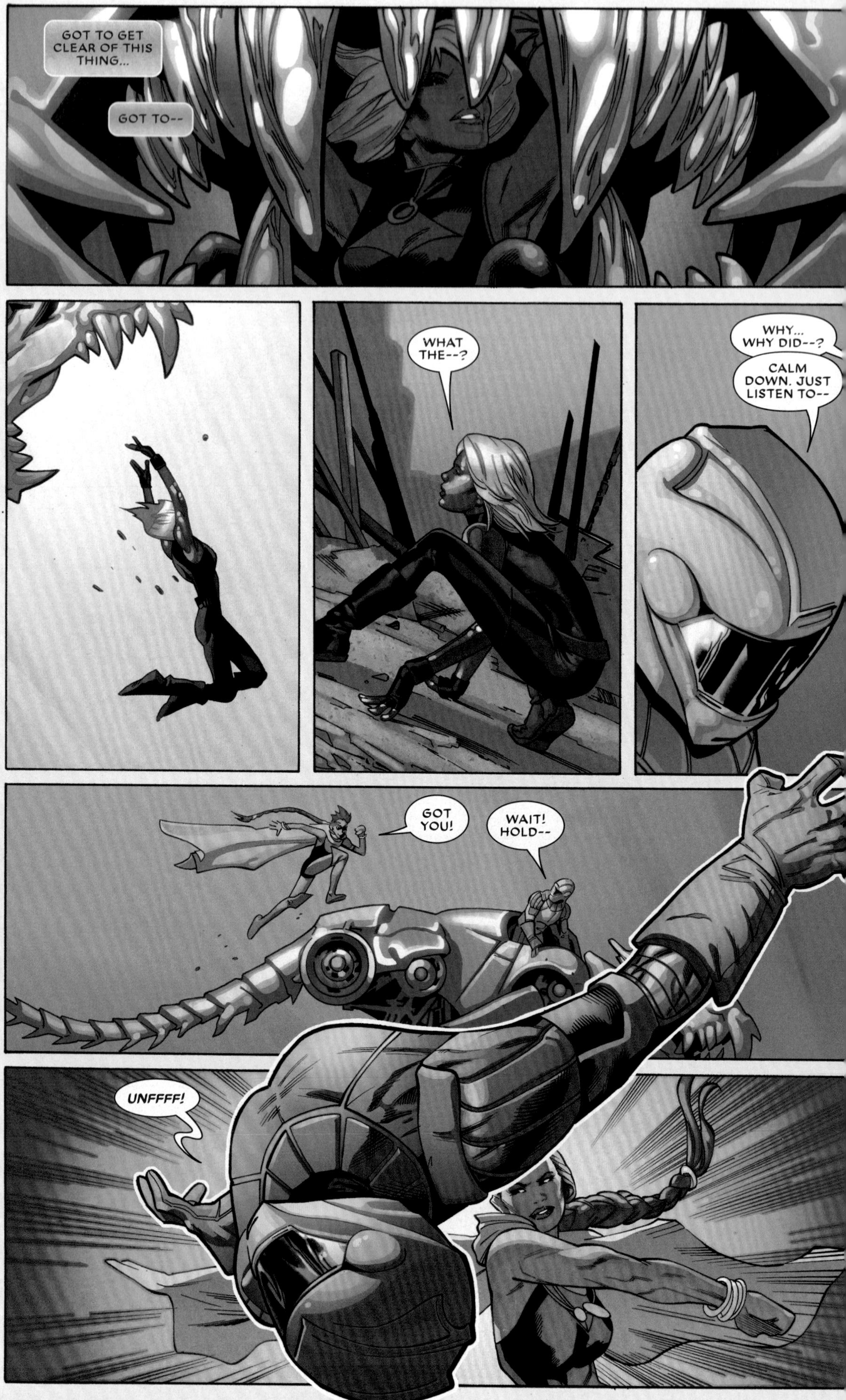
GOT TO GET CLEAR OF THIS THING...
GOT TO--
WHAT THE--?
WHY... WHY DID--?
CALM DOWN. JUST LISTEN TO--
GOT YOU!
WAIT! HOLD--
UNFFFF!

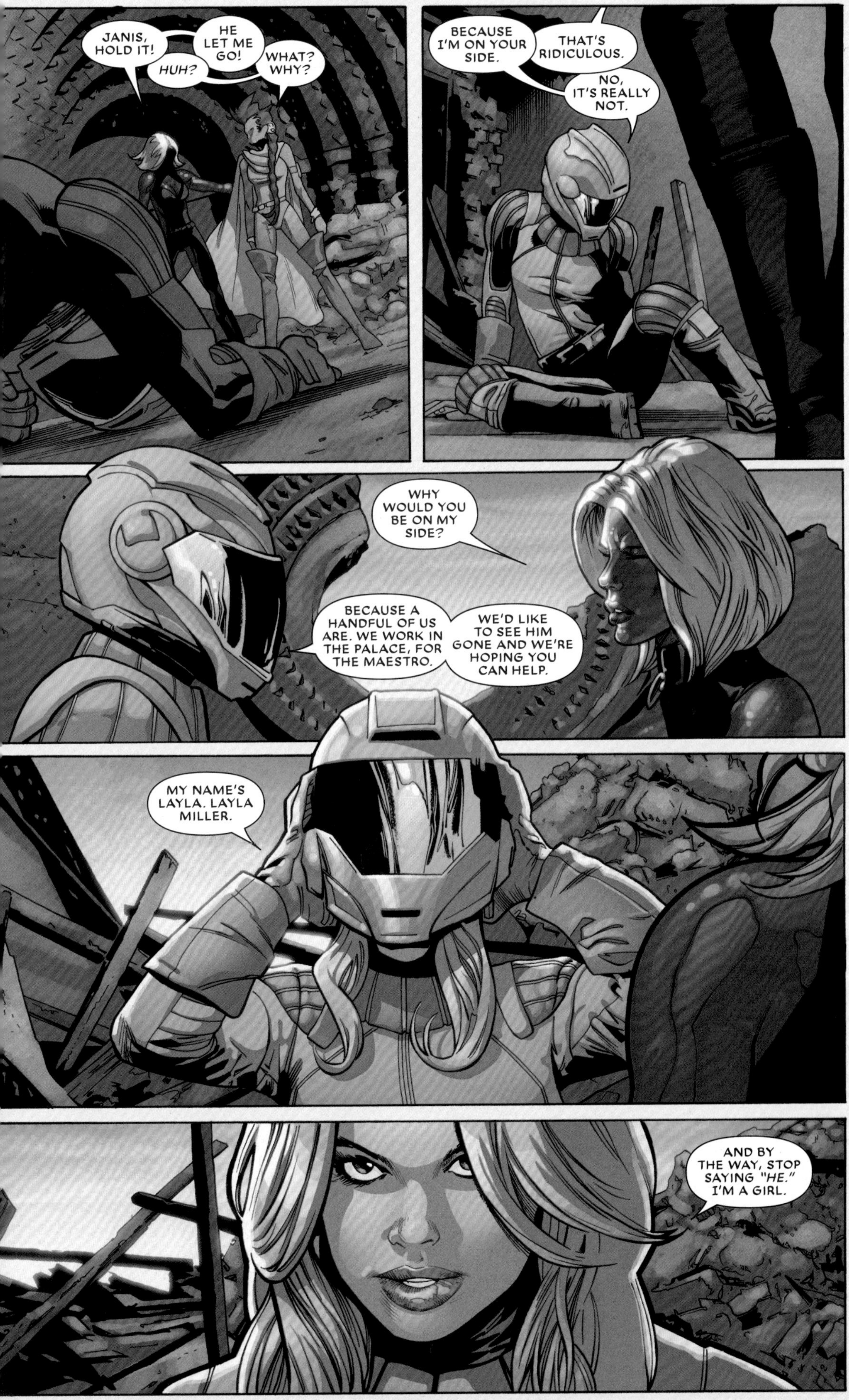
JANIS, HOLD IT!
HE LET ME GO!
HUH?
WHAT? WHY?
BECAUSE I'M ON YOUR SIDE.
THAT'S RIDICULOUS.
NO, IT'S REALLY NOT.
WHY WOULD YOU BE ON MY SIDE?
BECAUSE A HANDFUL OF US ARE. WE WORK IN THE PALACE, FOR THE MAESTRO.
WE'D LIKE TO SEE HIM GONE AND WE'RE HOPING YOU CAN HELP.
MY NAME'S LAYLA. LAYLA MILLER.
AND BY THE WAY, STOP SAYING *"HE."* I'M A GIRL.

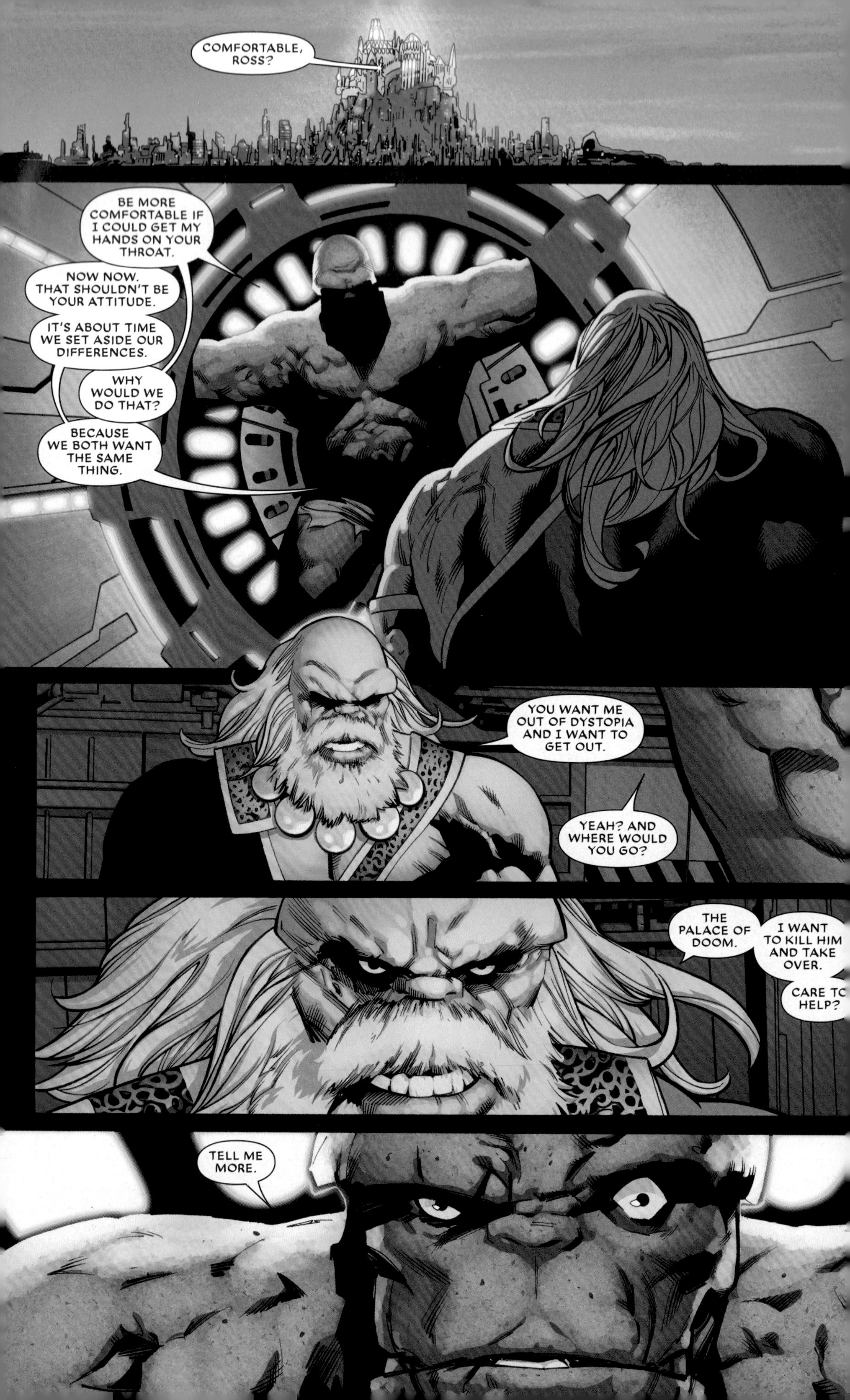
COMFORTABLE, ROSS?
BE MORE COMFORTABLE IF I COULD GET MY HANDS ON YOUR THROAT.
NOW NOW. THAT SHOULDN'T BE YOUR ATTITUDE.
IT'S ABOUT TIME WE SET ASIDE OUR DIFFERENCES.
WHY WOULD WE DO THAT?
BECAUSE WE BOTH WANT THE SAME THING.
YOU WANT ME OUT OF DYSTOPIA AND I WANT TO GET OUT.
YEAH? AND WHERE WOULD YOU GO?
THE PALACE OF DOOM.
I WANT TO KILL HIM AND TAKE OVER.
CARE TO HELP?
TELL ME MORE.

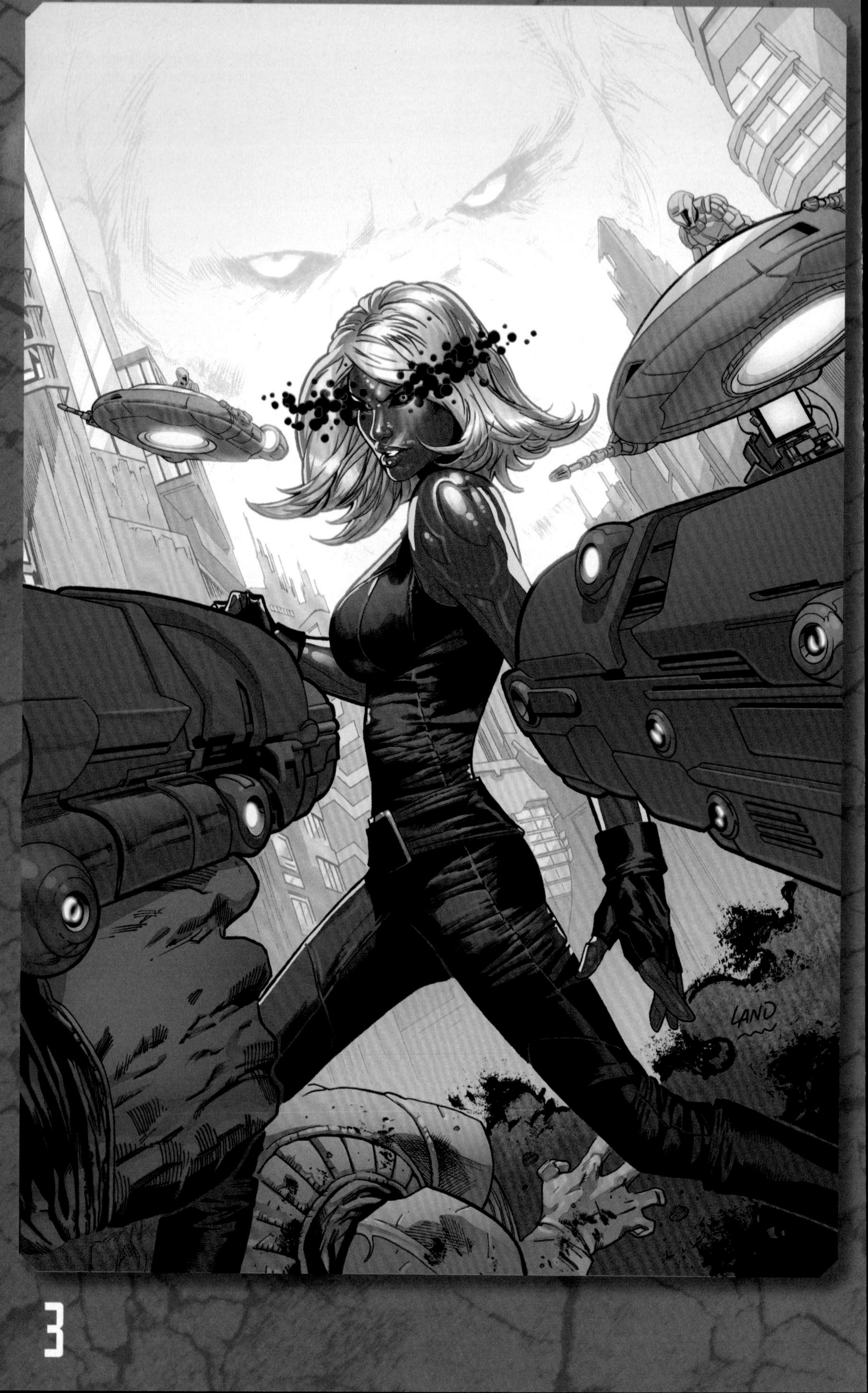
LAND

3

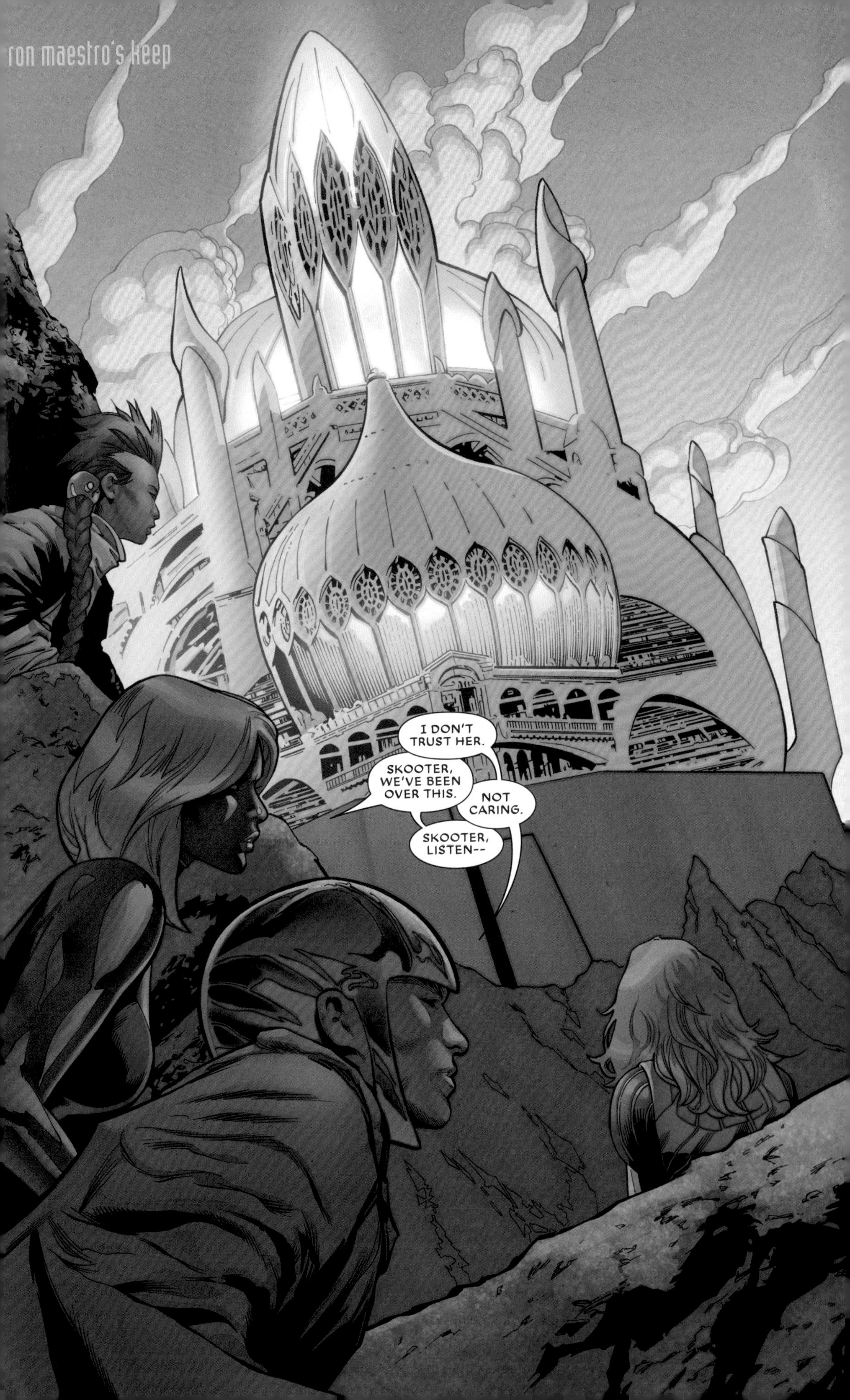
ron maestro's keep
I DON'T TRUST HER.
SKOOTER, WE'VE BEEN OVER THIS.
NOT CARING.
SKOOTER, LISTEN--

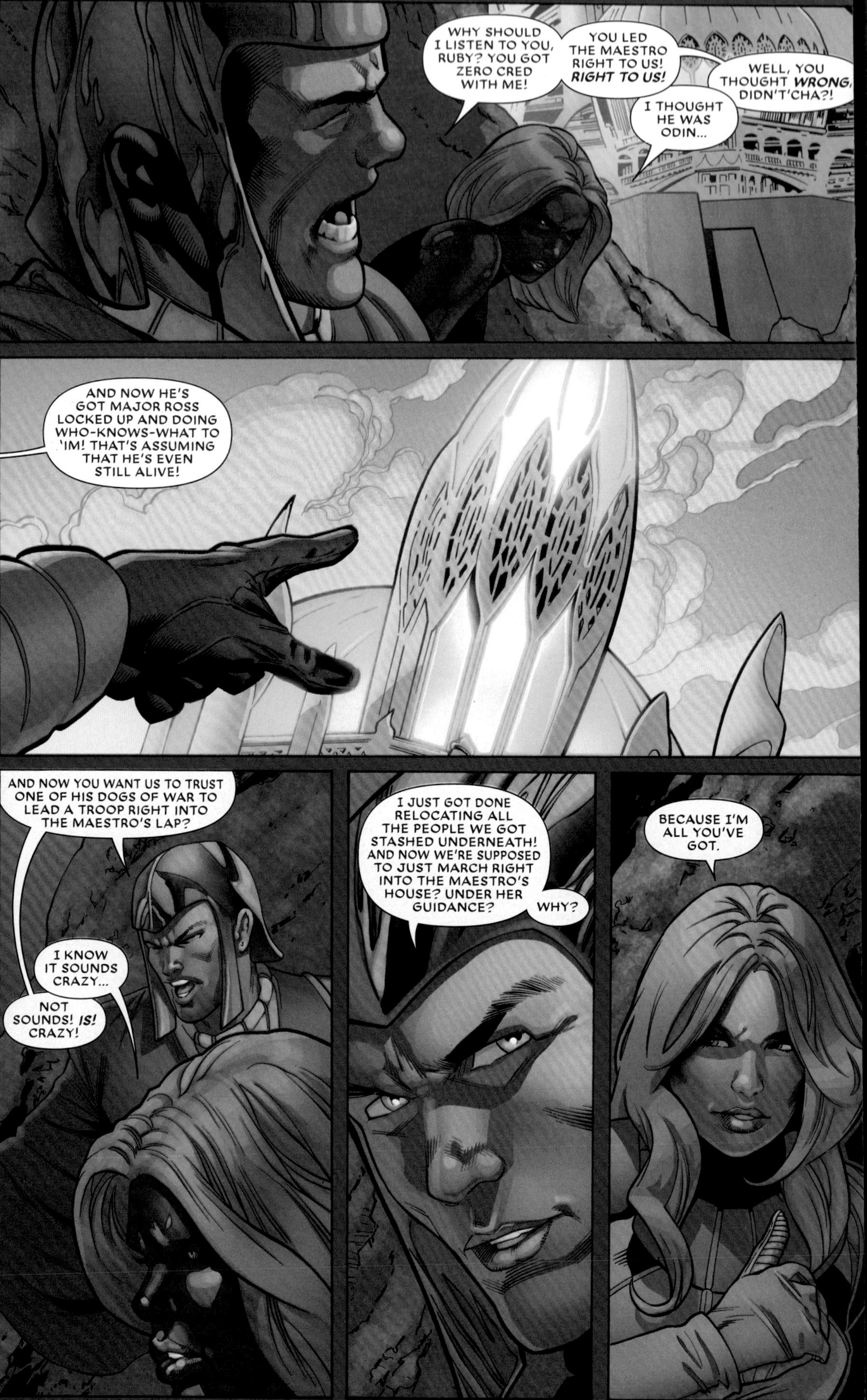
WHY SHOULD I LISTEN TO YOU, RUBY? YOU GOT ZERO CRED WITH ME!
YOU LED THE MAESTRO RIGHT TO US! RIGHT TO US!
I THOUGHT HE WAS ODIN...
WELL, YOU THOUGHT WRONG, DIDN'T'CHA?!
AND NOW HE'S GOT MAJOR ROSS LOCKED UP AND DOING WHO-KNOWS-WHAT TO 'IM! THAT'S ASSUMING THAT HE'S EVEN STILL ALIVE!
AND NOW YOU WANT US TO TRUST ONE OF HIS DOGS OF WAR TO LEAD A TROOP RIGHT INTO THE MAESTRO'S LAP?
I KNOW IT SOUNDS CRAZY...
NOT SOUNDS! IS! CRAZY!
I JUST GOT DONE RELOCATING ALL THE PEOPLE WE GOT STASHED UNDERNEATH! AND NOW WE'RE SUPPOSED TO JUST MARCH RIGHT INTO THE MAESTRO'S HOUSE? UNDER HER GUIDANCE?
WHY?
BECAUSE I'M ALL YOU'VE GOT.

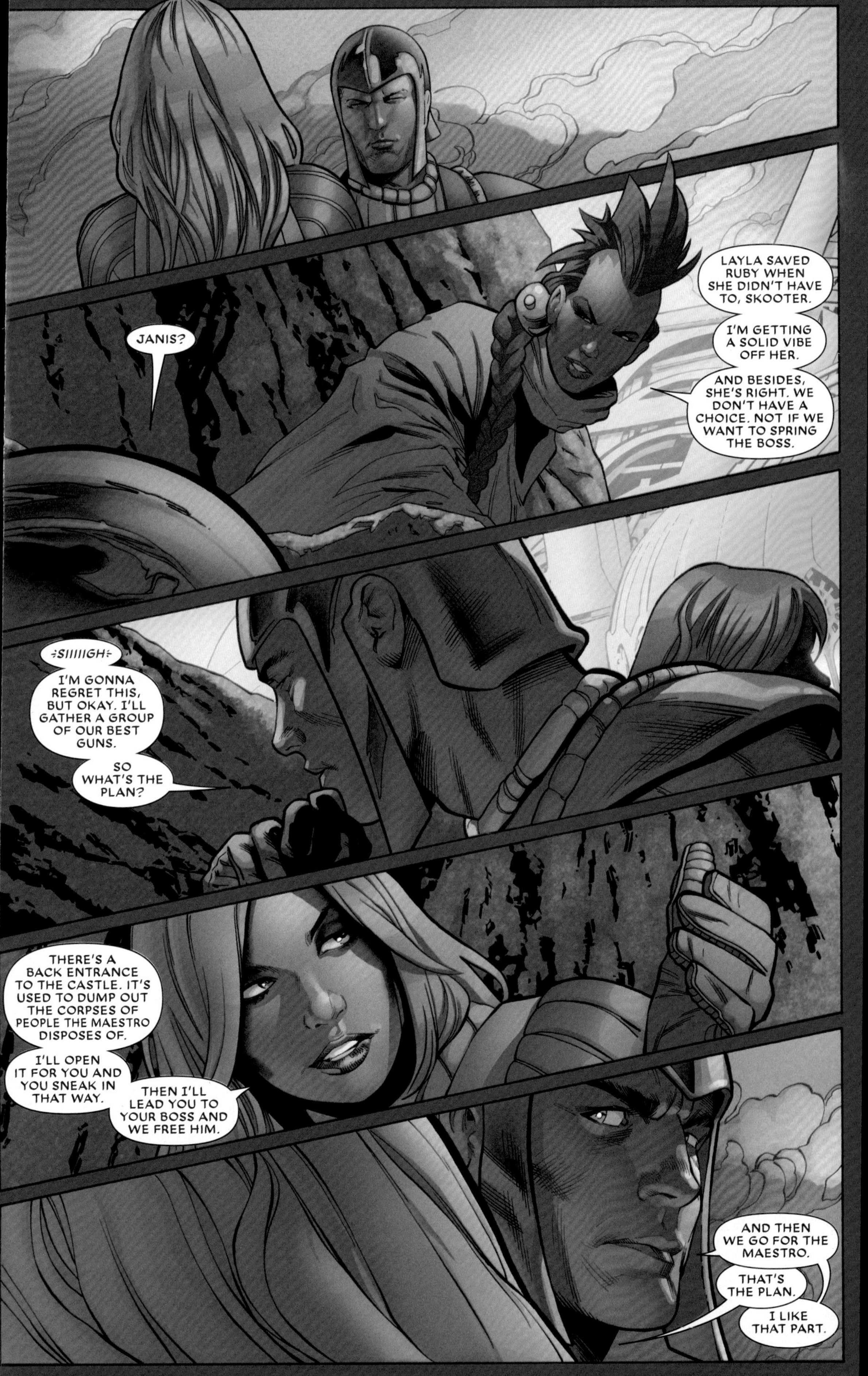

LAYLA SAVED RUBY WHEN SHE DIDN'T HAVE TO, SKOOTER.
JANIS?
I'M GETTING A SOLID VIBE OFF HER.
AND BESIDES, SHE'S RIGHT. WE DON'T HAVE A CHOICE. NOT IF WE WANT TO SPRING THE BOSS.
SIIIIIGH
I'M GONNA REGRET THIS, BUT OKAY. I'LL GATHER A GROUP OF OUR BEST GUNS.
SO WHAT'S THE PLAN?
THERE'S A BACK ENTRANCE TO THE CASTLE. IT'S USED TO DUMP OUT THE CORPSES OF PEOPLE THE MAESTRO DISPOSES OF.
I'LL OPEN IT FOR YOU AND YOU SNEAK IN THAT WAY.
THEN I'LL LEAD YOU TO YOUR BOSS AND WE FREE HIM.
AND THEN WE GO FOR THE MAESTRO.
THAT'S THE PLAN.
I LIKE THAT PART.

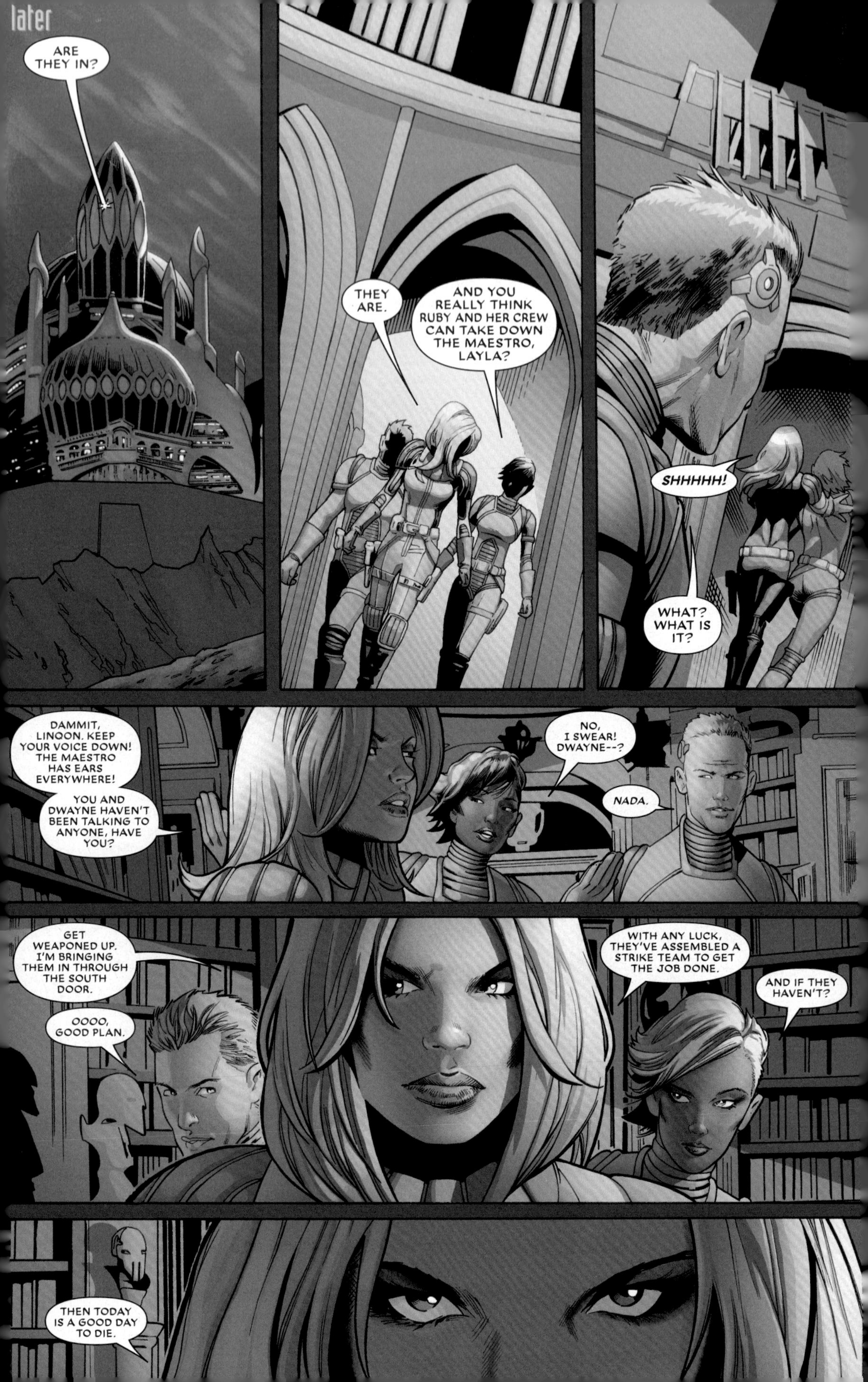
later
ARE THEY IN?
THEY ARE.
AND YOU REALLY THINK RUBY AND HER CREW CAN TAKE DOWN THE MAESTRO, LAYLA?
SHHHHH!
WHAT? WHAT IS IT?
DAMMIT, LINOON. KEEP YOUR VOICE DOWN! THE MAESTRO HAS EARS EVERYWHERE!
YOU AND DWAYNE HAVEN'T BEEN TALKING TO ANYONE, HAVE YOU?
NO, I SWEAR! DWAYNE--?
NADA.
GET WEAPONED UP. I'M BRINGING THEM IN THROUGH THE SOUTH DOOR.
OOOO, GOOD PLAN.
WITH ANY LUCK, THEY'VE ASSEMBLED A STRIKE TEAM TO GET THE JOB DONE.
AND IF THEY HAVEN'T?
THEN TODAY IS A GOOD DAY TO DIE.

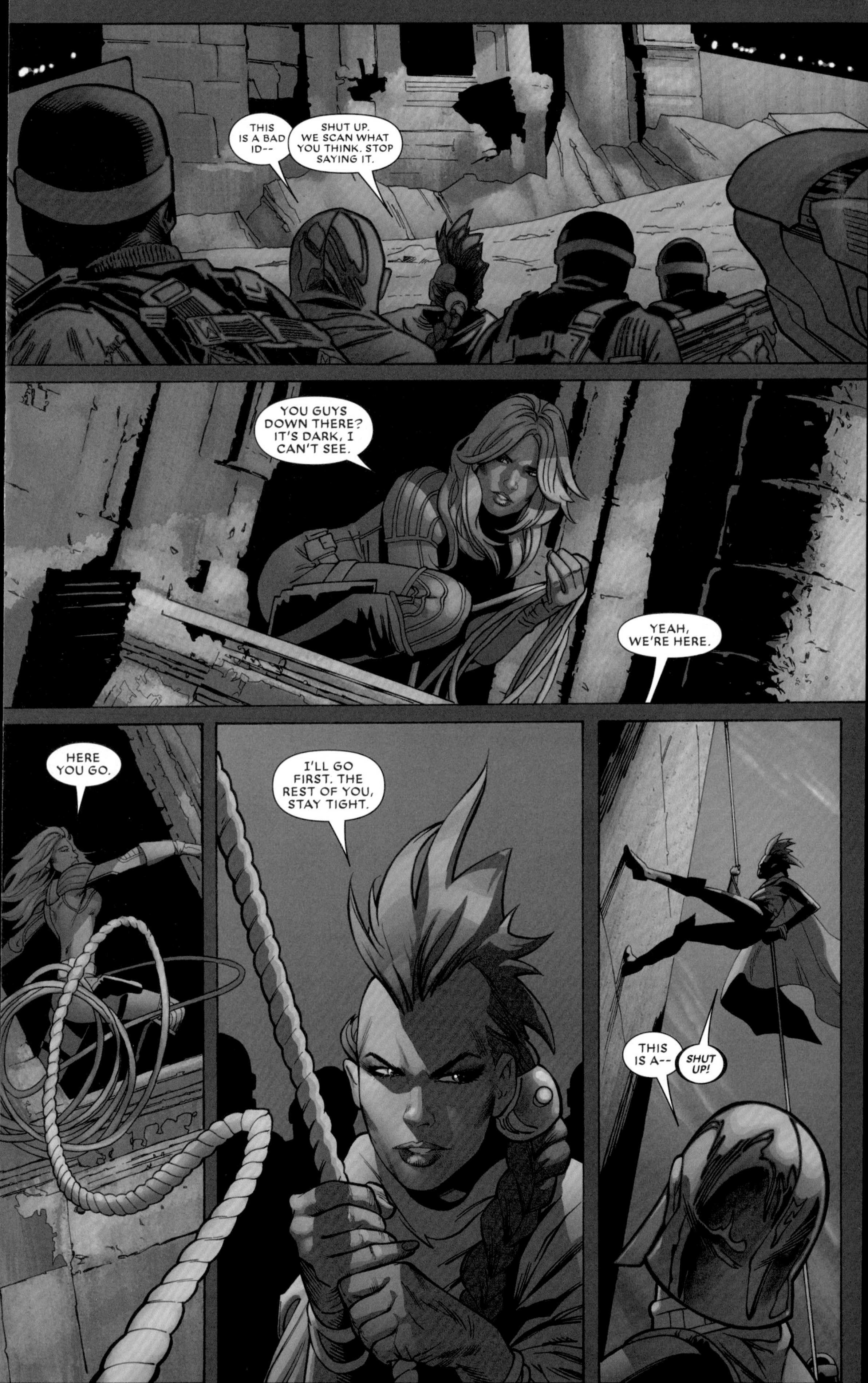
THIS IS A BAD ID--
SHUT UP. WE SCAN WHAT YOU THINK. STOP SAYING IT.
YOU GUYS DOWN THERE? IT'S DARK, I CAN'T SEE.
YEAH, WE'RE HERE.
HERE YOU GO.
I'LL GO FIRST. THE REST OF YOU, STAY TIGHT.
THIS IS A--
SHUT UP!

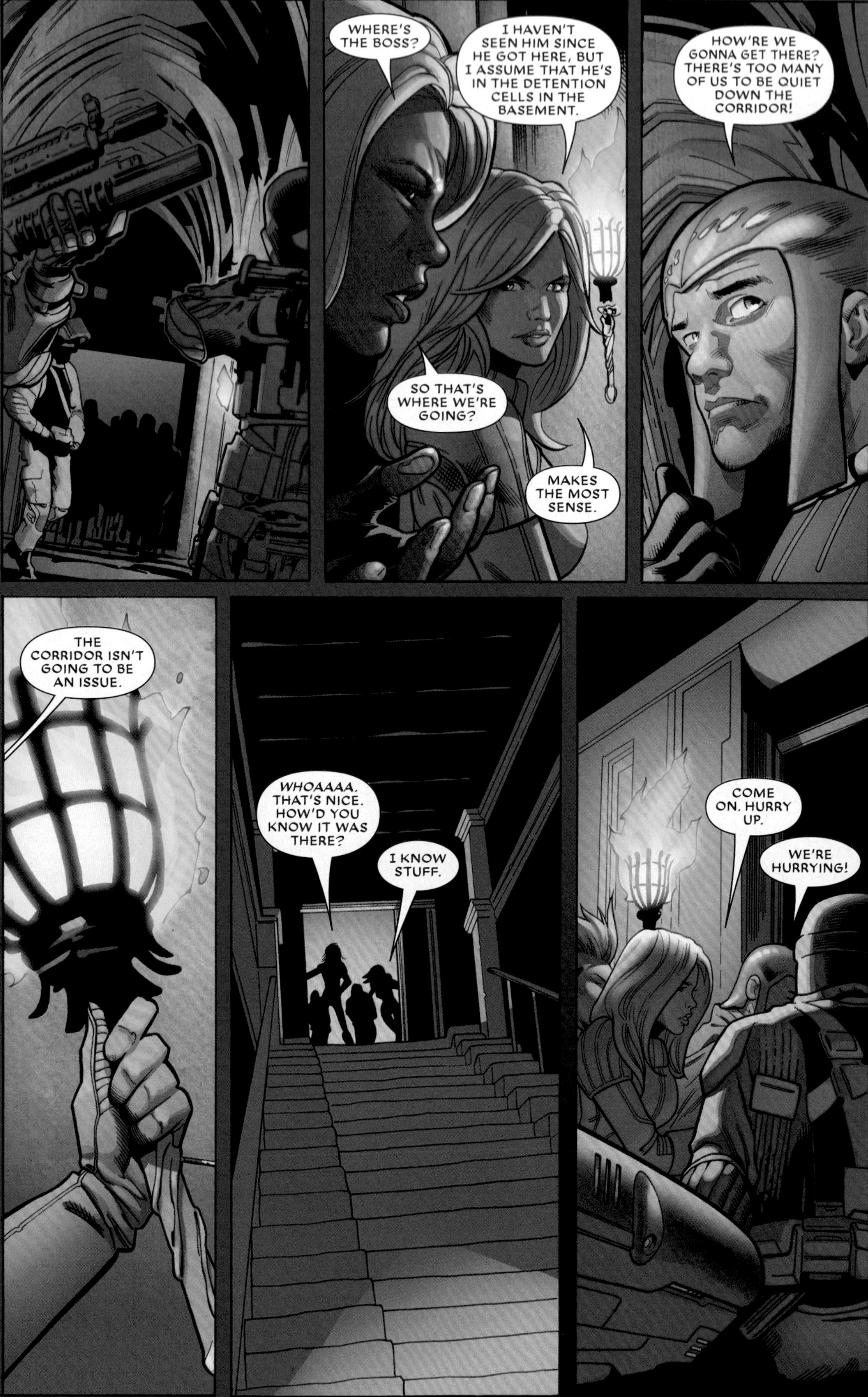
WHERE'S THE BOSS?
I HAVEN'T SEEN HIM SINCE HE GOT HERE, BUT I ASSUME THAT HE'S IN THE DETENTION CELLS IN THE BASEMENT.
SO THAT'S WHERE WE'RE GOING?
MAKES THE MOST SENSE.
HOW'RE WE GONNA GET THERE? THERE'S TOO MANY OF US TO BE QUIET DOWN THE CORRIDOR!
THE CORRIDOR ISN'T GOING TO BE AN ISSUE.
WHOAAAA. THAT'S NICE. HOW'D YOU KNOW IT WAS THERE?
I KNOW STUFF.
COME ON. HURRY UP.
WE'RE HURRYING!

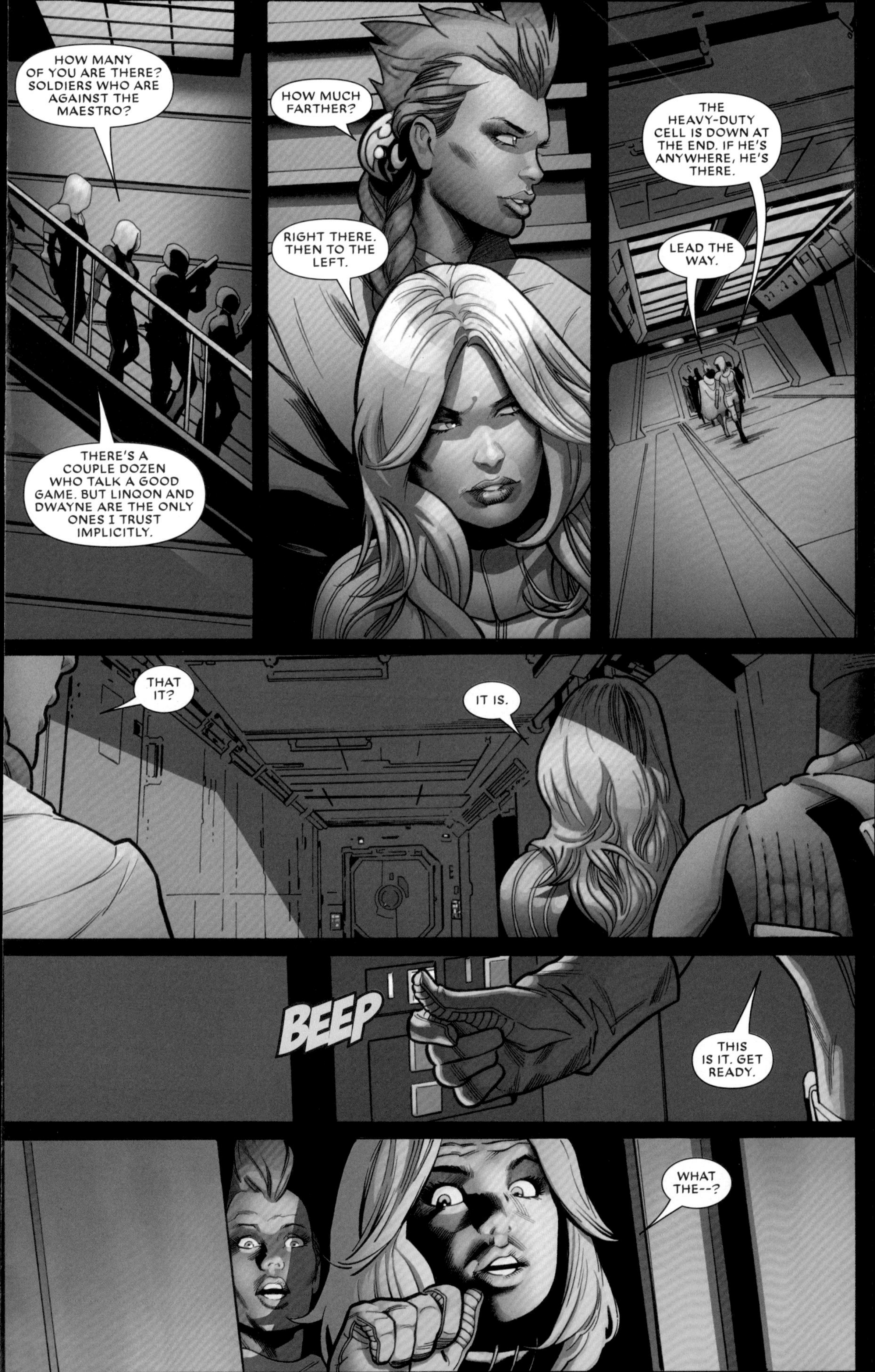
HOW MANY OF YOU ARE THERE? SOLDIERS WHO ARE AGAINST THE MAESTRO?
THERE'S A COUPLE DOZEN WHO TALK A GOOD GAME. BUT LINQON AND DWAYNE ARE THE ONLY ONES I TRUST IMPLICITLY.
HOW MUCH FARTHER?
RIGHT THERE. THEN TO THE LEFT.
THE HEAVY-DUTY CELL IS DOWN AT THE END. IF HE'S ANYWHERE, HE'S THERE.
LEAD THE WAY.
THAT IT?
IT IS.
BEEP
THIS IS IT. GET READY.
WHAT THE--?

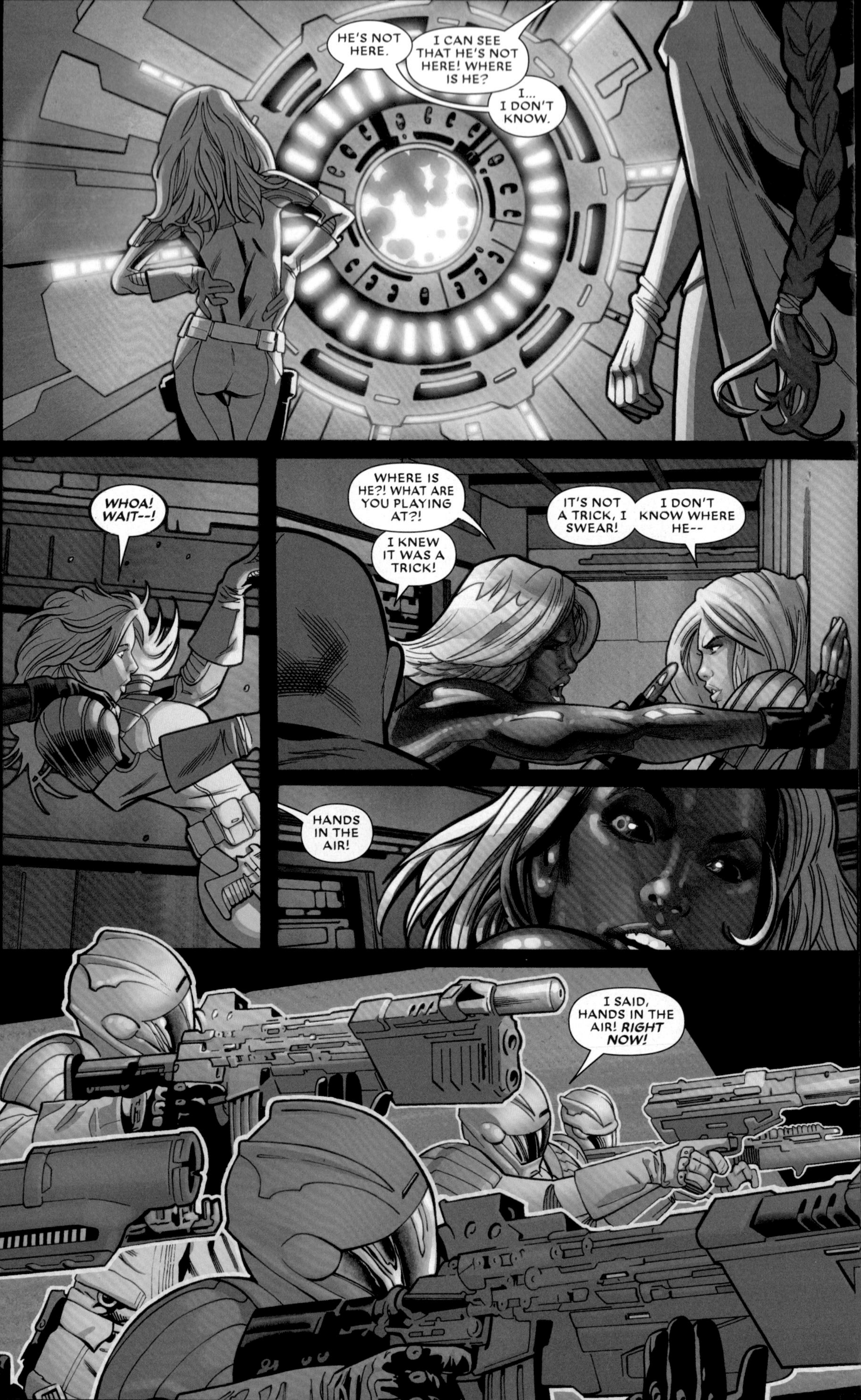
HE'S NOT HERE.
I CAN SEE THAT HE'S NOT HERE! WHERE IS HE?
I... I DON'T KNOW.
WHOA! WAIT--!
WHERE IS HE?! WHAT ARE YOU PLAYING AT?!
I KNEW IT WAS A TRICK!
IT'S NOT A TRICK, I SWEAR!
I DON'T KNOW WHERE HE--
HANDS IN THE AIR!
I SAID, HANDS IN THE AIR! *RIGHT NOW!*

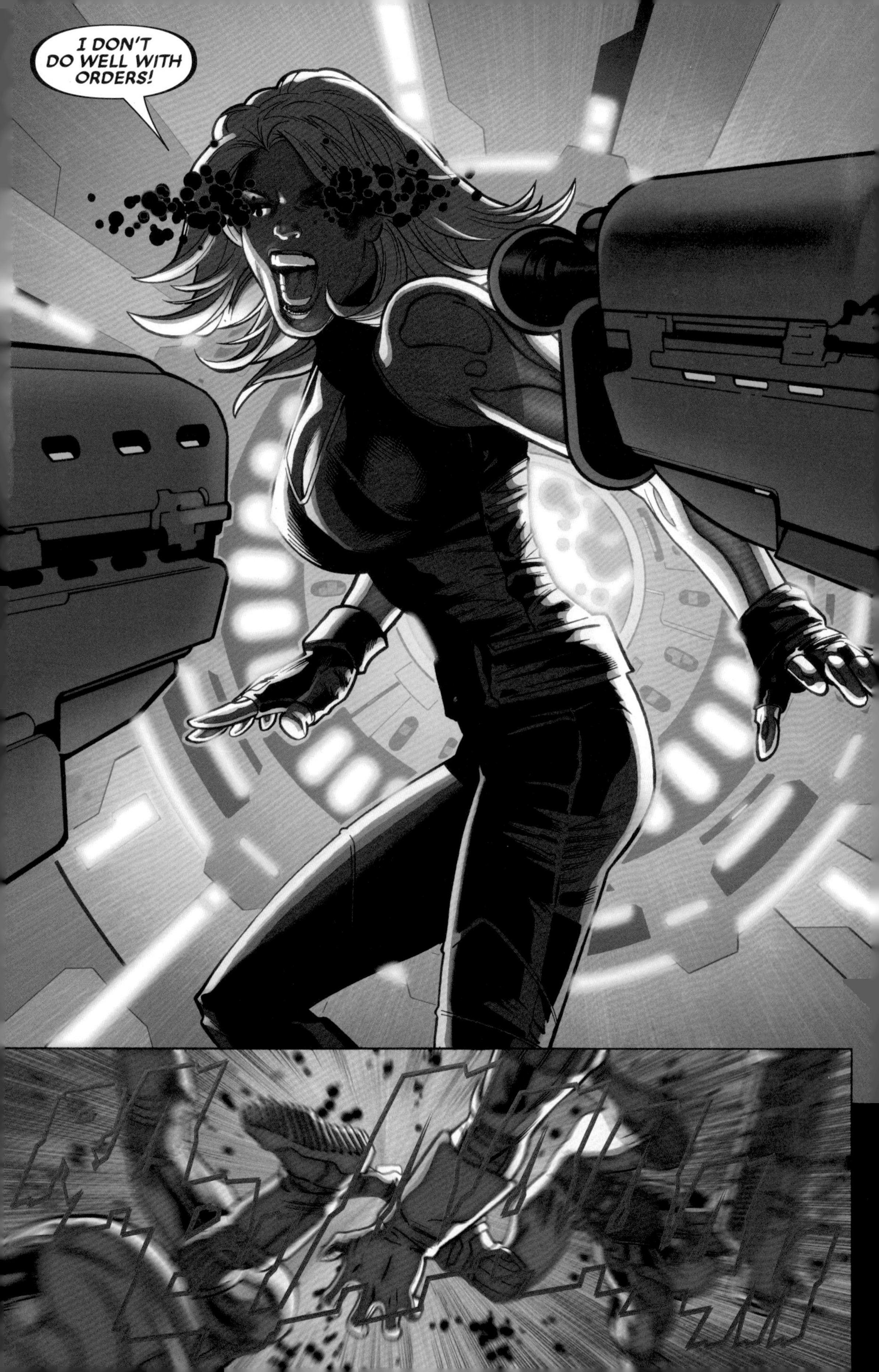
I DON'T DO WELL WITH ORDERS!

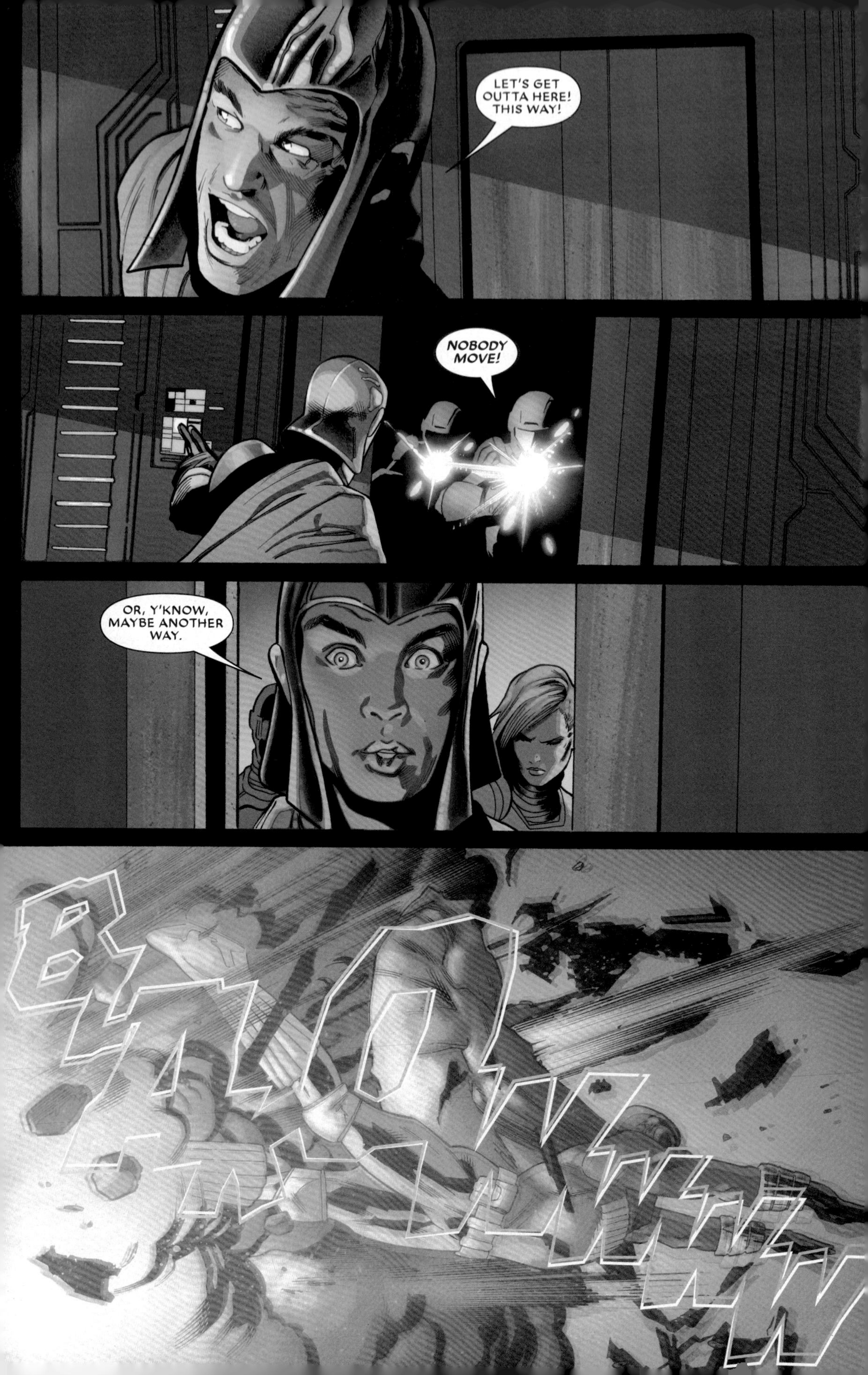
LET'S GET OUTTA HERE! THIS WAY!
NOBODY MOVE!
OR, Y'KNOW, MAYBE ANOTHER WAY.

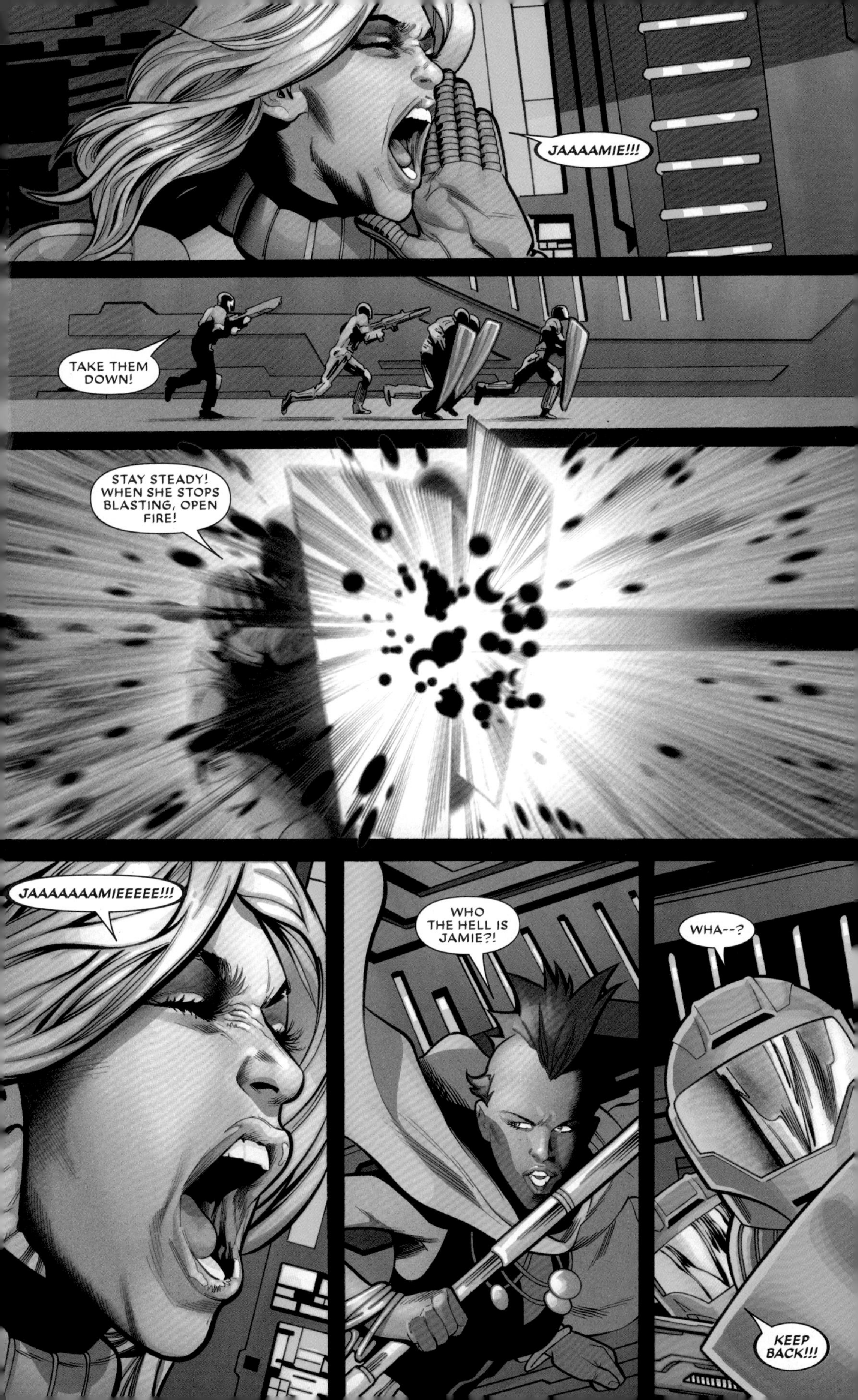
JAAAAMIE!!!
TAKE THEM DOWN!
STAY STEADY! WHEN SHE STOPS BLASTING, OPEN FIRE!
JAAAAAAAMIEEEEE!!!
WHO THE HELL IS JAMIE?!
WHA--?
KEEP BACK!!!

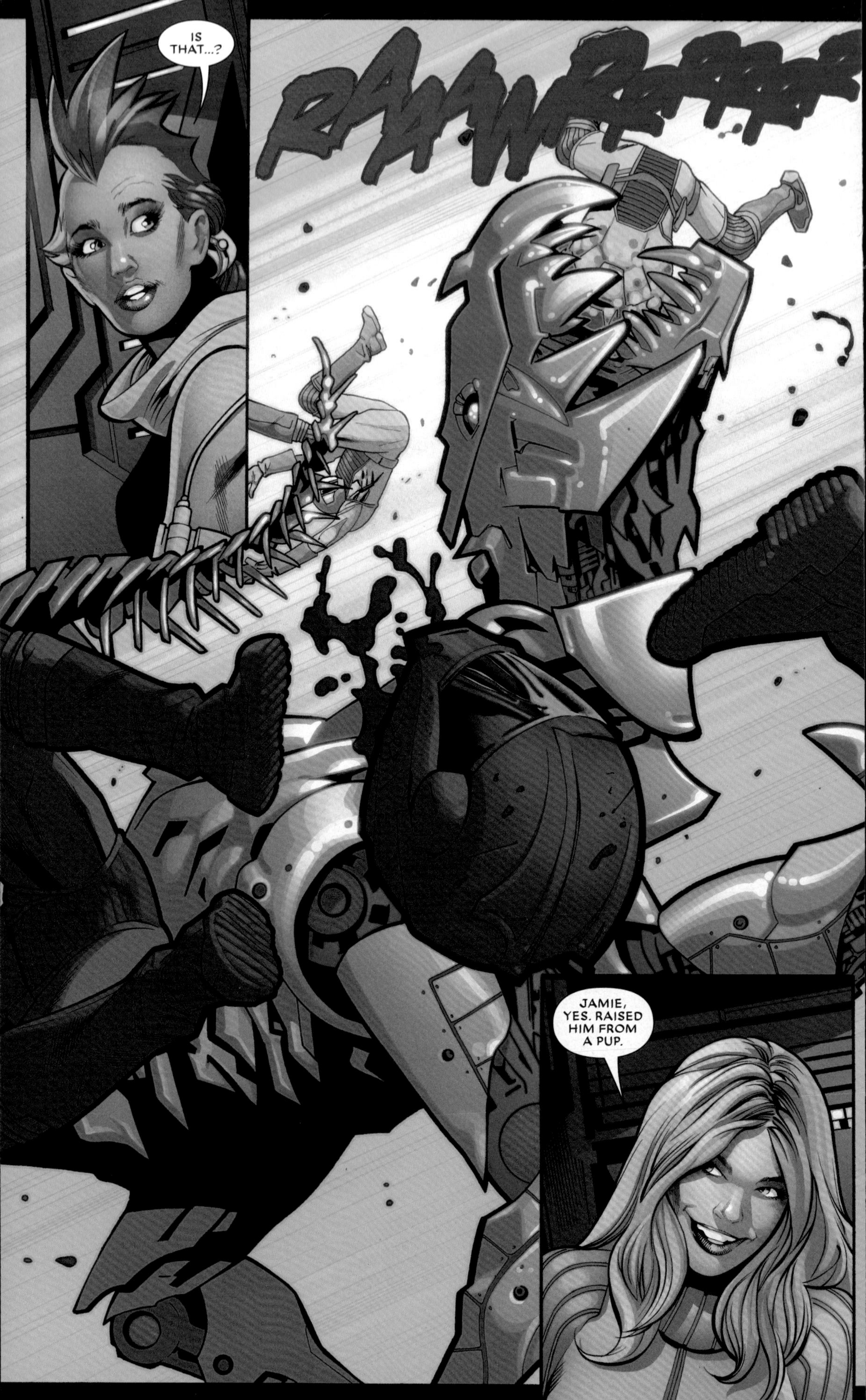
IS THAT...?
JAMIE, YES. RAISED HIM FROM A PUP.

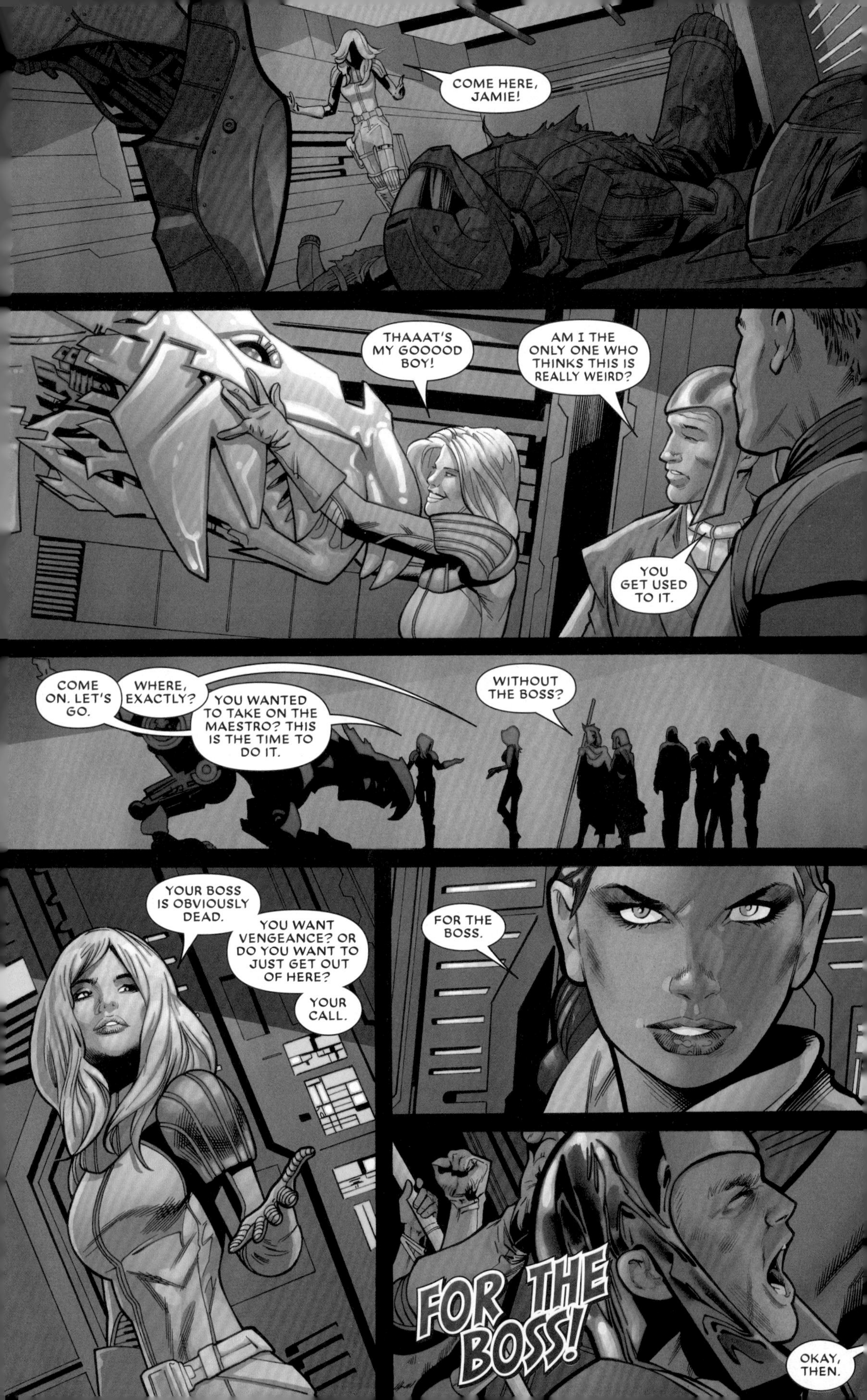
COME HERE, JAMIE!
THAAAT'S MY GOOOOD BOY!
AM I THE ONLY ONE WHO THINKS THIS IS REALLY WEIRD?
YOU GET USED TO IT.
COME ON. LET'S GO.
WHERE, EXACTLY?
YOU WANTED TO TAKE ON THE MAESTRO? THIS IS THE TIME TO DO IT.
WITHOUT THE BOSS?
YOUR BOSS IS OBVIOUSLY DEAD.
YOU WANT VENGEANCE? OR DO YOU WANT TO JUST GET OUT OF HERE?
YOUR CALL.
FOR THE BOSS.
FOR THE BOSS!
OKAY, THEN.

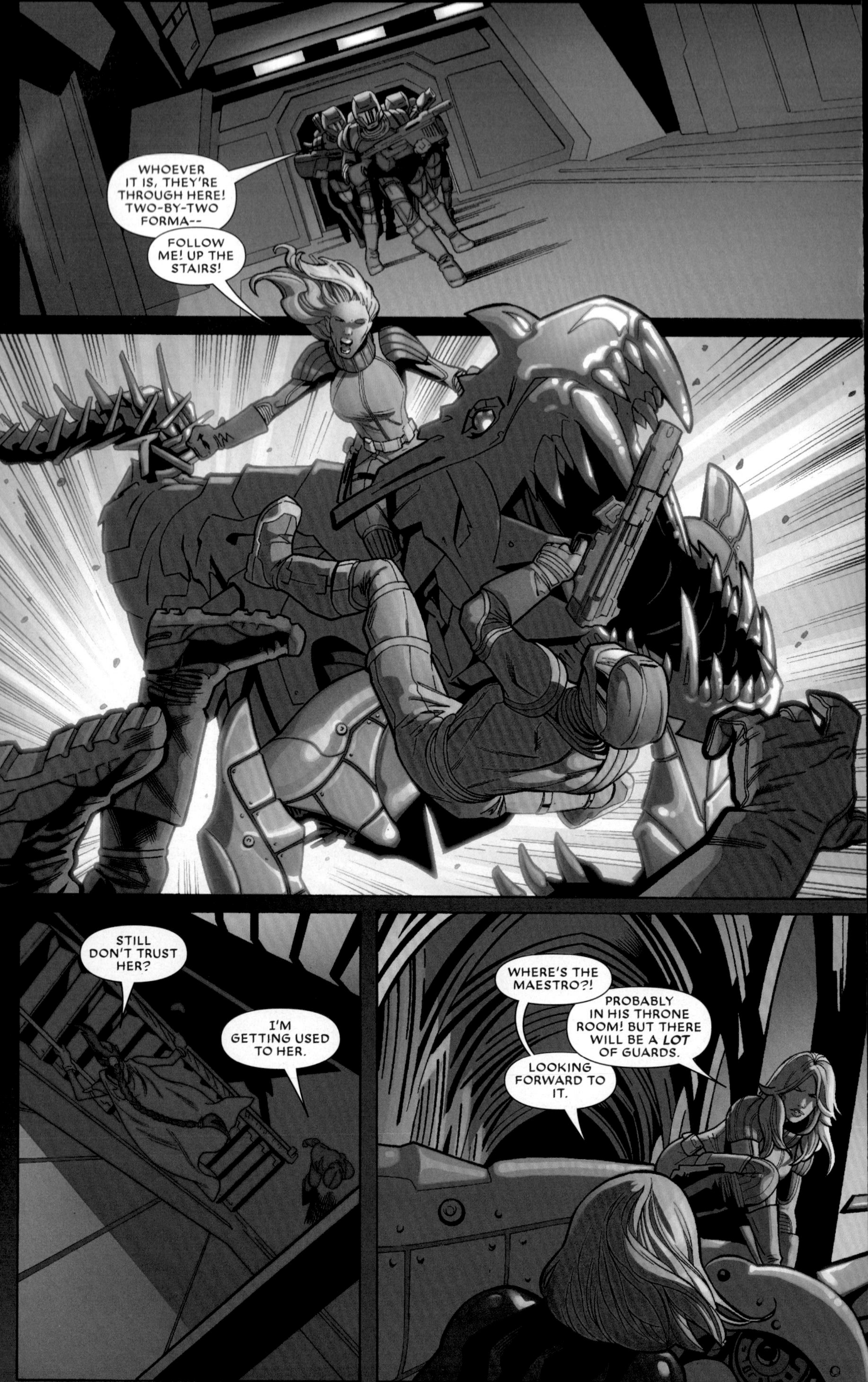
WHOEVER IT IS, THEY'RE THROUGH HERE! TWO-BY-TWO FORMA--
FOLLOW ME! UP THE STAIRS!
STILL DON'T TRUST HER?
I'M GETTING USED TO HER.
WHERE'S THE MAESTRO?!
PROBABLY IN HIS THRONE ROOM! BUT THERE WILL BE A *LOT* OF GUARDS.
LOOKING FORWARD TO IT.

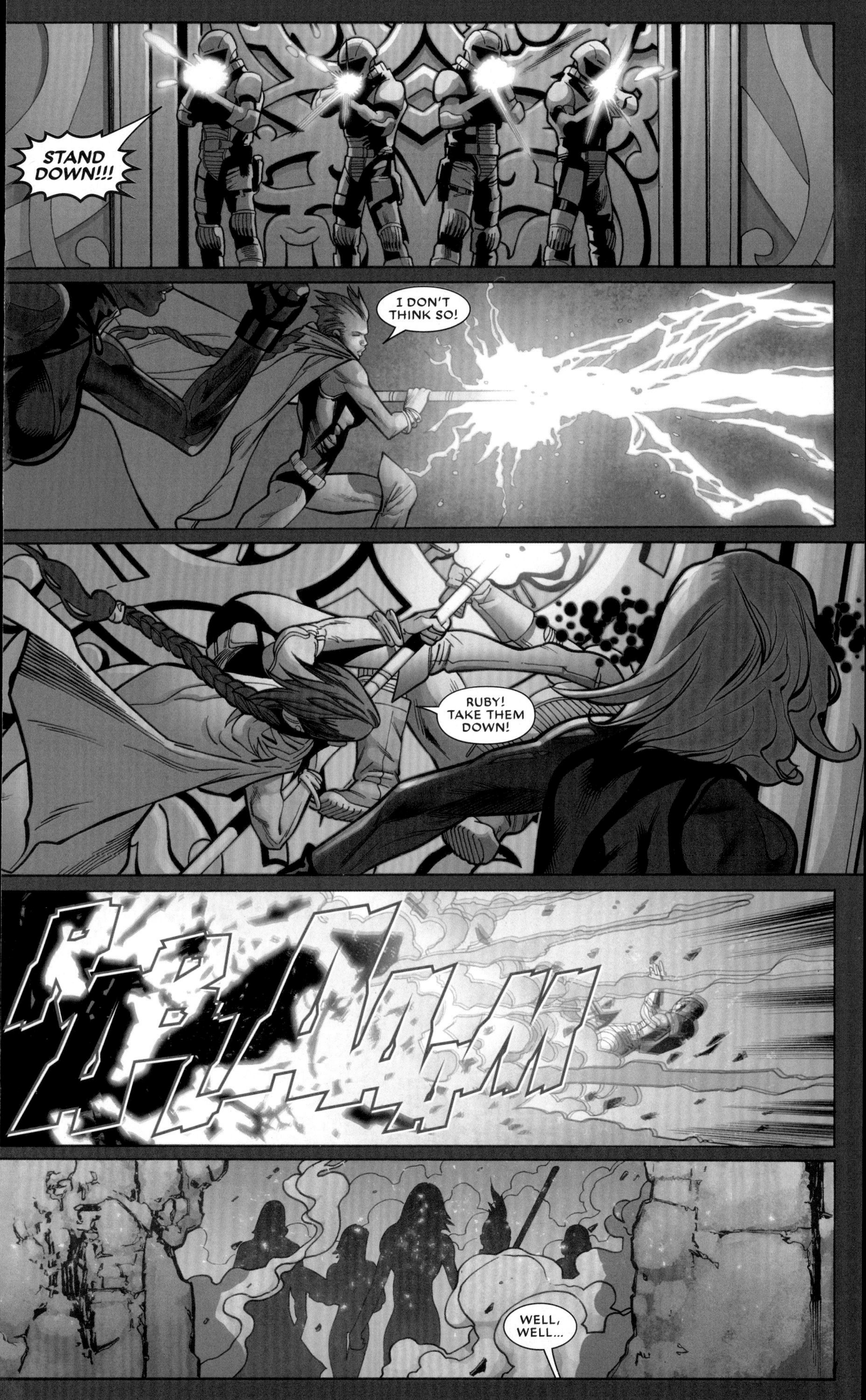
STAND DOWN!!!
I DON'T THINK SO!
RUBY! TAKE THEM DOWN!
WELL, WELL...

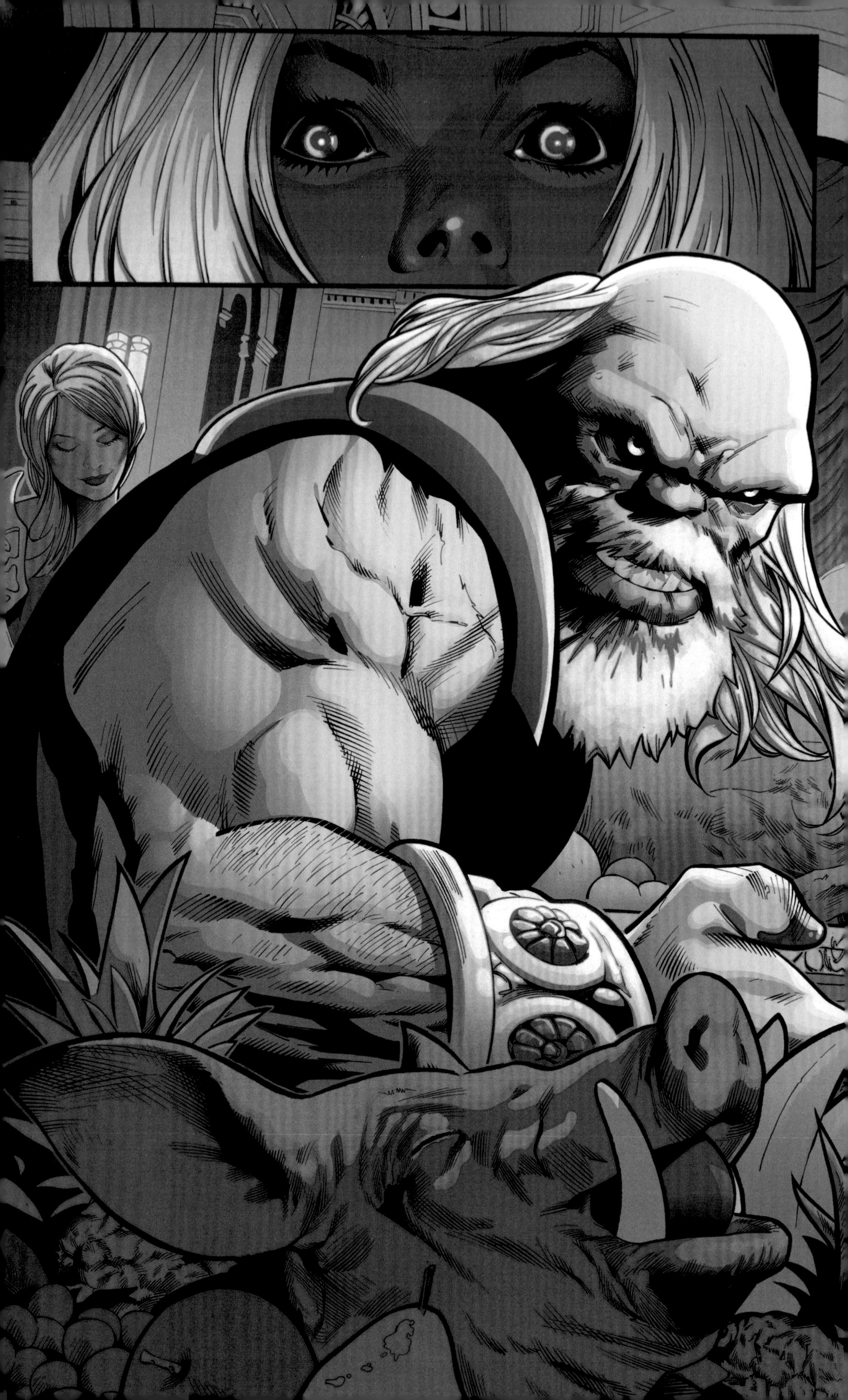

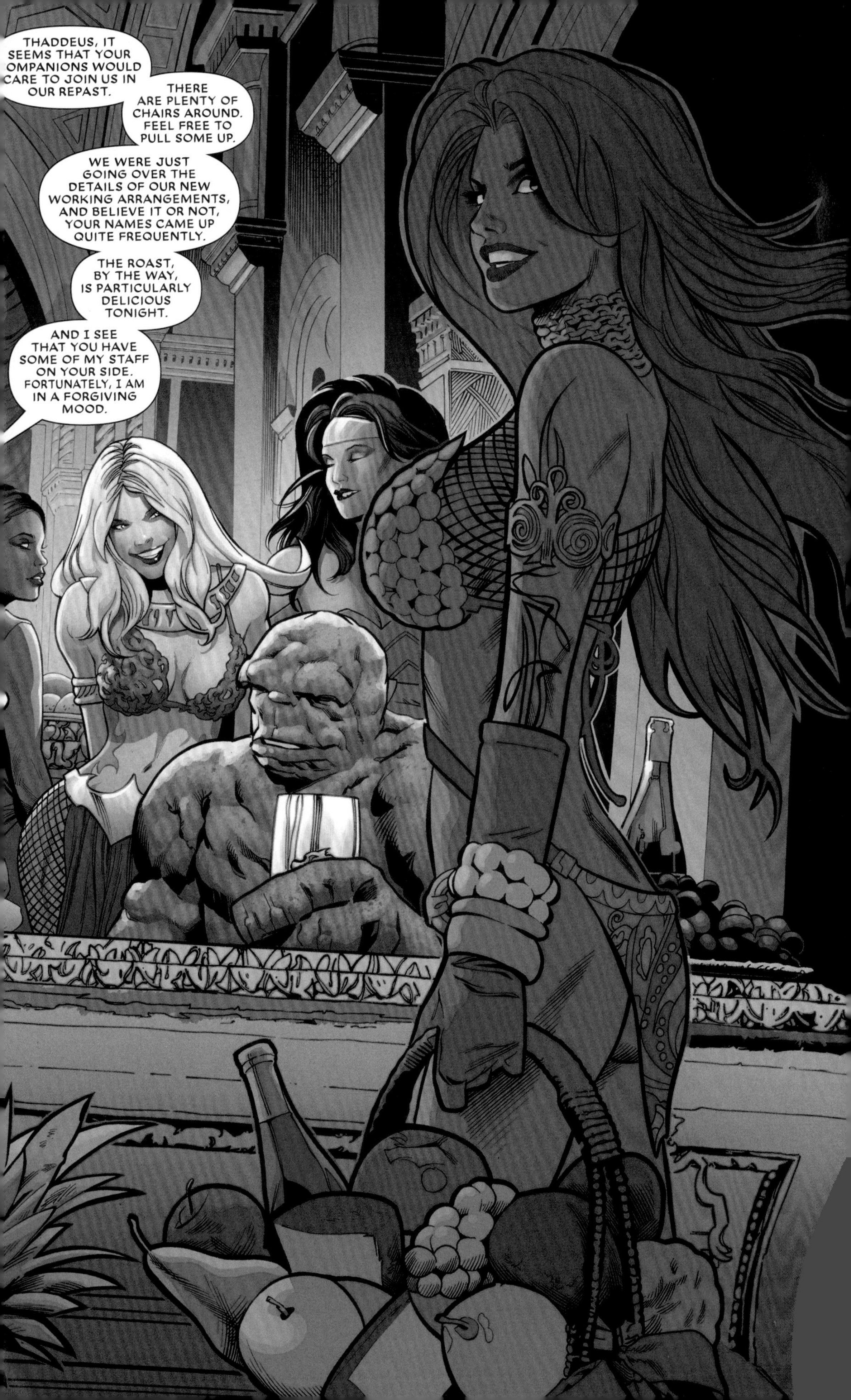
THADDEUS, IT SEEMS THAT YOUR OMPANIONS WOULD CARE TO JOIN US IN OUR REPAST.
THERE ARE PLENTY OF CHAIRS AROUND. FEEL FREE TO PULL SOME UP.
WE WERE JUST GOING OVER THE DETAILS OF OUR NEW WORKING ARRANGEMENTS, AND BELIEVE IT OR NOT, YOUR NAMES CAME UP QUITE FREQUENTLY.
THE ROAST, BY THE WAY, IS PARTICULARLY DELICIOUS TONIGHT.
AND I SEE THAT YOU HAVE SOME OF MY STAFF ON YOUR SIDE. FORTUNATELY, I AM IN A FORGIVING MOOD.

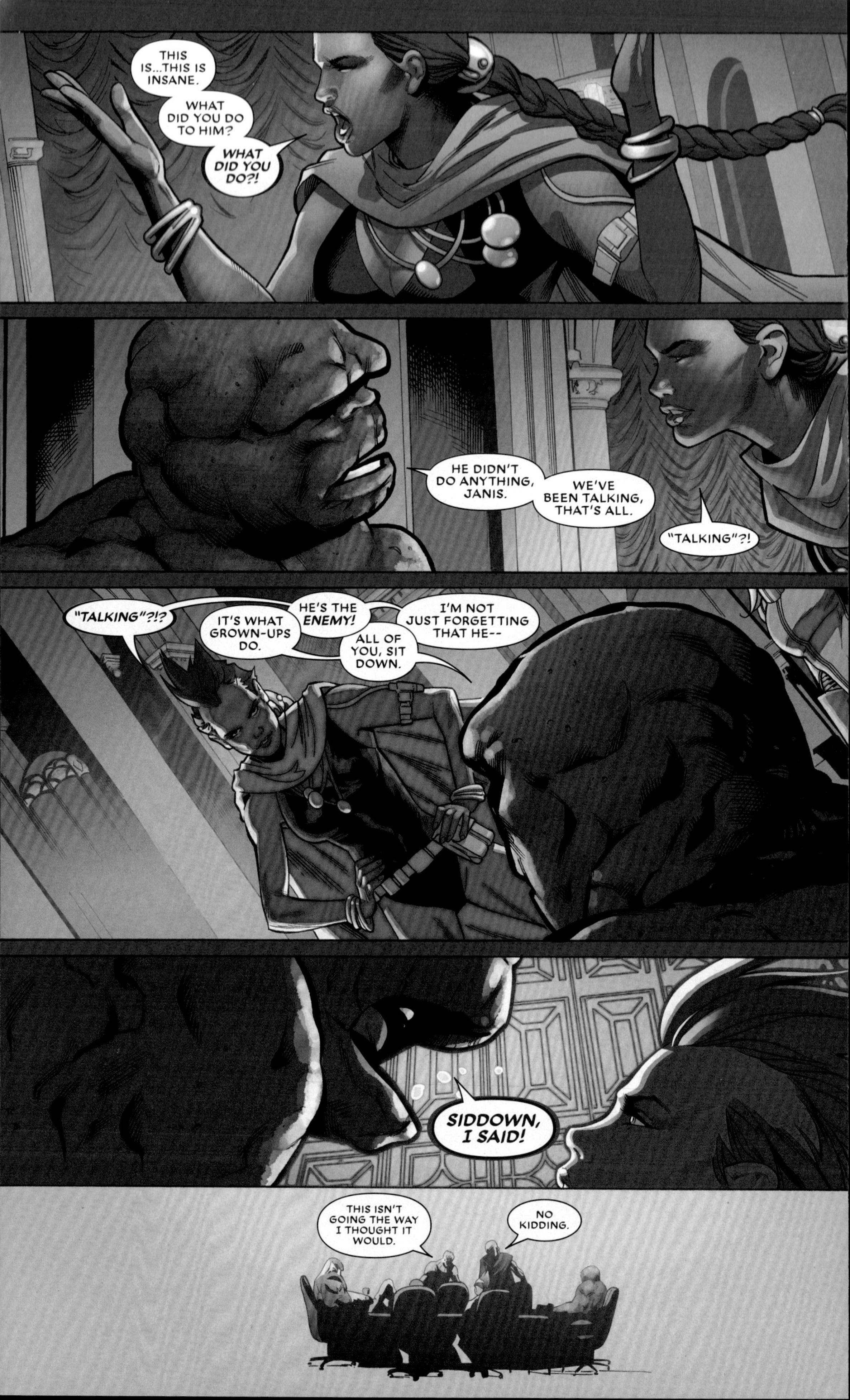
THIS IS...THIS IS INSANE.
WHAT DID YOU DO TO HIM?
WHAT DID YOU DO?!
HE DIDN'T DO ANYTHING, JANIS.
WE'VE BEEN TALKING, THAT'S ALL.
"TALKING"?!
"TALKING"?!?
IT'S WHAT GROWN-UPS DO.
HE'S THE ENEMY!
I'M NOT JUST FORGETTING THAT HE--
ALL OF YOU, SIT DOWN.
SIDDOWN, I SAID!
THIS ISN'T GOING THE WAY I THOUGHT IT WOULD.
NO KIDDING.

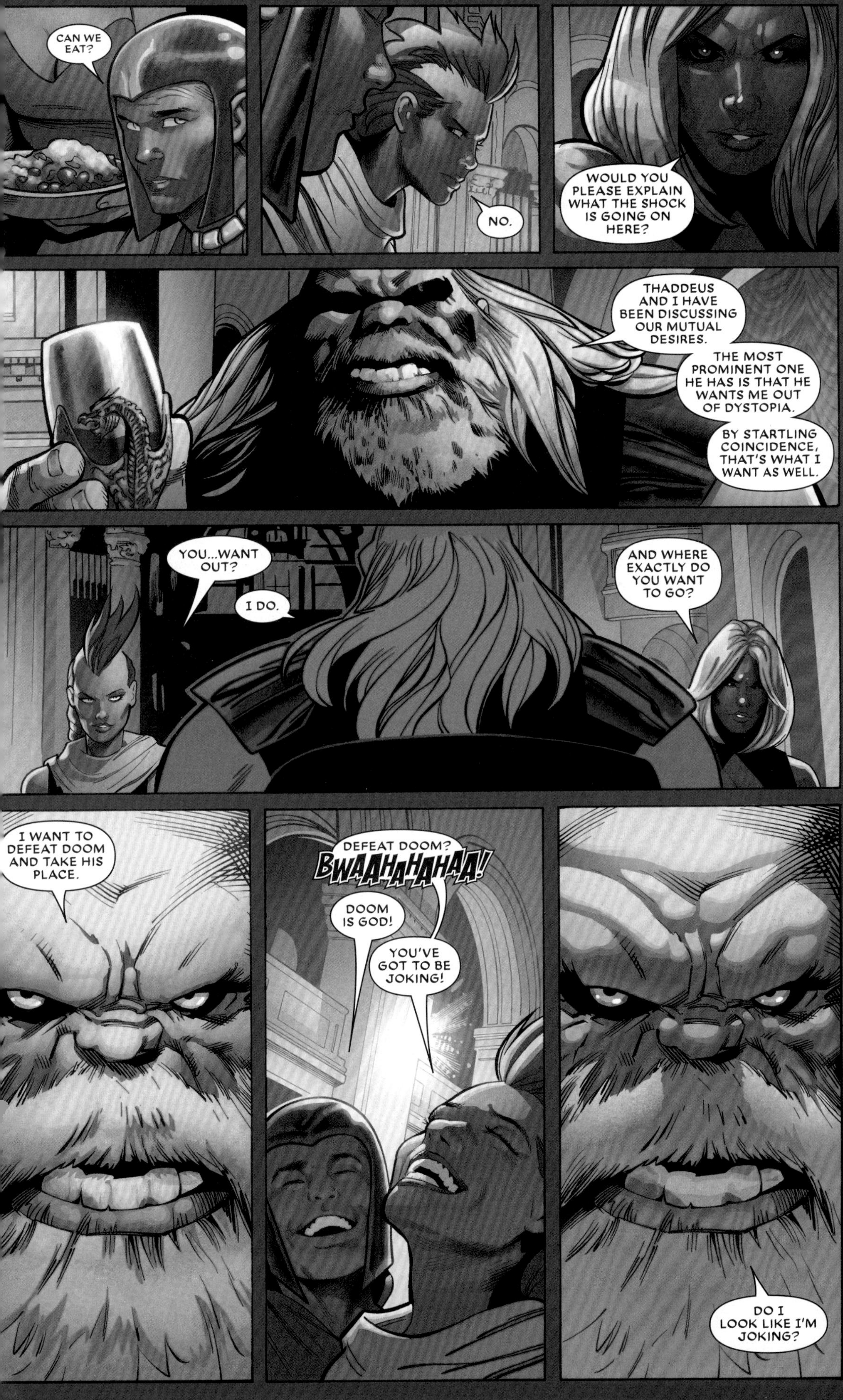
CAN WE EAT?
NO.
WOULD YOU PLEASE EXPLAIN WHAT THE SHOCK IS GOING ON HERE?
THADDEUS AND I HAVE BEEN DISCUSSING OUR MUTUAL DESIRES.
THE MOST PROMINENT ONE HE HAS IS THAT HE WANTS ME OUT OF DYSTOPIA.
BY STARTLING COINCIDENCE, THAT'S WHAT I WANT AS WELL.
YOU...WANT OUT?
I DO.
AND WHERE EXACTLY DO YOU WANT TO GO?
I WANT TO DEFEAT DOOM AND TAKE HIS PLACE.
DEFEAT DOOM?
BWAAHAHAHAA!
DOOM IS GOD!
YOU'VE GOT TO BE JOKING!
DO I LOOK LIKE I'M JOKING?

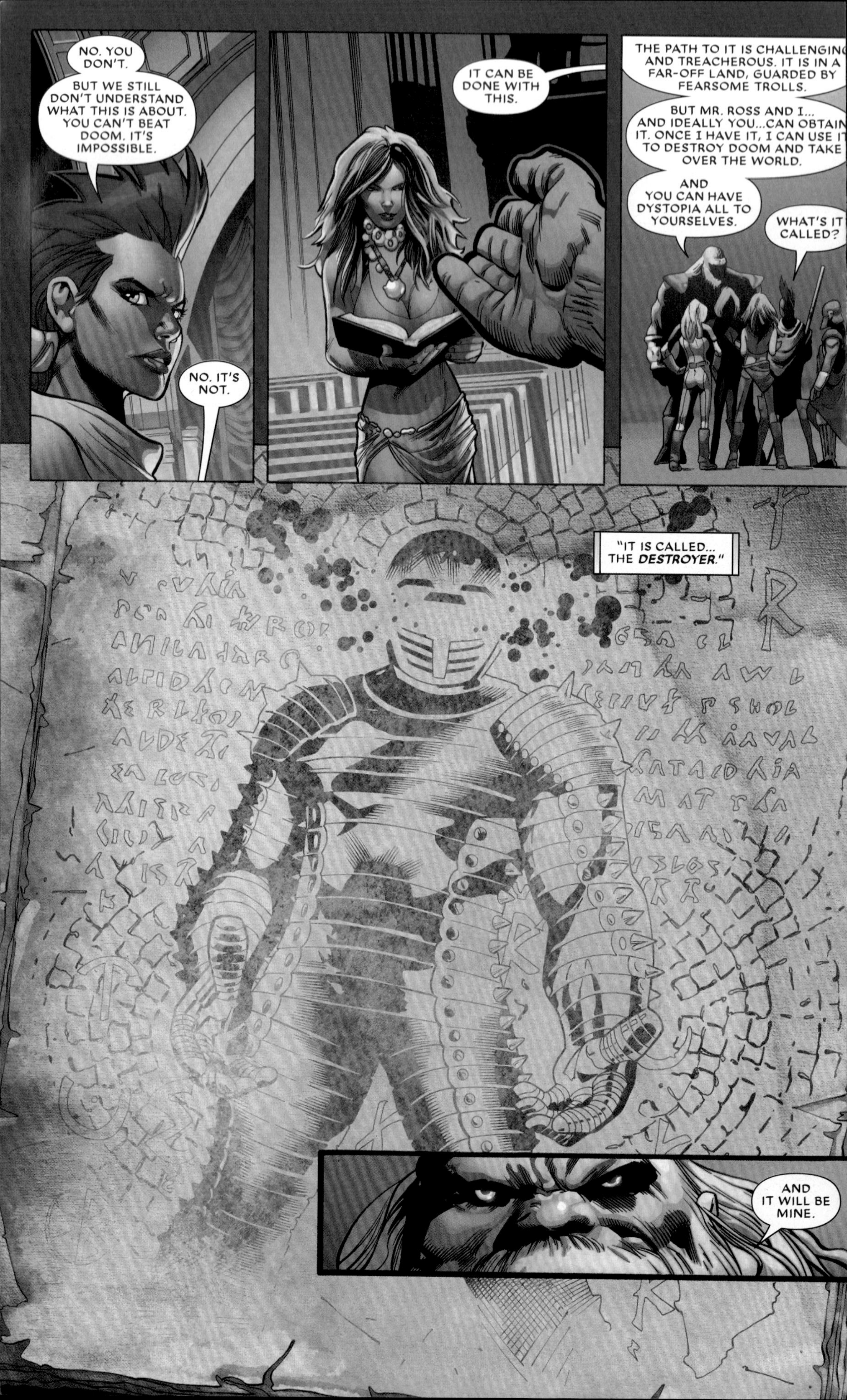
NO. YOU DON'T.
BUT WE STILL DON'T UNDERSTAND WHAT THIS IS ABOUT. YOU CAN'T BEAT DOOM. IT'S IMPOSSIBLE.
NO. IT'S NOT.
IT CAN BE DONE WITH THIS.
THE PATH TO IT IS CHALLENGING AND TREACHEROUS. IT IS IN A FAR-OFF LAND, GUARDED BY FEARSOME TROLLS.
BUT MR. ROSS AND I... AND IDEALLY YOU...CAN OBTAIN IT. ONCE I HAVE IT, I CAN USE IT TO DESTROY DOOM AND TAKE OVER THE WORLD.
AND YOU CAN HAVE DYSTOPIA ALL TO YOURSELVES.
WHAT'S IT CALLED?
"IT IS CALLED... THE DESTROYER."
AND IT WILL BE MINE.

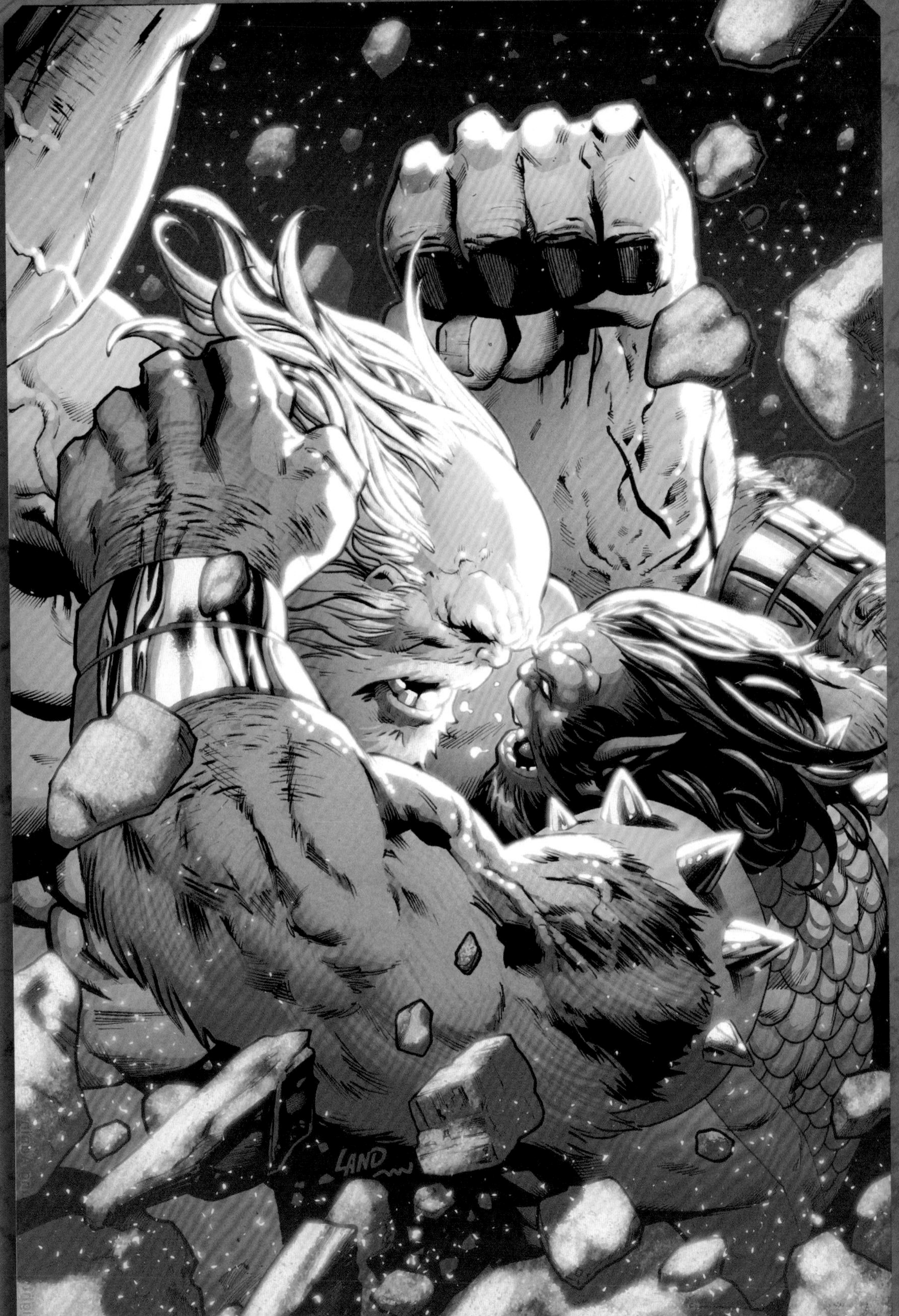
LAND

4

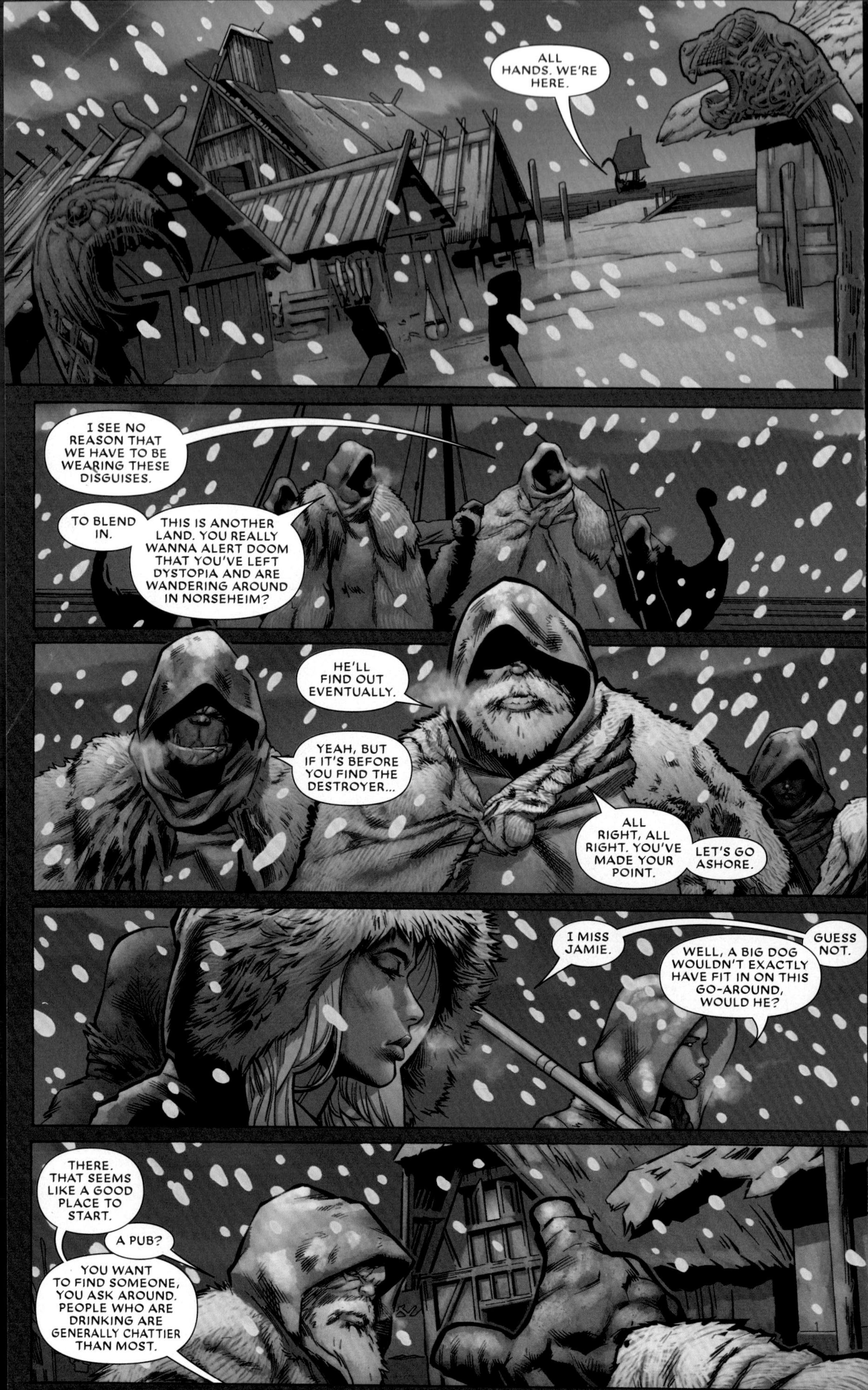
ALL HANDS. WE'RE HERE.
I SEE NO REASON THAT WE HAVE TO BE WEARING THESE DISGUISES.
TO BLEND IN.
THIS IS ANOTHER LAND. YOU REALLY WANNA ALERT DOOM THAT YOU'VE LEFT DYSTOPIA AND ARE WANDERING AROUND IN NORSEHEIM?
HE'LL FIND OUT EVENTUALLY.
YEAH, BUT IF IT'S BEFORE YOU FIND THE DESTROYER...
ALL RIGHT, ALL RIGHT. YOU'VE MADE YOUR POINT.
LET'S GO ASHORE.
I MISS JAMIE.
GUESS NOT.
WELL, A BIG DOG WOULDN'T EXACTLY HAVE FIT IN ON THIS GO-AROUND, WOULD HE?
THERE. THAT SEEMS LIKE A GOOD PLACE TO START.
A PUB?
YOU WANT TO FIND SOMEONE, YOU ASK AROUND. PEOPLE WHO ARE DRINKING ARE GENERALLY CHATTIER THAN MOST.

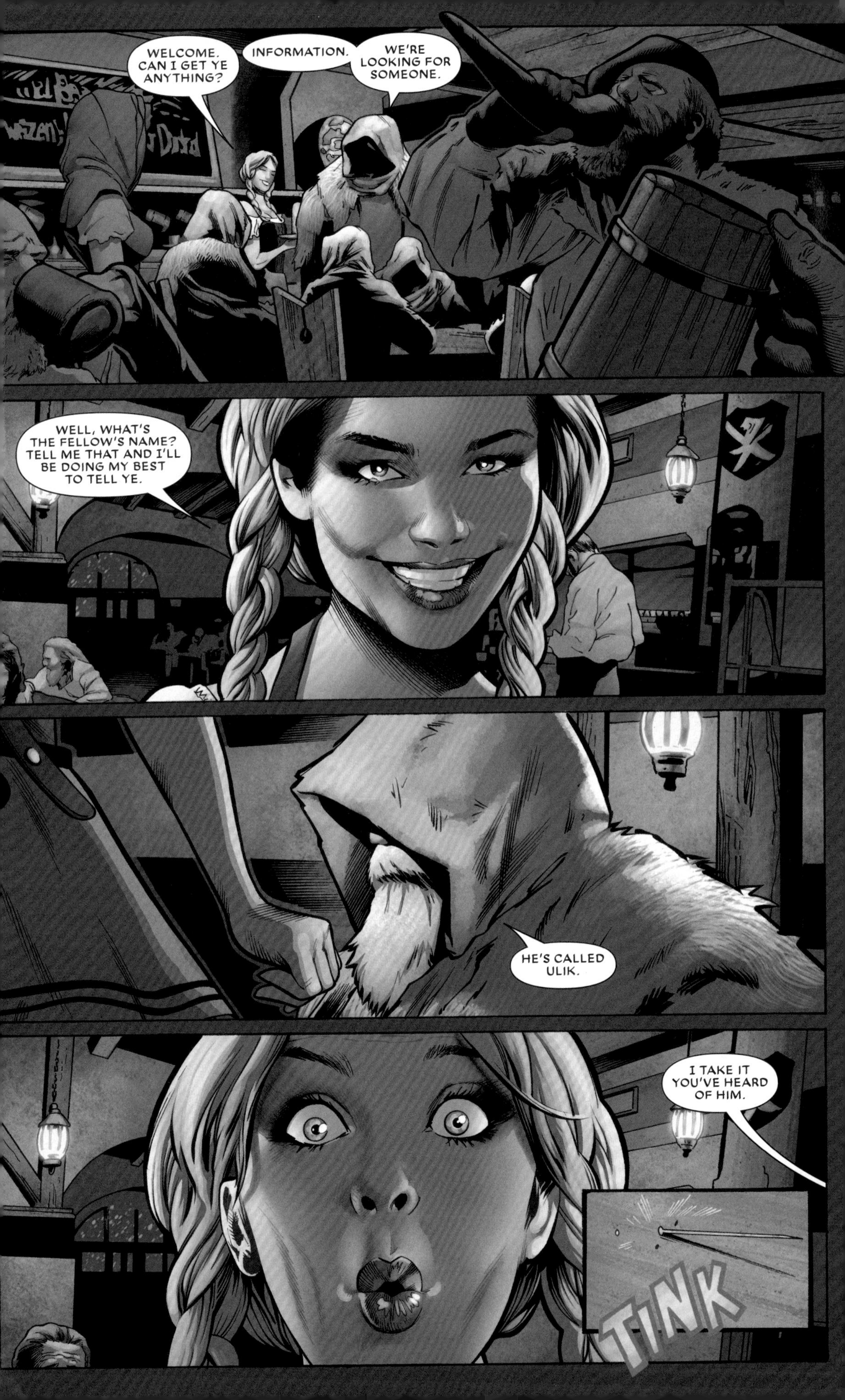
WELCOME. CAN I GET YE ANYTHING?
INFORMATION.
WE'RE LOOKING FOR SOMEONE.
WELL, WHAT'S THE FELLOW'S NAME? TELL ME THAT AND I'LL BE DOING MY BEST TO TELL YE.
HE'S CALLED ULIK.
I TAKE IT YOU'VE HEARD OF HIM.
TINK

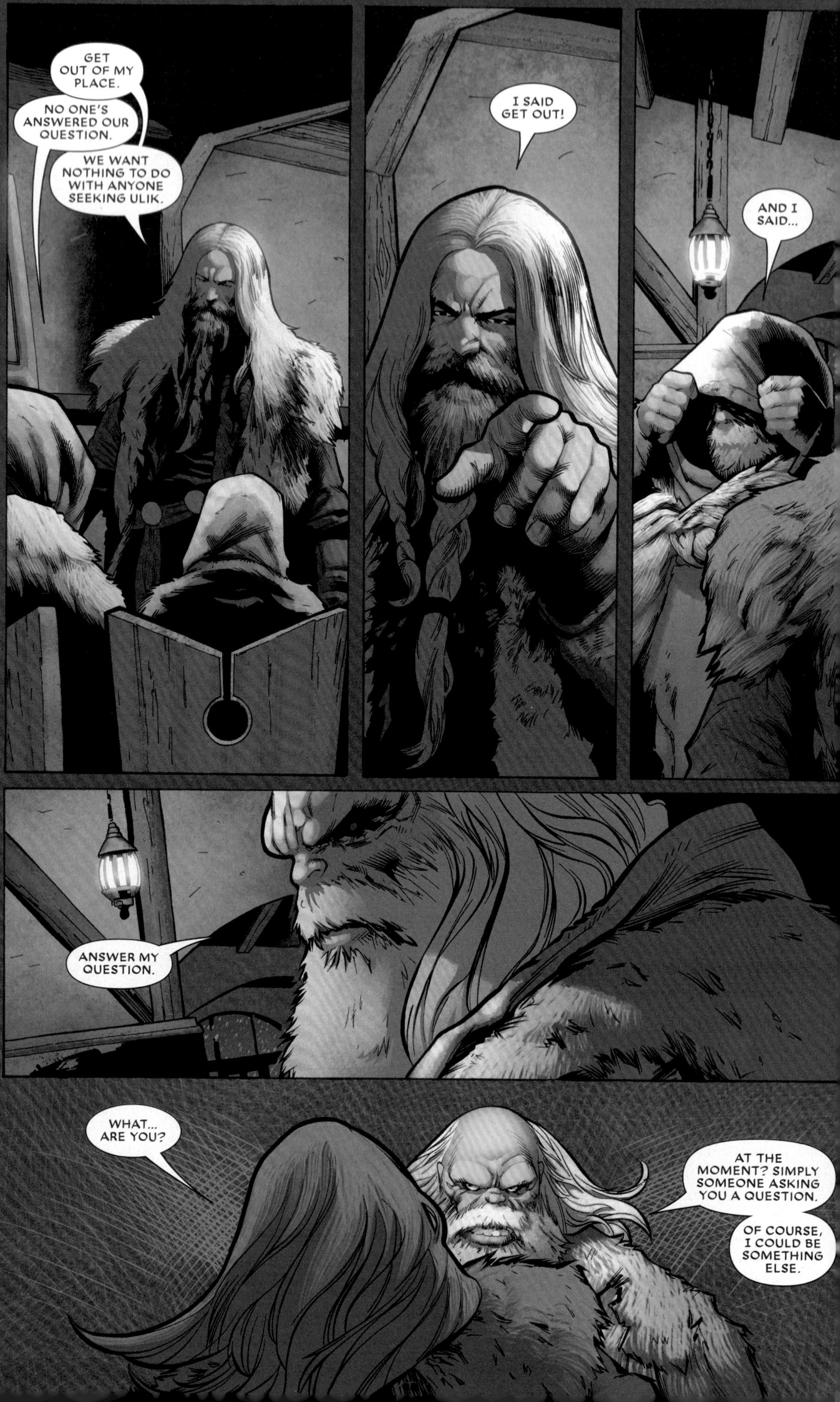
GET OUT OF MY PLACE.
NO ONE'S ANSWERED OUR QUESTION.
WE WANT NOTHING TO DO WITH ANYONE SEEKING ULIK.
I SAID GET OUT!
AND I SAID...
ANSWER MY QUESTION.
WHAT... ARE YOU?
AT THE MOMENT? SIMPLY SOMEONE ASKING YOU A QUESTION.
OF COURSE, I COULD BE SOMETHING ELSE.

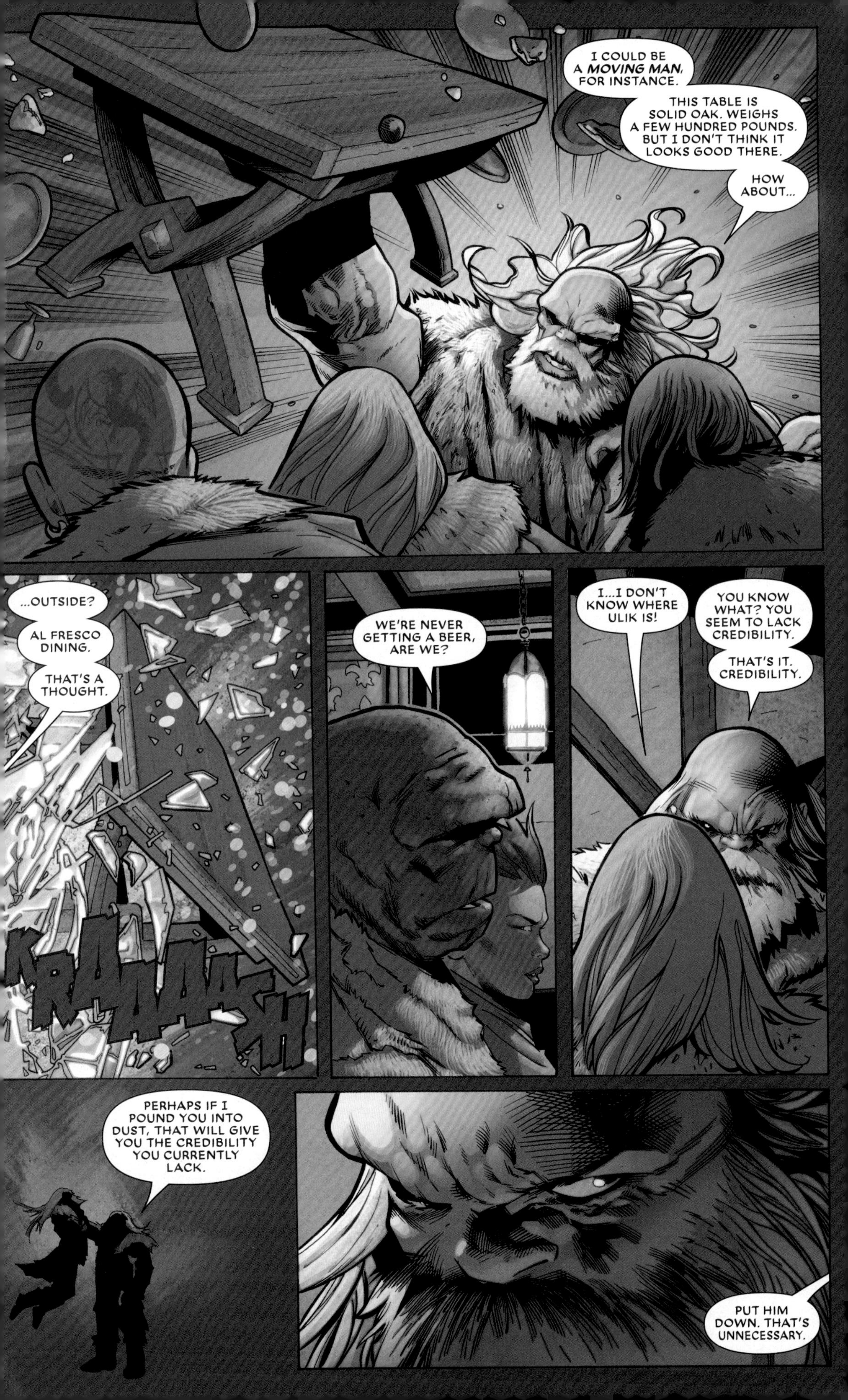
I COULD BE A *MOVING MAN*, FOR INSTANCE.
THIS TABLE IS SOLID OAK. WEIGHS A FEW HUNDRED POUNDS. BUT I DON'T THINK IT LOOKS GOOD THERE.
HOW ABOUT...
...OUTSIDE?
AL FRESCO DINING.
THAT'S A THOUGHT.
KRAAAASH
WE'RE NEVER GETTING A BEER, ARE WE?
I...I DON'T KNOW WHERE ULIK IS!
YOU KNOW WHAT? YOU SEEM TO LACK CREDIBILITY.
THAT'S IT. CREDIBILITY.
PERHAPS IF I POUND YOU INTO DUST, THAT WILL GIVE YOU THE CREDIBILITY YOU CURRENTLY LACK.
PUT HIM DOWN. THAT'S UNNECESSARY.

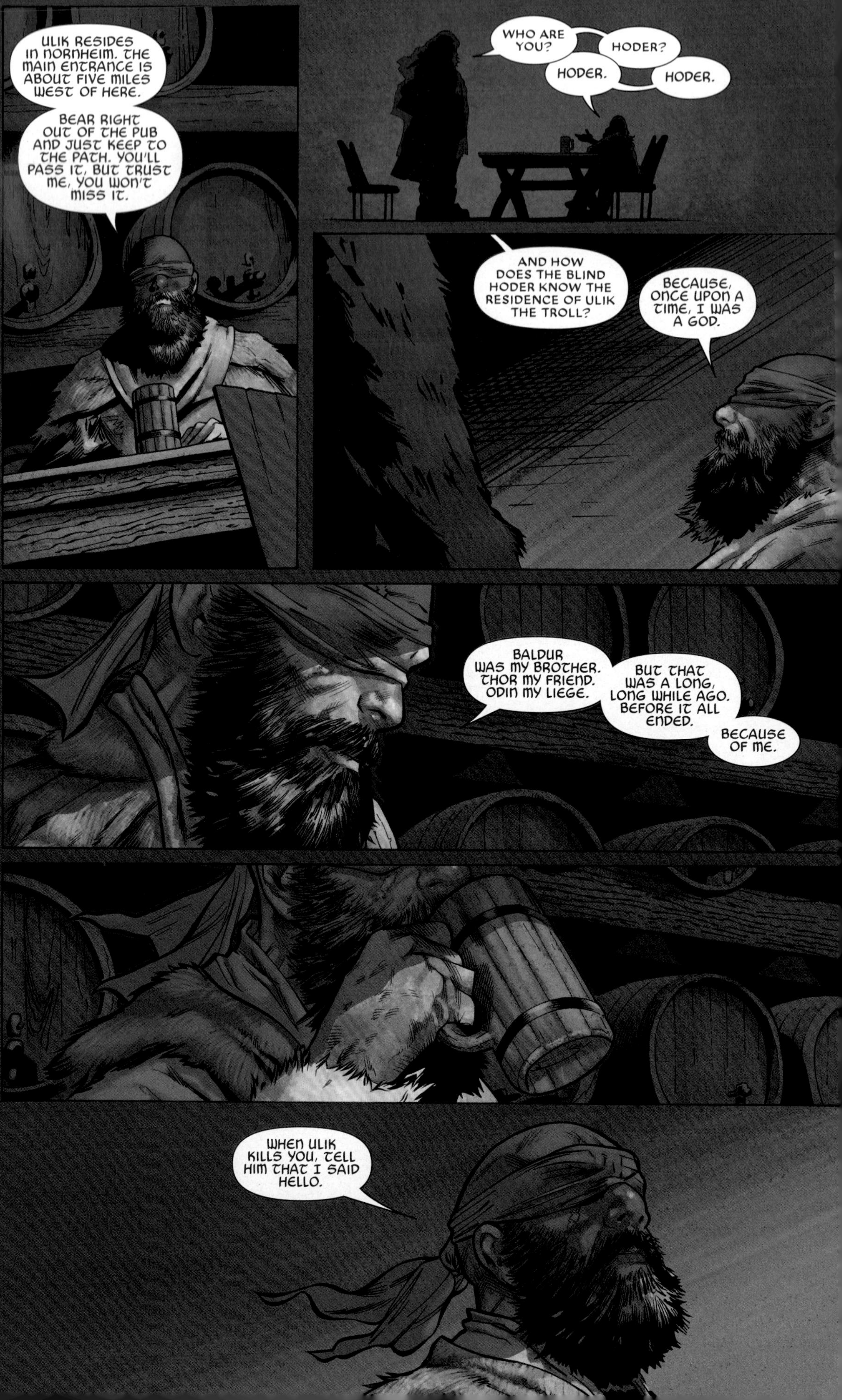
ULIK RESIDES IN NORNHEIM. THE MAIN ENTRANCE IS ABOUT FIVE MILES WEST OF HERE.
BEAR RIGHT OUT OF THE PUB AND JUST KEEP TO THE PATH. YOU'LL PASS IT, BUT TRUST ME, YOU WON'T MISS IT.
WHO ARE YOU?
HODER.
HODER?
HODER.
AND HOW DOES THE BLIND HODER KNOW THE RESIDENCE OF ULIK THE TROLL?
BECAUSE, ONCE UPON A TIME, I WAS A GOD.
BALDUR WAS MY BROTHER. THOR MY FRIEND. ODIN MY LIEGE.
BUT THAT WAS A LONG, LONG WHILE AGO. BEFORE IT ALL ENDED.
BECAUSE OF ME.
WHEN ULIK KILLS YOU, TELL HIM THAT I SAID HELLO.

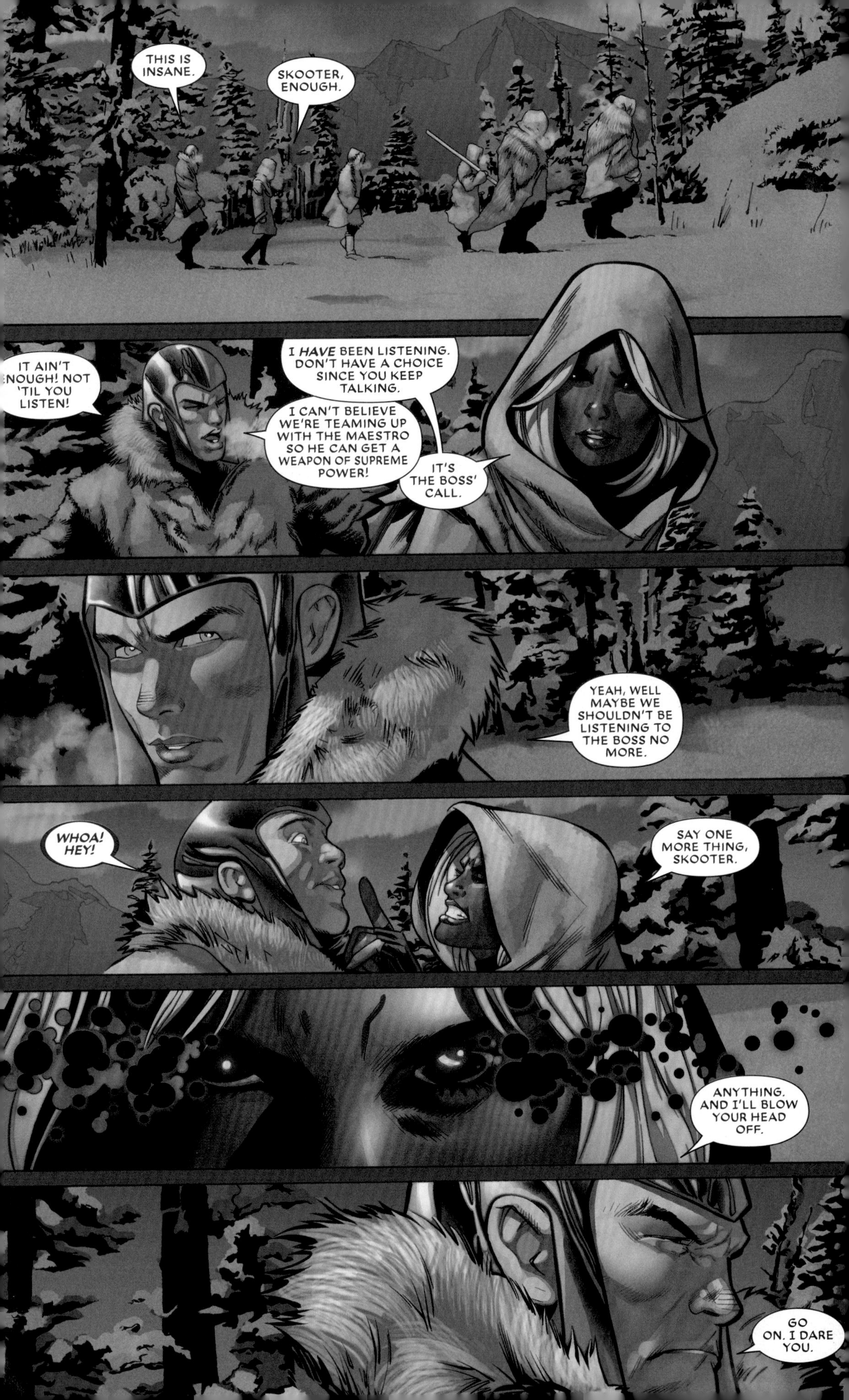
THIS IS INSANE.
SKOOTER, ENOUGH.
IT AIN'T ENOUGH! NOT 'TIL YOU LISTEN!
I HAVE BEEN LISTENING. DON'T HAVE A CHOICE SINCE YOU KEEP TALKING.
I CAN'T BELIEVE WE'RE TEAMING UP WITH THE MAESTRO SO HE CAN GET A WEAPON OF SUPREME POWER!
IT'S THE BOSS' CALL.
YEAH, WELL MAYBE WE SHOULDN'T BE LISTENING TO THE BOSS NO MORE.
WHOA! HEY!
SAY ONE MORE THING, SKOOTER.
ANYTHING. AND I'LL BLOW YOUR HEAD OFF.
GO ON. I DARE YOU.

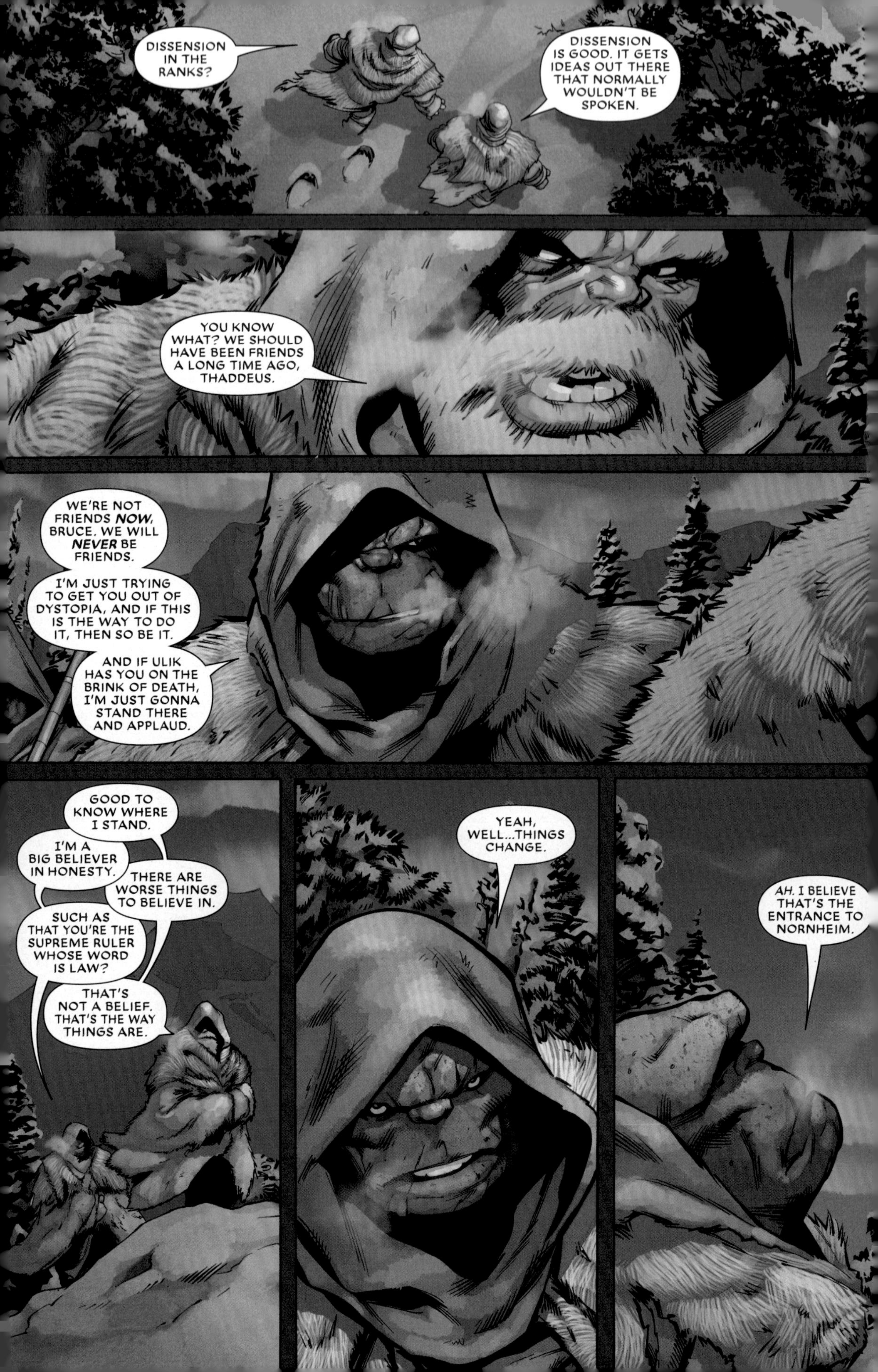
DISSENSION IN THE RANKS?
DISSENSION IS GOOD. IT GETS IDEAS OUT THERE THAT NORMALLY WOULDN'T BE SPOKEN.
YOU KNOW WHAT? WE SHOULD HAVE BEEN FRIENDS A LONG TIME AGO, THADDEUS.
WE'RE NOT FRIENDS NOW, BRUCE. WE WILL NEVER BE FRIENDS.
I'M JUST TRYING TO GET YOU OUT OF DYSTOPIA, AND IF THIS IS THE WAY TO DO IT, THEN SO BE IT.
AND IF ULIK HAS YOU ON THE BRINK OF DEATH, I'M JUST GONNA STAND THERE AND APPLAUD.
GOOD TO KNOW WHERE I STAND.
I'M A BIG BELIEVER IN HONESTY.
THERE ARE WORSE THINGS TO BELIEVE IN.
SUCH AS THAT YOU'RE THE SUPREME RULER WHOSE WORD IS LAW?
THAT'S NOT A BELIEF. THAT'S THE WAY THINGS ARE.
YEAH, WELL...THINGS CHANGE.
AH. I BELIEVE THAT'S THE ENTRANCE TO NORNHEIM.

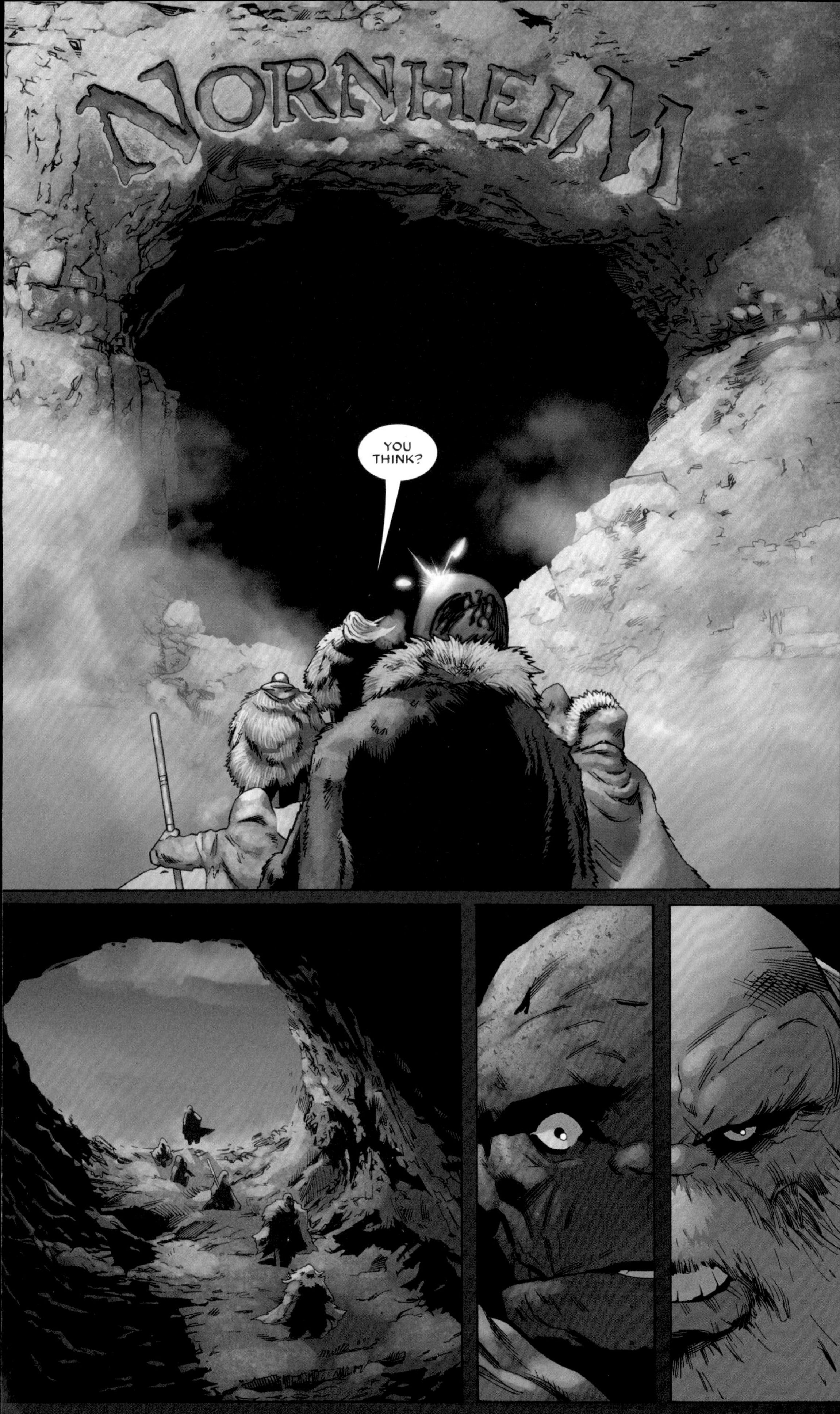
NORNHEIM
YOU THINK?

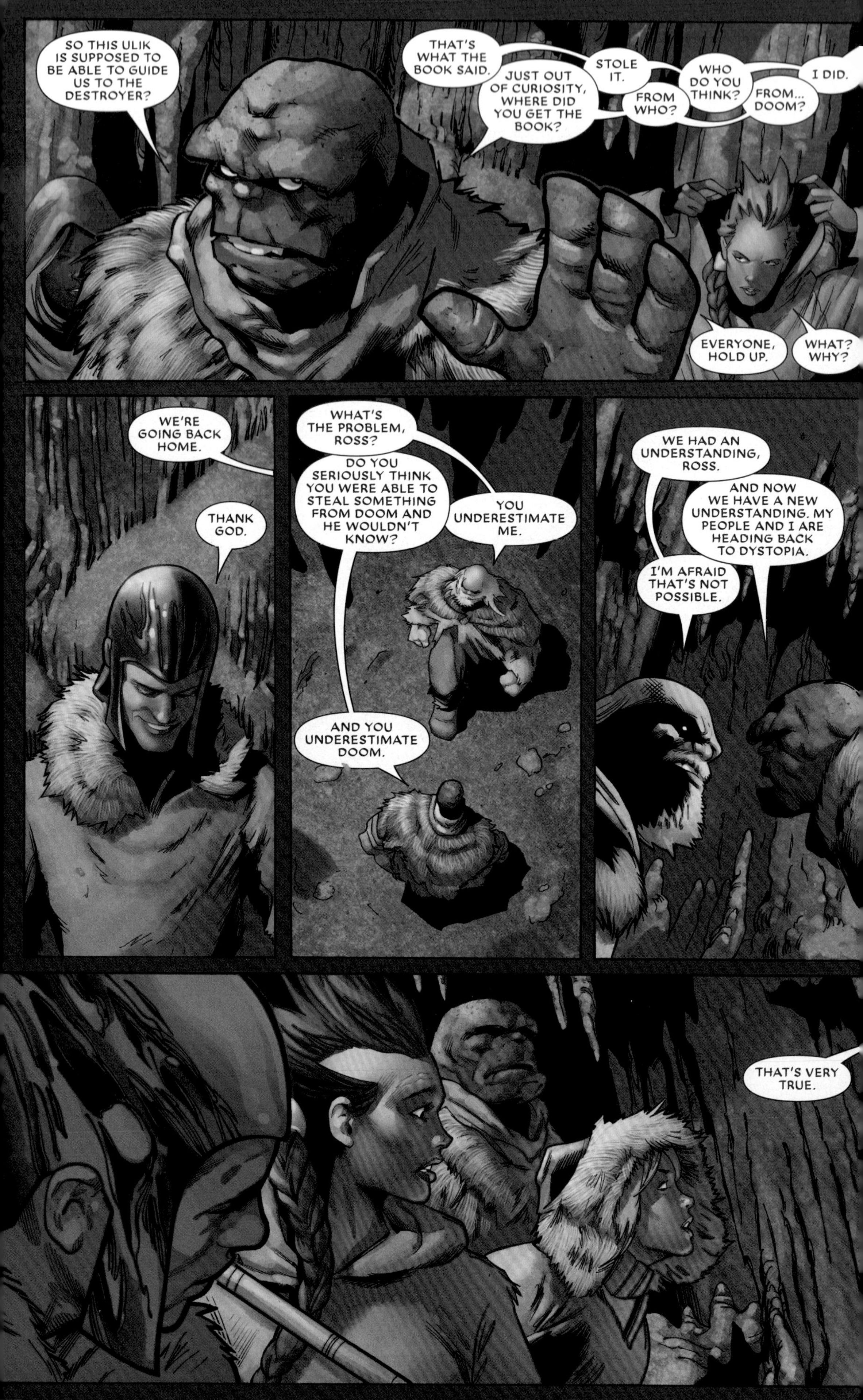
SO THIS ULIK IS SUPPOSED TO BE ABLE TO GUIDE US TO THE DESTROYER?
THAT'S WHAT THE BOOK SAID.
JUST OUT OF CURIOSITY, WHERE DID YOU GET THE BOOK?
STOLE IT.
FROM WHO?
WHO DO YOU THINK?
FROM... DOOM?
I DID.
EVERYONE, HOLD UP.
WHAT? WHY?
WE'RE GOING BACK HOME.
THANK GOD.
WHAT'S THE PROBLEM, ROSS?
DO YOU SERIOUSLY THINK YOU WERE ABLE TO STEAL SOMETHING FROM DOOM AND HE WOULDN'T KNOW?
YOU UNDERESTIMATE ME.
AND YOU UNDERESTIMATE DOOM.
WE HAD AN UNDERSTANDING, ROSS.
AND NOW WE HAVE A NEW UNDERSTANDING. MY PEOPLE AND I ARE HEADING BACK TO DYSTOPIA.
I'M AFRAID THAT'S NOT POSSIBLE.
THAT'S VERY TRUE.

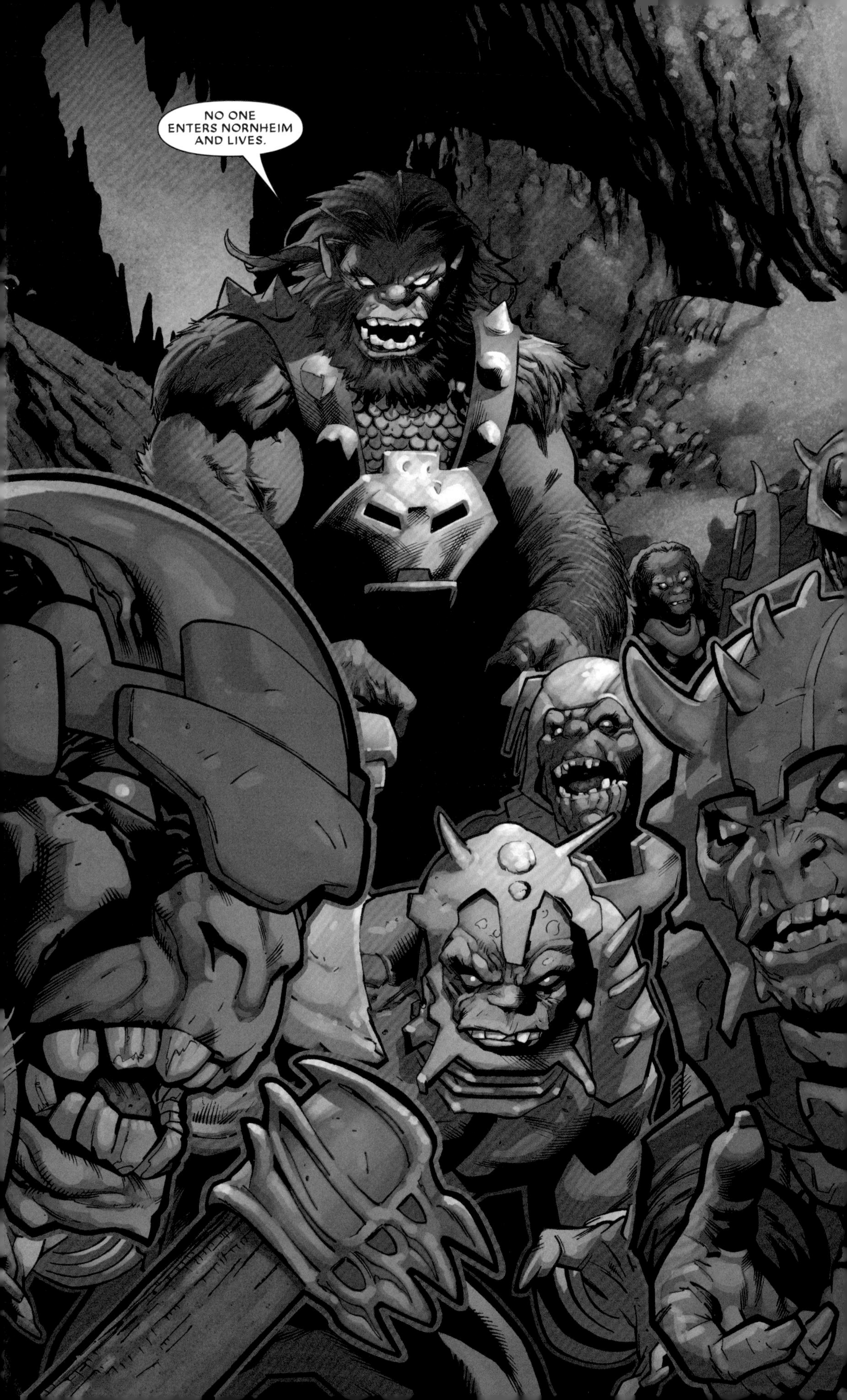
NO ONE ENTERS NORNHEIM AND LIVES.

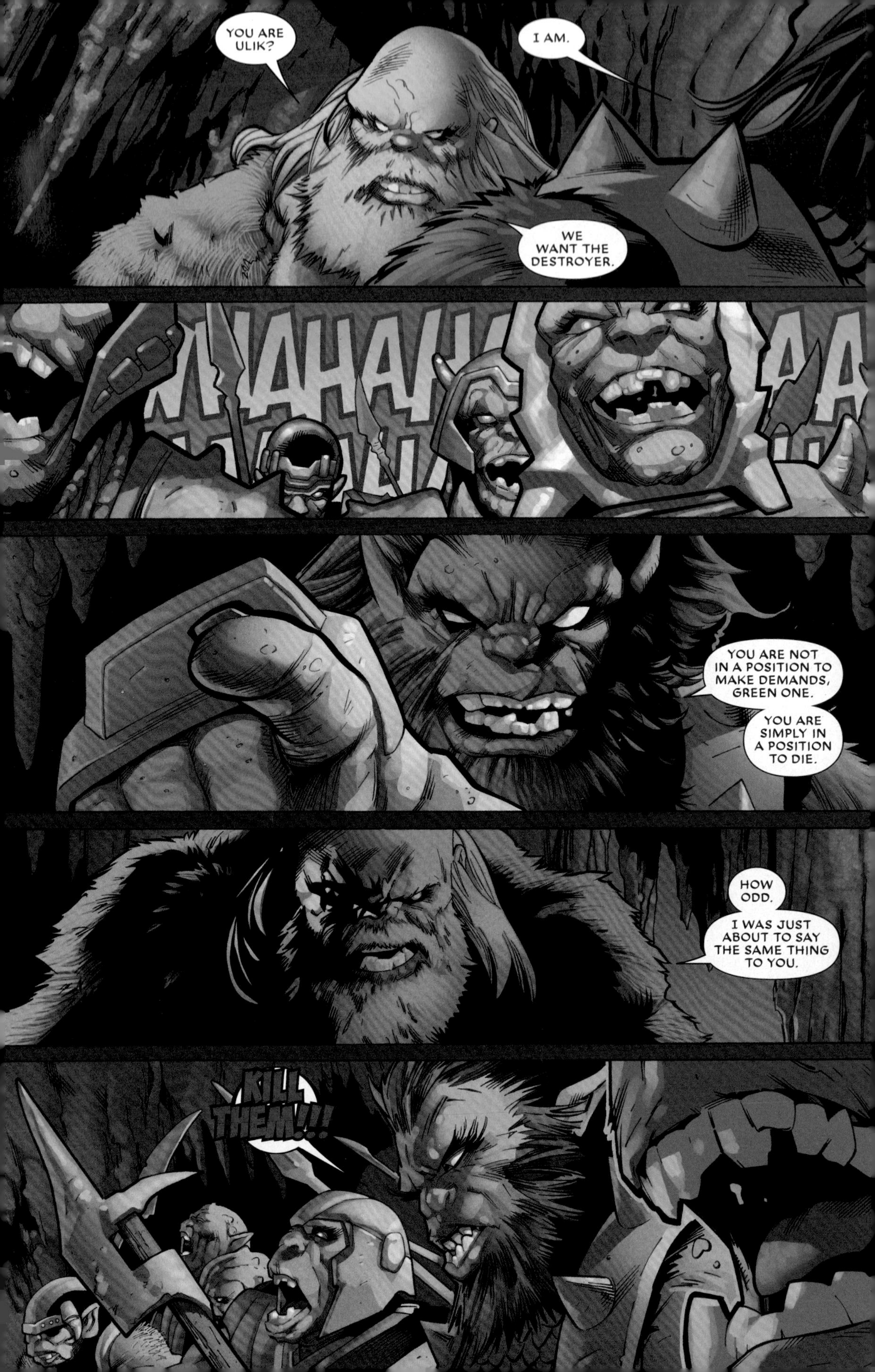
YOU ARE ULIK?
I AM.
WE WANT THE DESTROYER.
HAHAHAHAHAHAA
YOU ARE NOT IN A POSITION TO MAKE DEMANDS, GREEN ONE.
YOU ARE SIMPLY IN A POSITION TO DIE.
HOW ODD.
I WAS JUST ABOUT TO SAY THE SAME THING TO YOU.
KILL THEM!!!

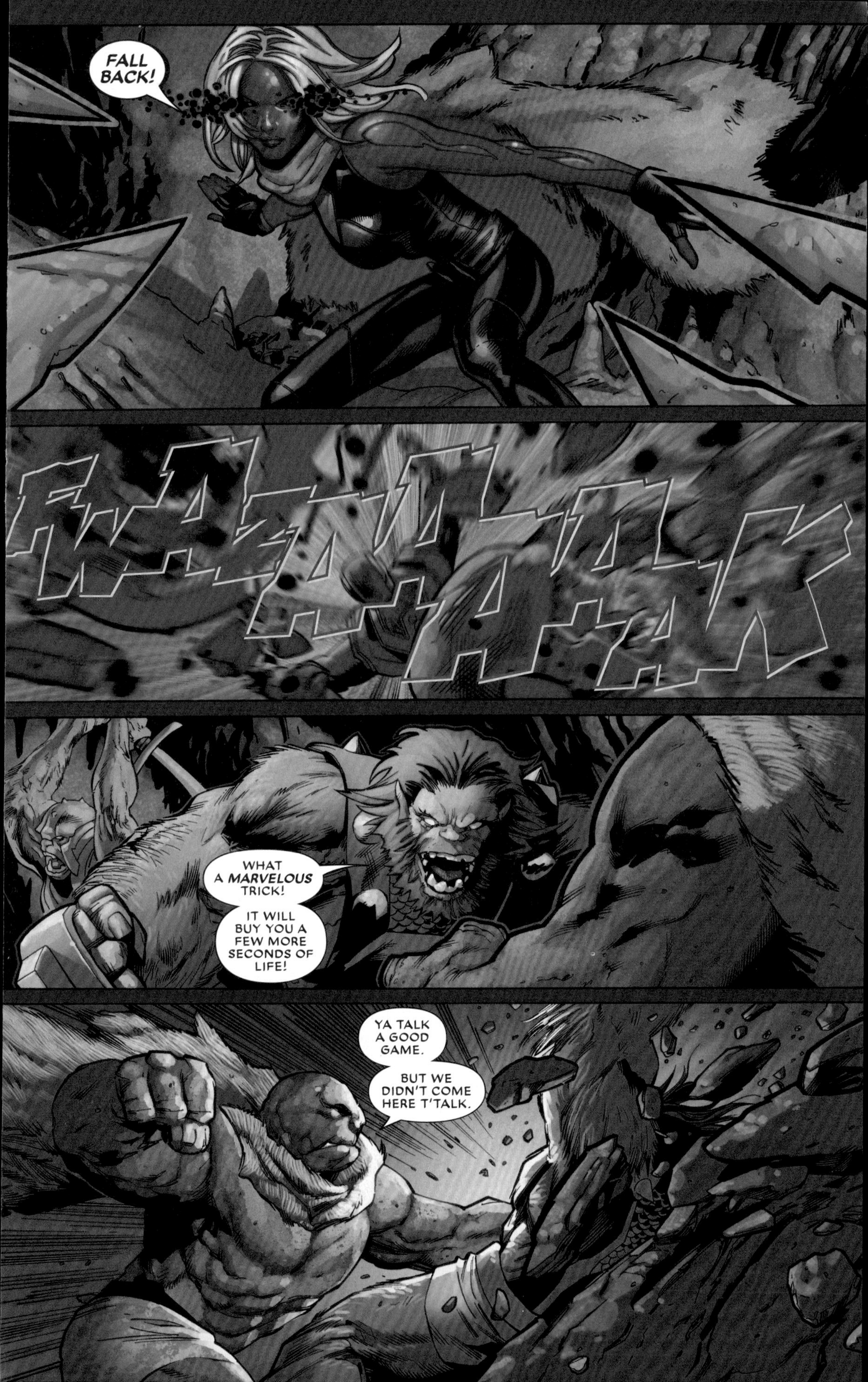
FALL BACK!
FWAAAAKK
WHAT A *MARVELOUS* TRICK!
IT WILL BUY YOU A FEW MORE SECONDS OF LIFE!
YA TALK A GOOD GAME.
BUT WE DIDN'T COME HERE T'TALK.

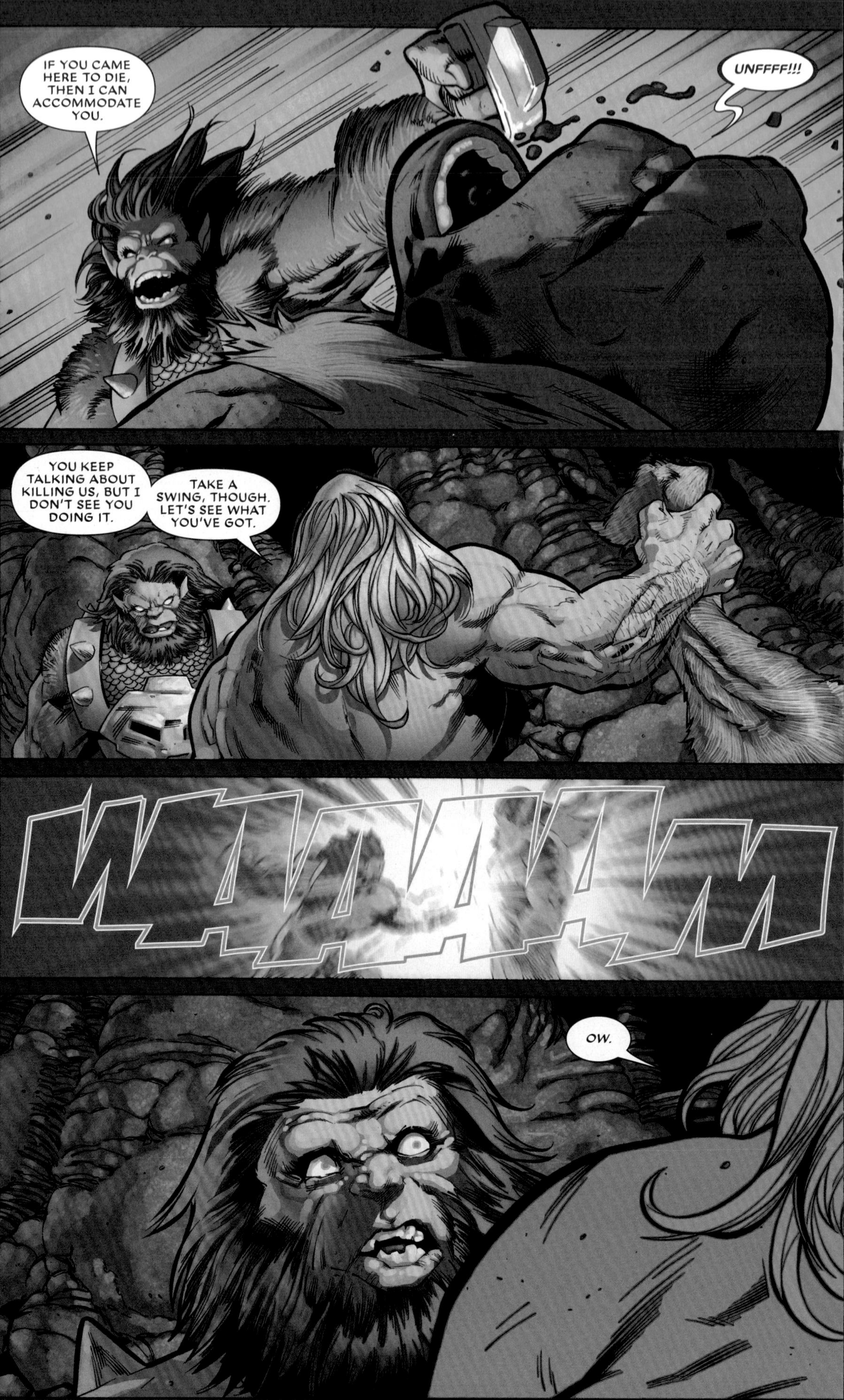
IF YOU CAME HERE TO DIE, THEN I CAN ACCOMMODATE YOU.
UNFFFF!!!
YOU KEEP TALKING ABOUT KILLING US, BUT I DON'T SEE YOU DOING IT.
TAKE A SWING, THOUGH. LET'S SEE WHAT YOU'VE GOT.
WHAM
OW.

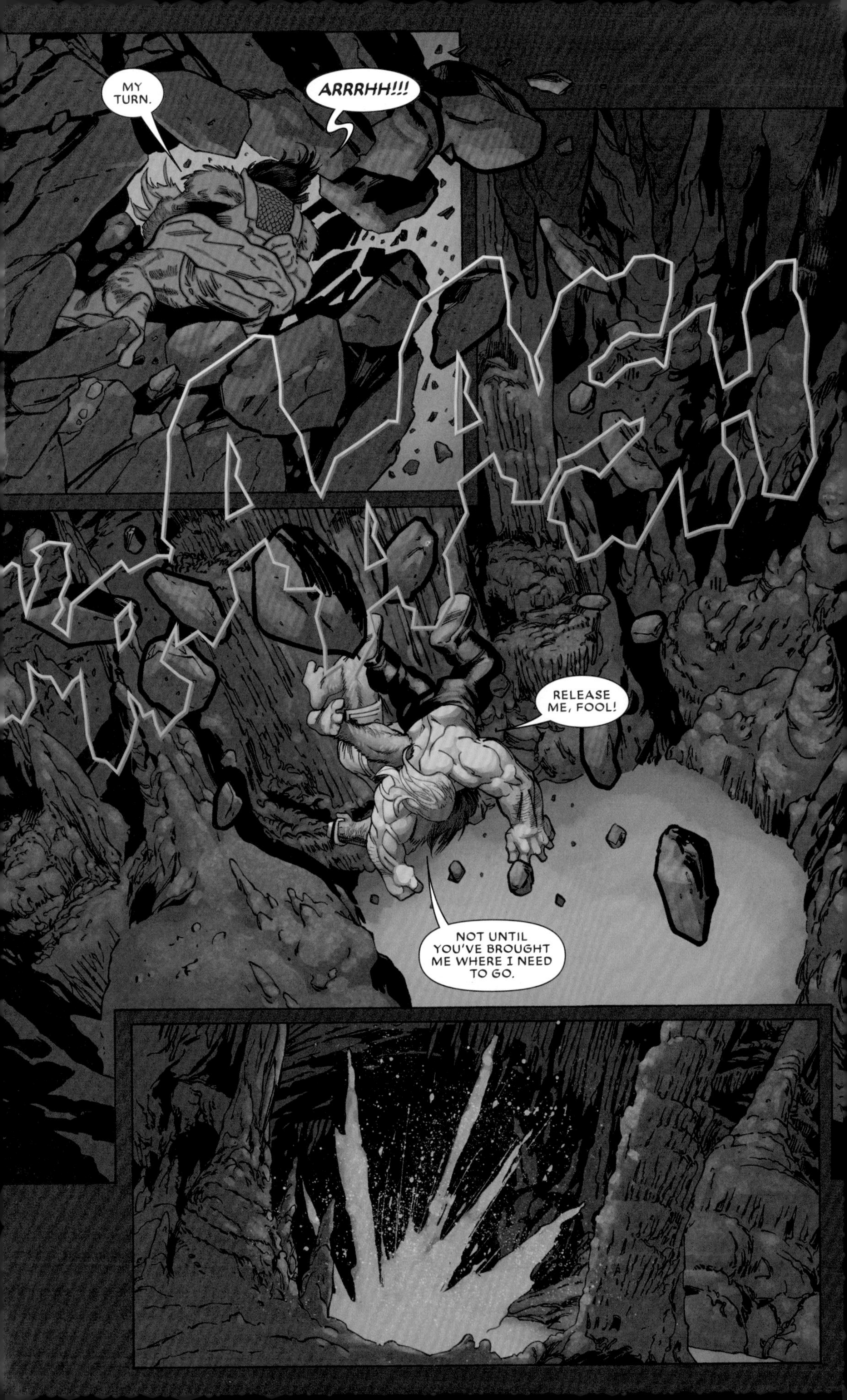
MY TURN.
ARRRHH!!!
RELEASE ME, FOOL!
NOT UNTIL YOU'VE BROUGHT ME WHERE I NEED TO GO.

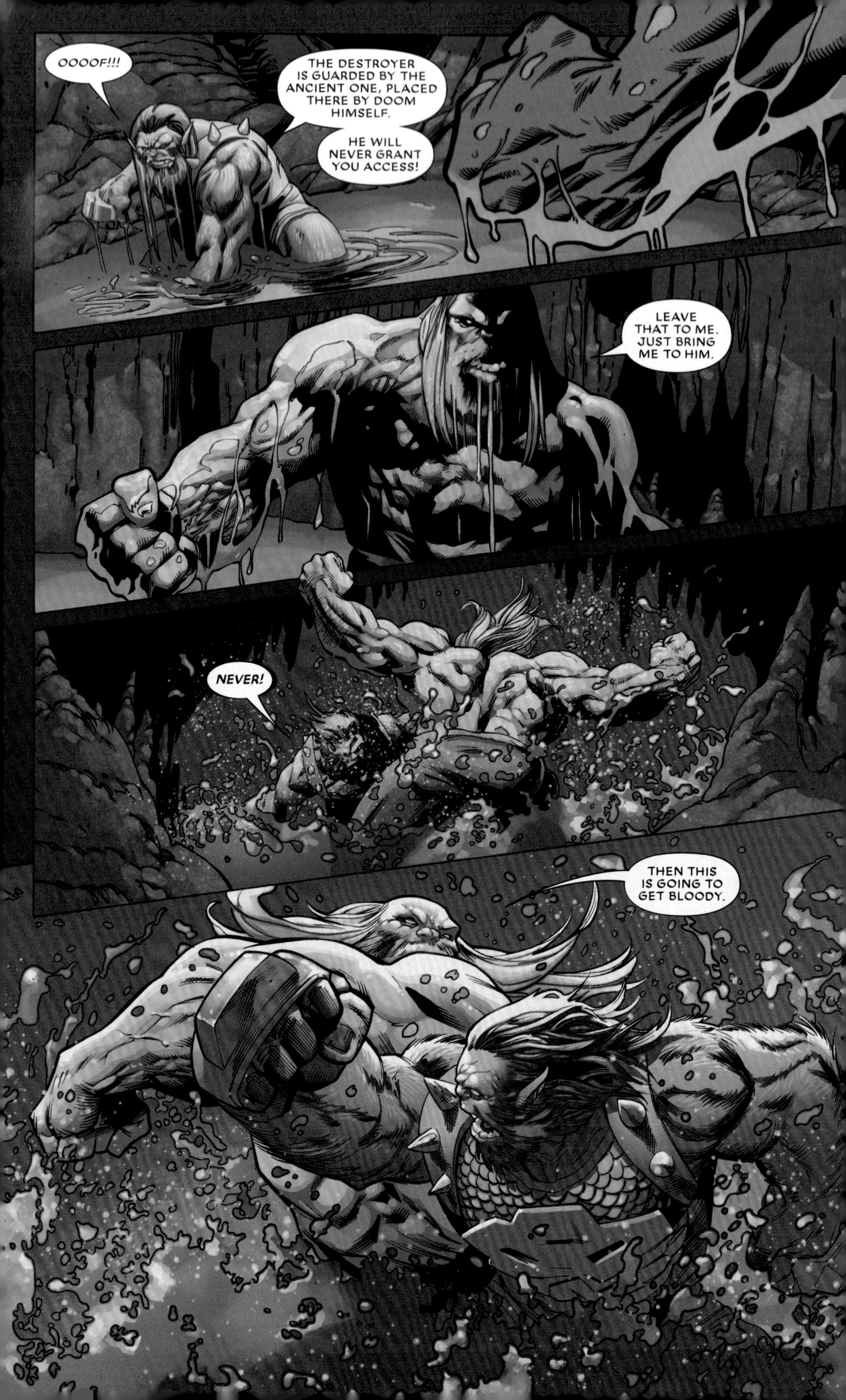
OOOOF!!!
THE DESTROYER IS GUARDED BY THE ANCIENT ONE, PLACED THERE BY DOOM HIMSELF.
HE WILL NEVER GRANT YOU ACCESS!
LEAVE THAT TO ME. JUST BRING ME TO HIM.
NEVER!
THEN THIS IS GOING TO GET BLOODY.

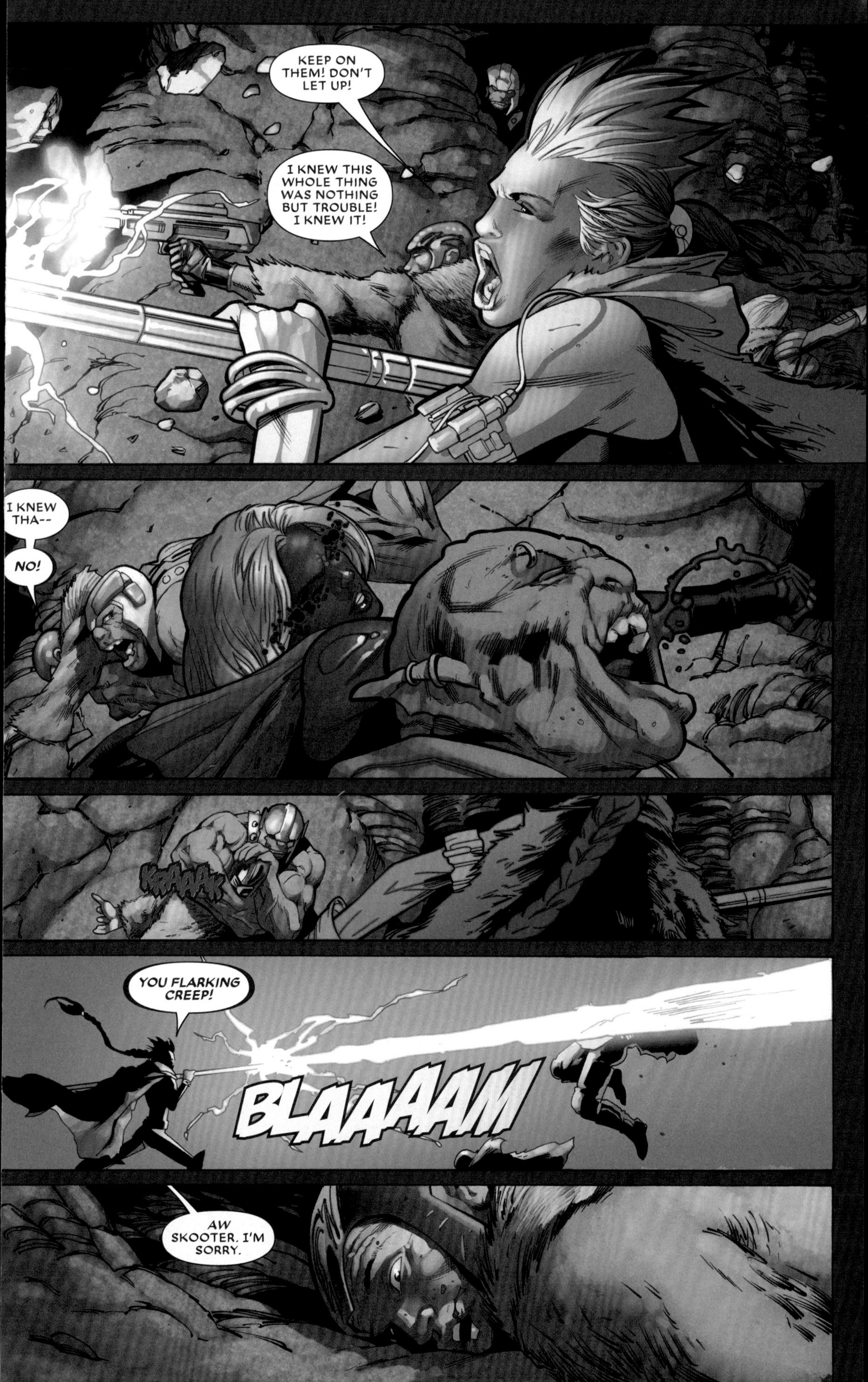
KEEP ON THEM! DON'T LET UP!
I KNEW THIS WHOLE THING WAS NOTHING BUT TROUBLE! I KNEW IT!
I KNEW THA--
NO!
KRAAAK
YOU FLARKING CREEP!
BLAAAAM
AW SKOOTER. I'M SORRY.

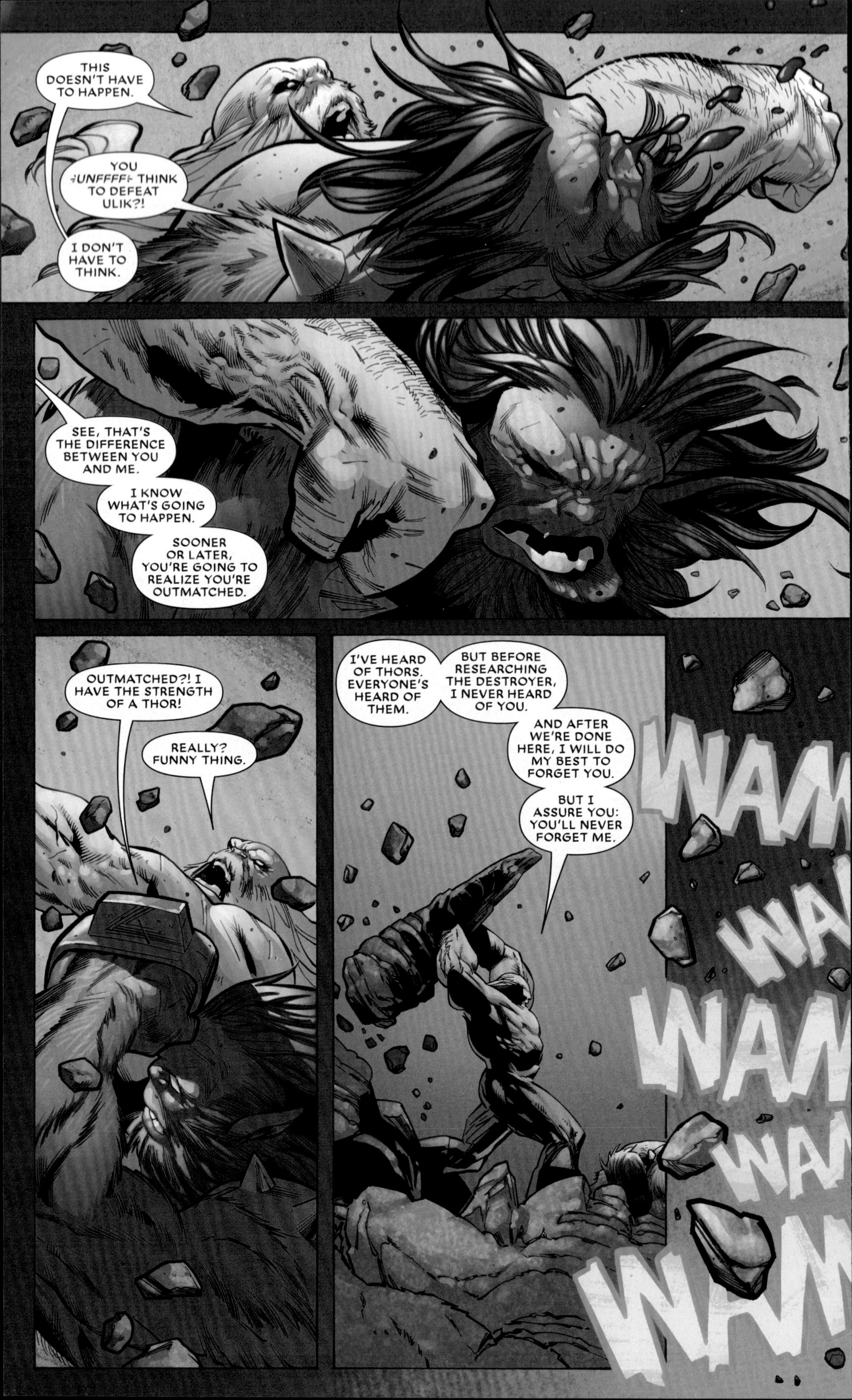
THIS DOESN'T HAVE TO HAPPEN.
YOU -UNFFFF- THINK TO DEFEAT ULIK?!
I DON'T HAVE TO THINK.
SEE, THAT'S THE DIFFERENCE BETWEEN YOU AND ME.
I KNOW WHAT'S GOING TO HAPPEN.
SOONER OR LATER, YOU'RE GOING TO REALIZE YOU'RE OUTMATCHED.
OUTMATCHED?! I HAVE THE STRENGTH OF A THOR!
REALLY? FUNNY THING.
I'VE HEARD OF THORS. EVERYONE'S HEARD OF THEM.
BUT BEFORE RESEARCHING THE DESTROYER, I NEVER HEARD OF YOU.
AND AFTER WE'RE DONE HERE, I WILL DO MY BEST TO FORGET YOU.
BUT I ASSURE YOU: YOU'LL NEVER FORGET ME.

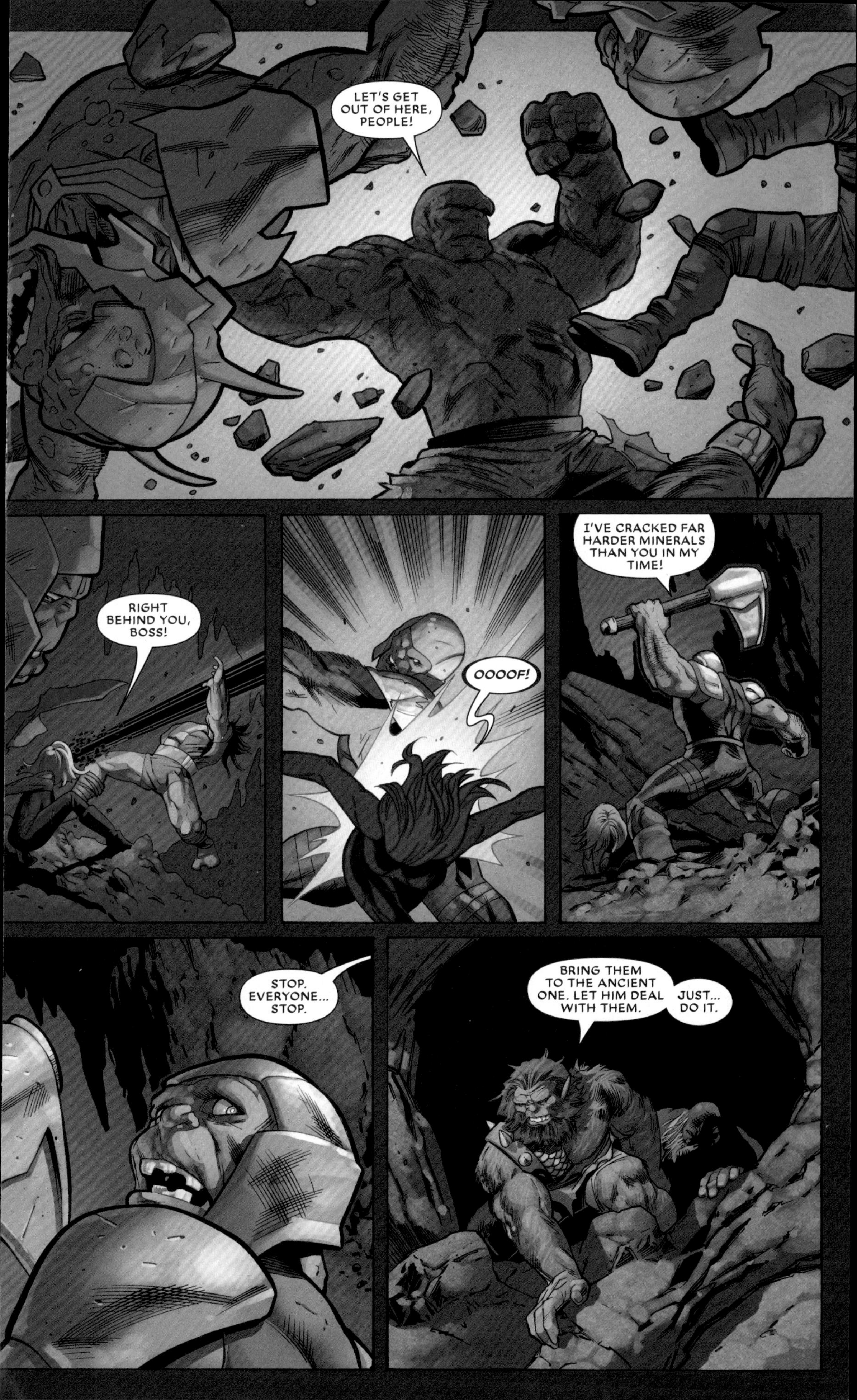
LET'S GET OUT OF HERE, PEOPLE!
RIGHT BEHIND YOU, BOSS!
OOOOF!
I'VE CRACKED FAR HARDER MINERALS THAN YOU IN MY TIME!
STOP. EVERYONE... STOP.
BRING THEM TO THE ANCIENT ONE. LET HIM DEAL WITH THEM.
JUST... DO IT.

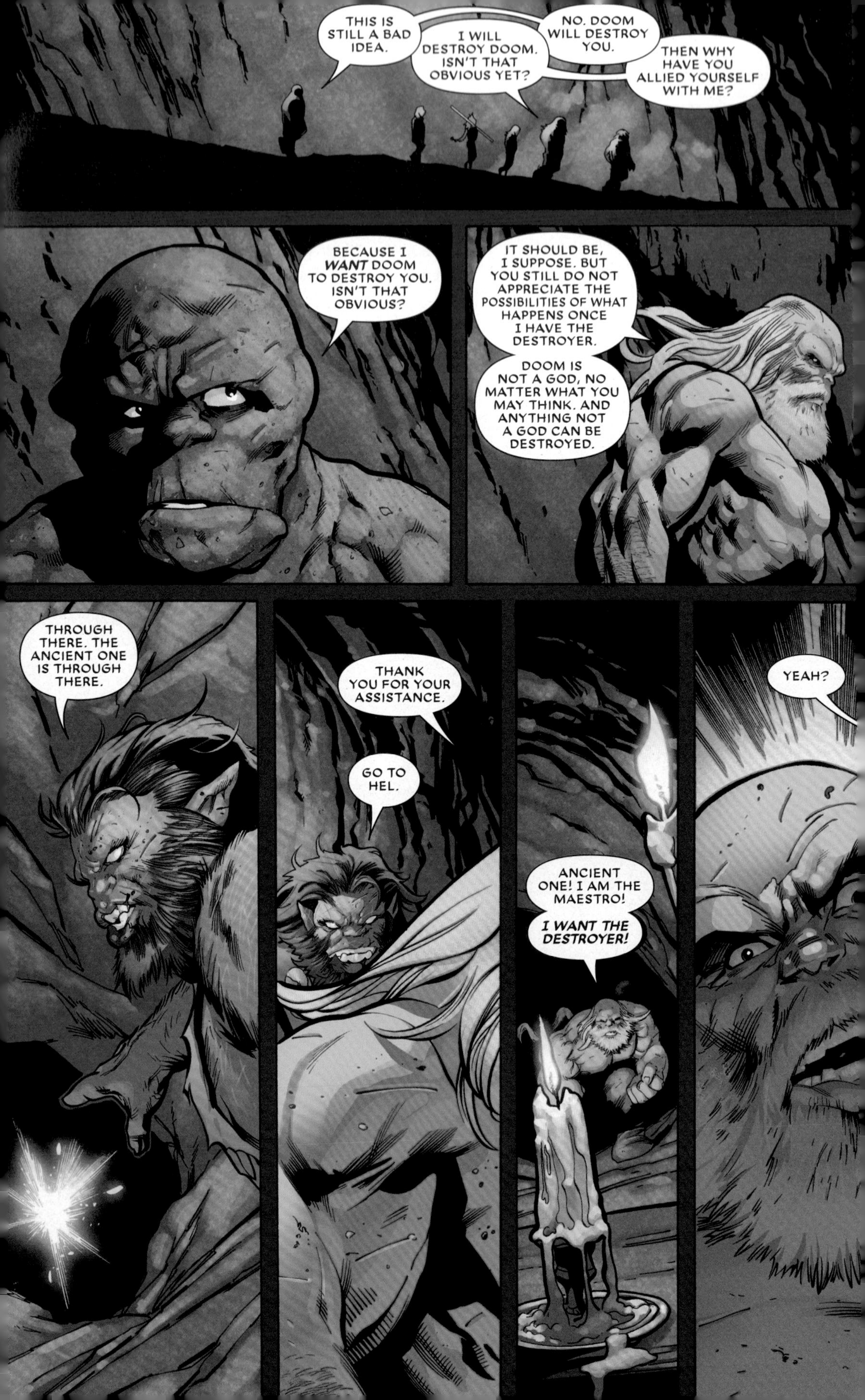
THIS IS STILL A BAD IDEA.
I WILL DESTROY DOOM. ISN'T THAT OBVIOUS YET?
NO. DOOM WILL DESTROY YOU.
THEN WHY HAVE YOU ALLIED YOURSELF WITH ME?
BECAUSE I *WANT* DOOM TO DESTROY YOU. ISN'T THAT OBVIOUS?
IT SHOULD BE, I SUPPOSE. BUT YOU STILL DO NOT APPRECIATE THE POSSIBILITIES OF WHAT HAPPENS ONCE I HAVE THE DESTROYER.
DOOM IS NOT A GOD, NO MATTER WHAT YOU MAY THINK. AND ANYTHING NOT A GOD CAN BE DESTROYED.
THROUGH THERE. THE ANCIENT ONE IS THROUGH THERE.
THANK YOU FOR YOUR ASSISTANCE.
GO TO HEL.
ANCIENT ONE! I AM THE MAESTRO!
I WANT THE DESTROYER!
YEAH?

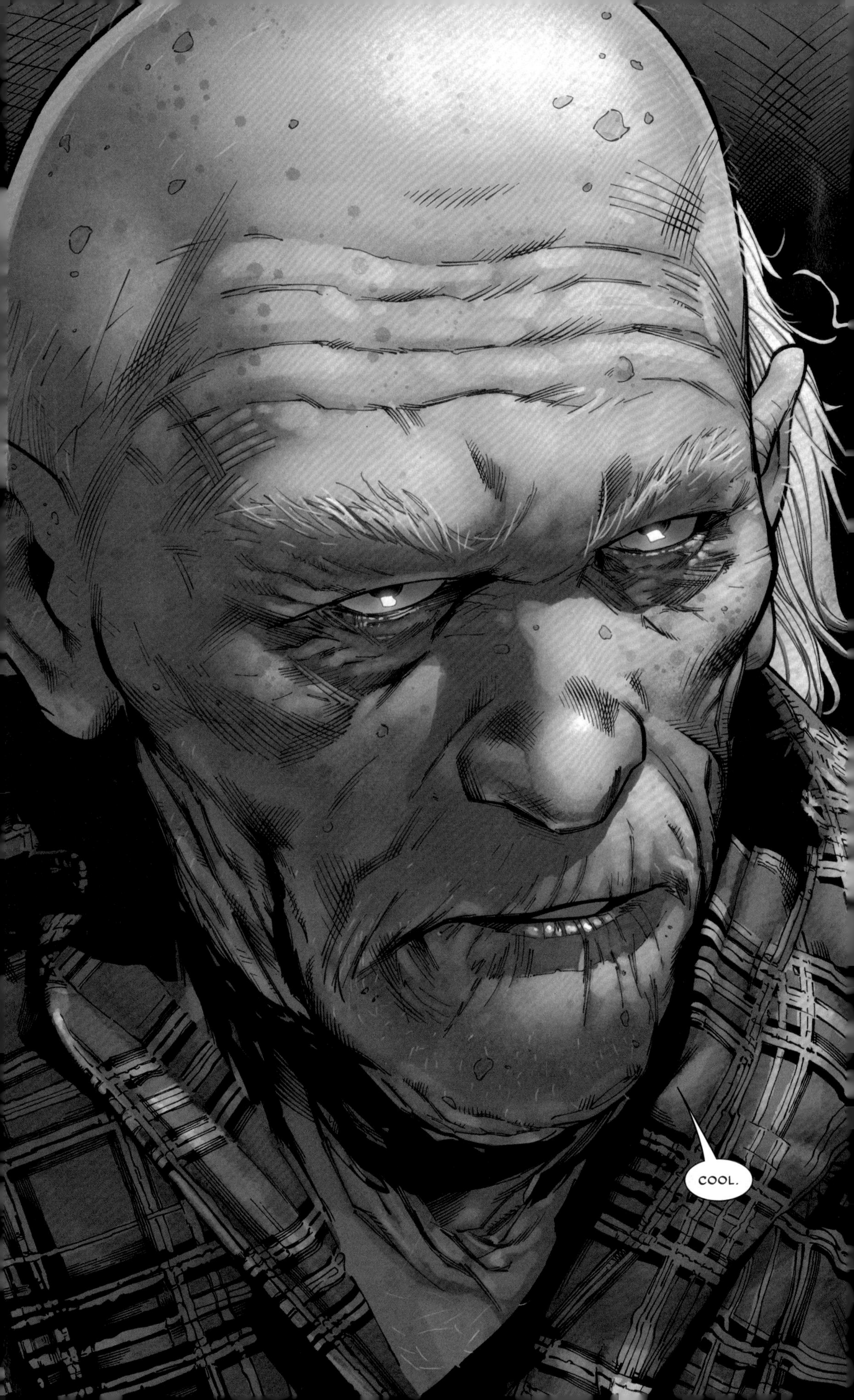
COOL.

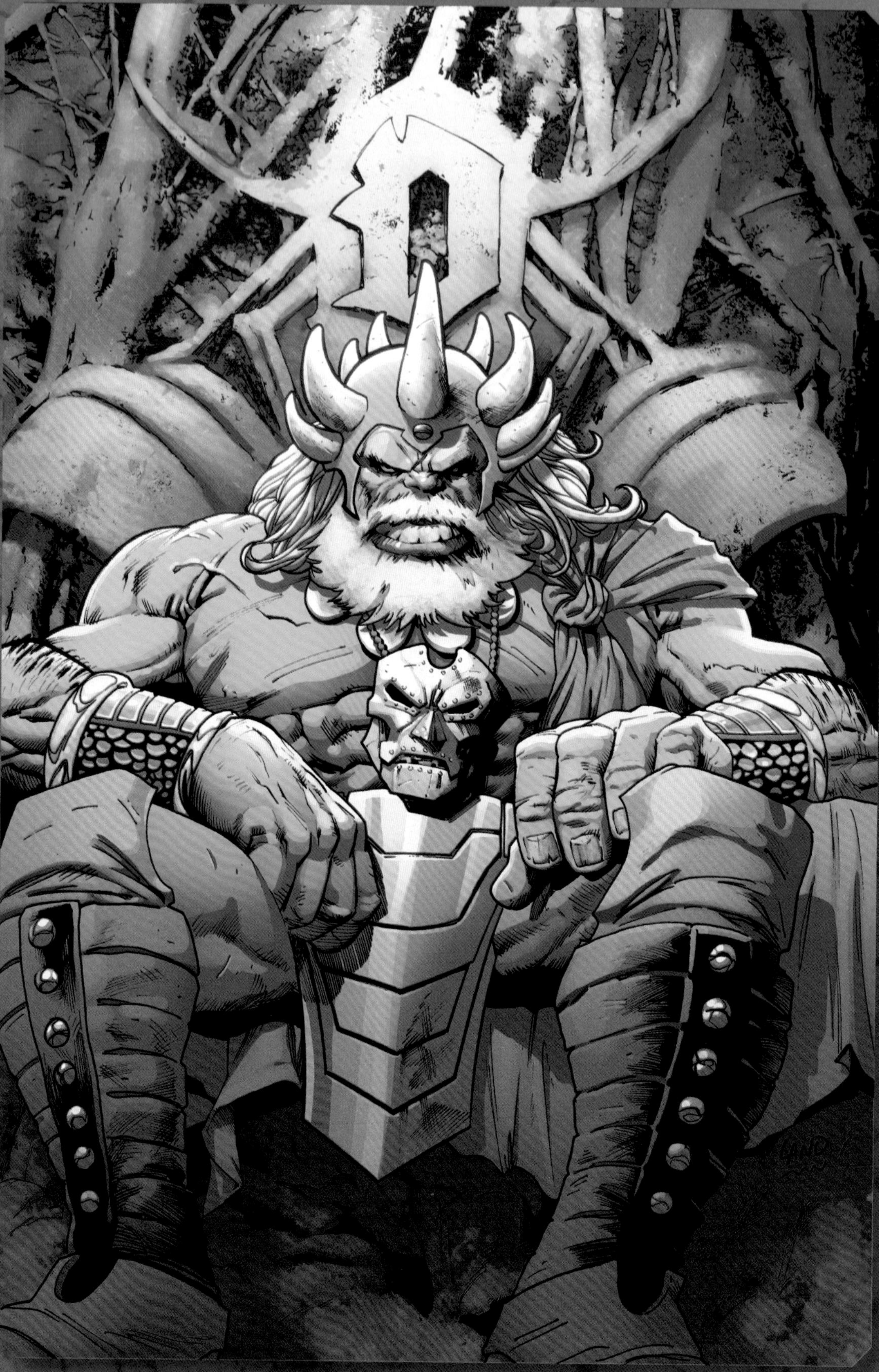

5

THE MULTIVERSE WAS DESTROYED!

THE HEROES OF EARTH-616 AND EARTH-1610 WERE POWERLESS TO SAVE IT!

NOW, ALL THAT REMAINS...IS BATTLEWORLD!

A MASSIVE, PATCHWORK PLANET COMPOSED OF THE FRAGMENTS OF WORLDS THAT NO LONGER EXIST, MAINTAINED BY THE IRON WILL OF ITS GOD AND MASTER, VICTOR VON DOOM!

EACH DOMAIN RULED BY POWERFUL BARONS, BUT NONE MORE TIGHTLY CONDUCTED THAN...

DYSTOPIA

SECRET WARS

OUR EXALTED BARON, THE MAESTRO, WELCOMES YOU TO HIS TROPHY ROOM OF CONQUERED OPPONENTS.

EXHIBITING THIS SEASON: HALL OF FOOTWEAR *PLEASE REMAIN QUIET AND RESPECTFUL!

WAR MACHINE REPULSOR BOOT

HERCULES SANDAL

QUICKSILVER CROSS-TRAINERS

EMMA FROST HIGH HEEL

BLACK GOLIATH BOOT

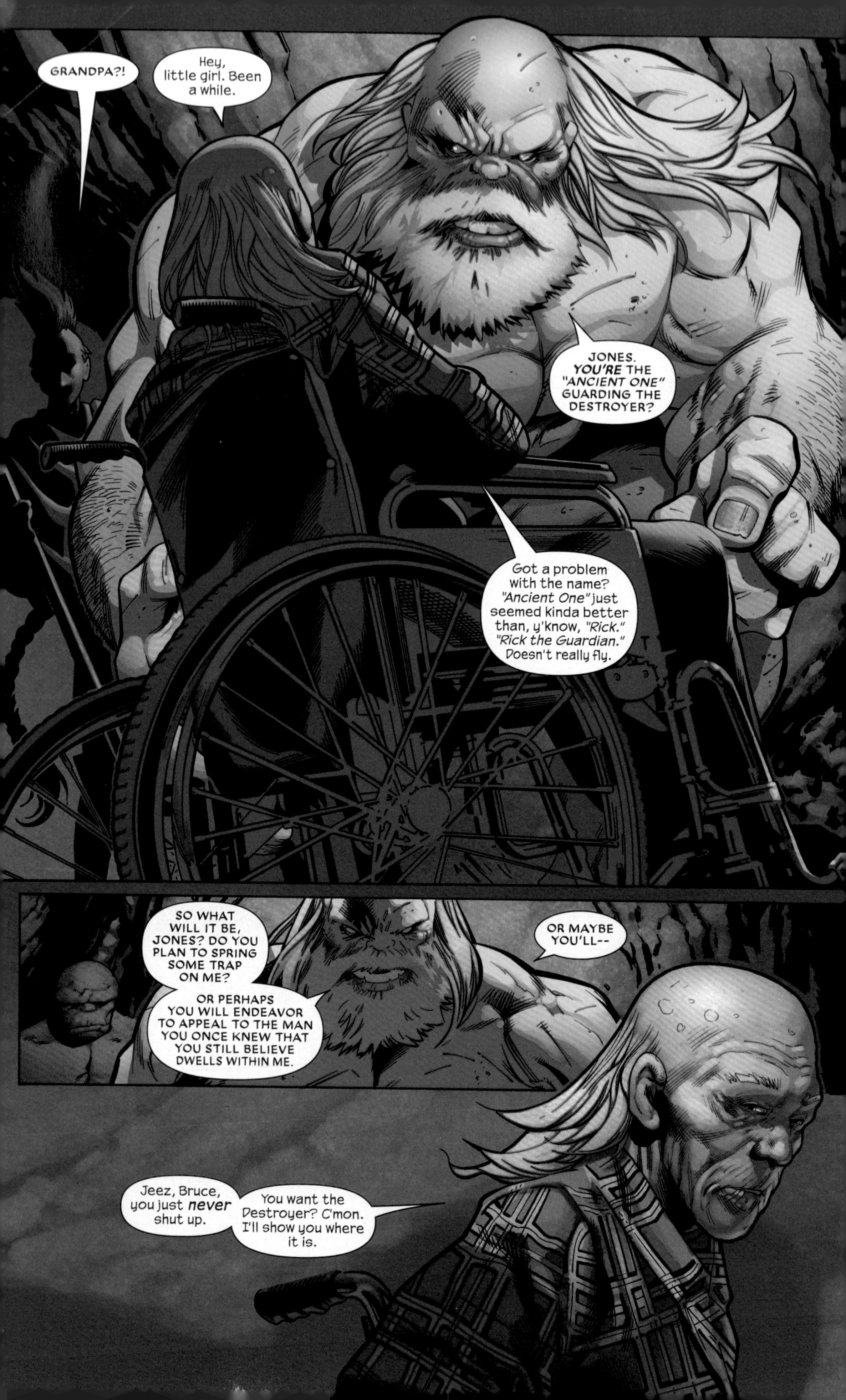
GRANDPA?!
Hey, little girl. Been a while.
JONES. *YOU'RE* THE "*ANCIENT ONE*" GUARDING THE DESTROYER?
Got a problem with the name? "*Ancient One*" just seemed kinda better than, y'know, "*Rick*." "*Rick the Guardian*." Doesn't really fly.
SO WHAT WILL IT BE, JONES? DO YOU PLAN TO SPRING SOME TRAP ON ME?
OR PERHAPS YOU WILL ENDEAVOR TO APPEAL TO THE MAN YOU ONCE KNEW THAT YOU STILL BELIEVE DWELLS WITHIN ME.
OR MAYBE YOU'LL--
Jeez, Bruce, you just ***never*** shut up.
You want the Destroyer? C'mon. I'll show you where it is.

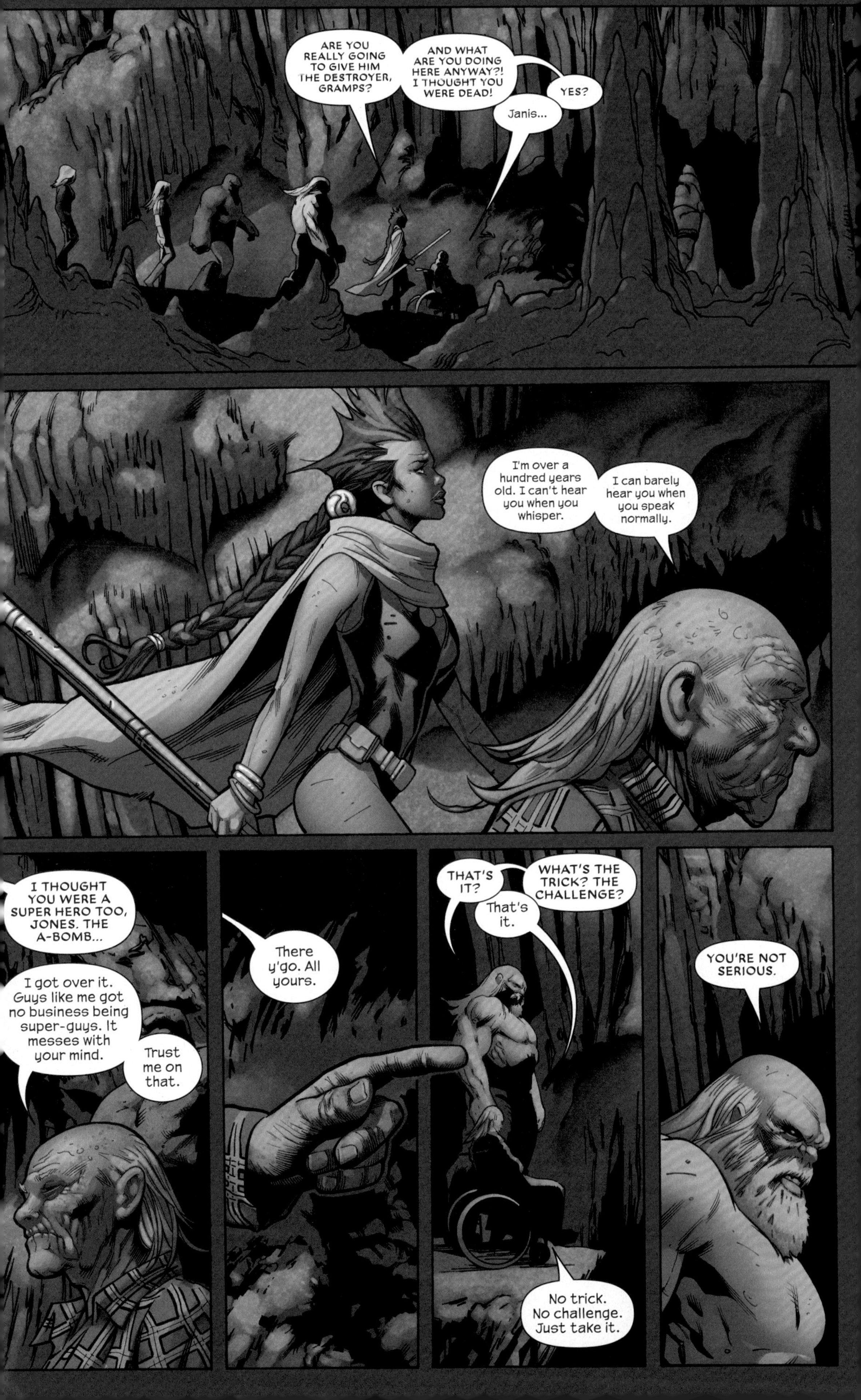
ARE YOU REALLY GOING TO GIVE HIM THE DESTROYER, GRAMPS?
AND WHAT ARE YOU DOING HERE ANYWAY?! I THOUGHT YOU WERE DEAD!
Janis...
YES?
I'm over a hundred years old. I can't hear you when you whisper.
I can barely hear you when you speak normally.
I THOUGHT YOU WERE A SUPER HERO TOO, JONES. THE A-BOMB...
I got over it. Guys like me got no business being super-guys. It messes with your mind.
Trust me on that.
There y'go. All yours.
THAT'S IT?
WHAT'S THE TRICK? THE CHALLENGE?
That's it.
No trick. No challenge. Just take it.
YOU'RE NOT SERIOUS.

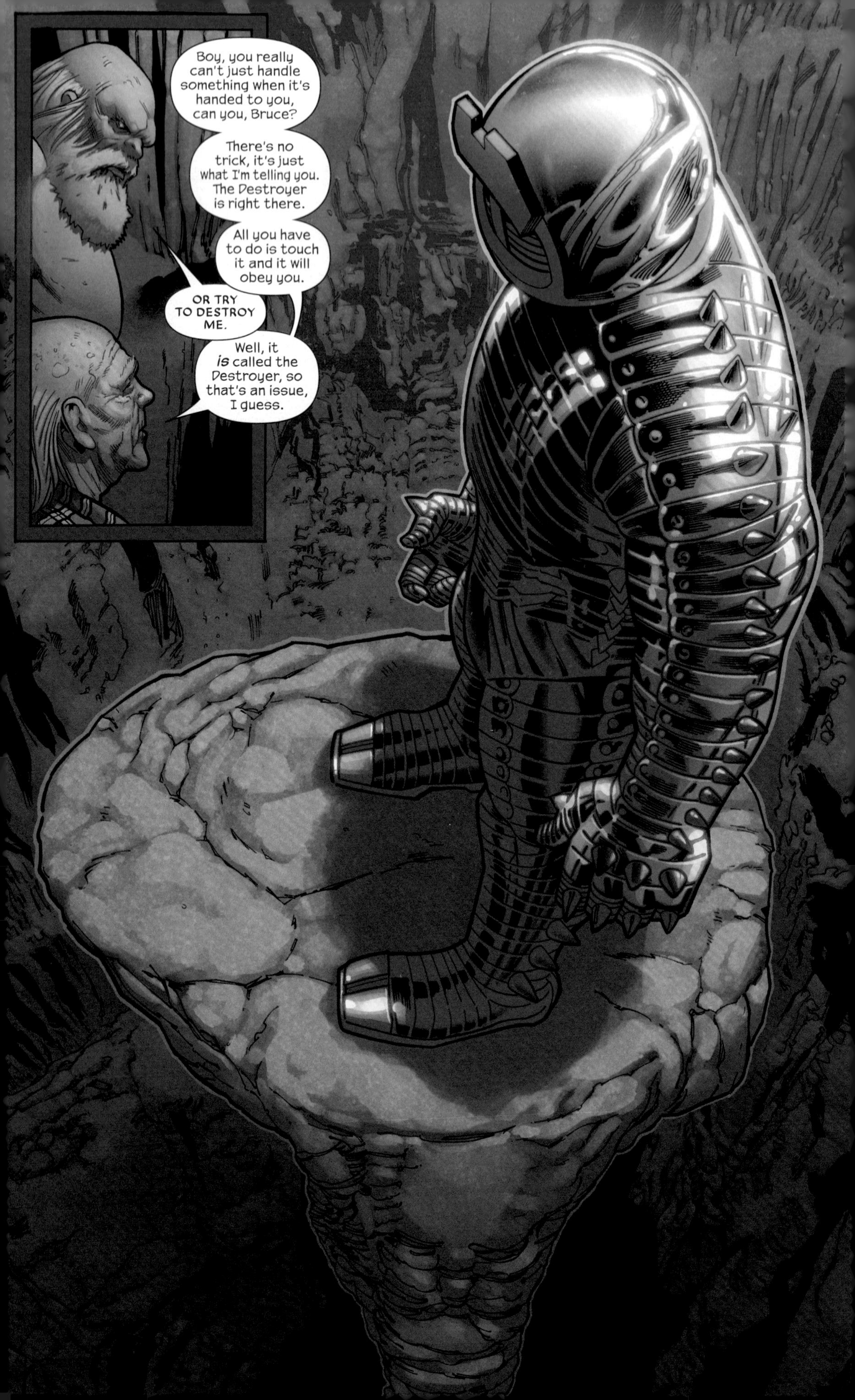
Boy, you really can't just handle something when it's handed to you, can you, Bruce?
There's no trick, it's just what I'm telling you. The Destroyer is right there.
All you have to do is touch it and it will obey you.
OR TRY TO DESTROY ME.
Well, it *is* called the Destroyer, so that's an issue, I guess.

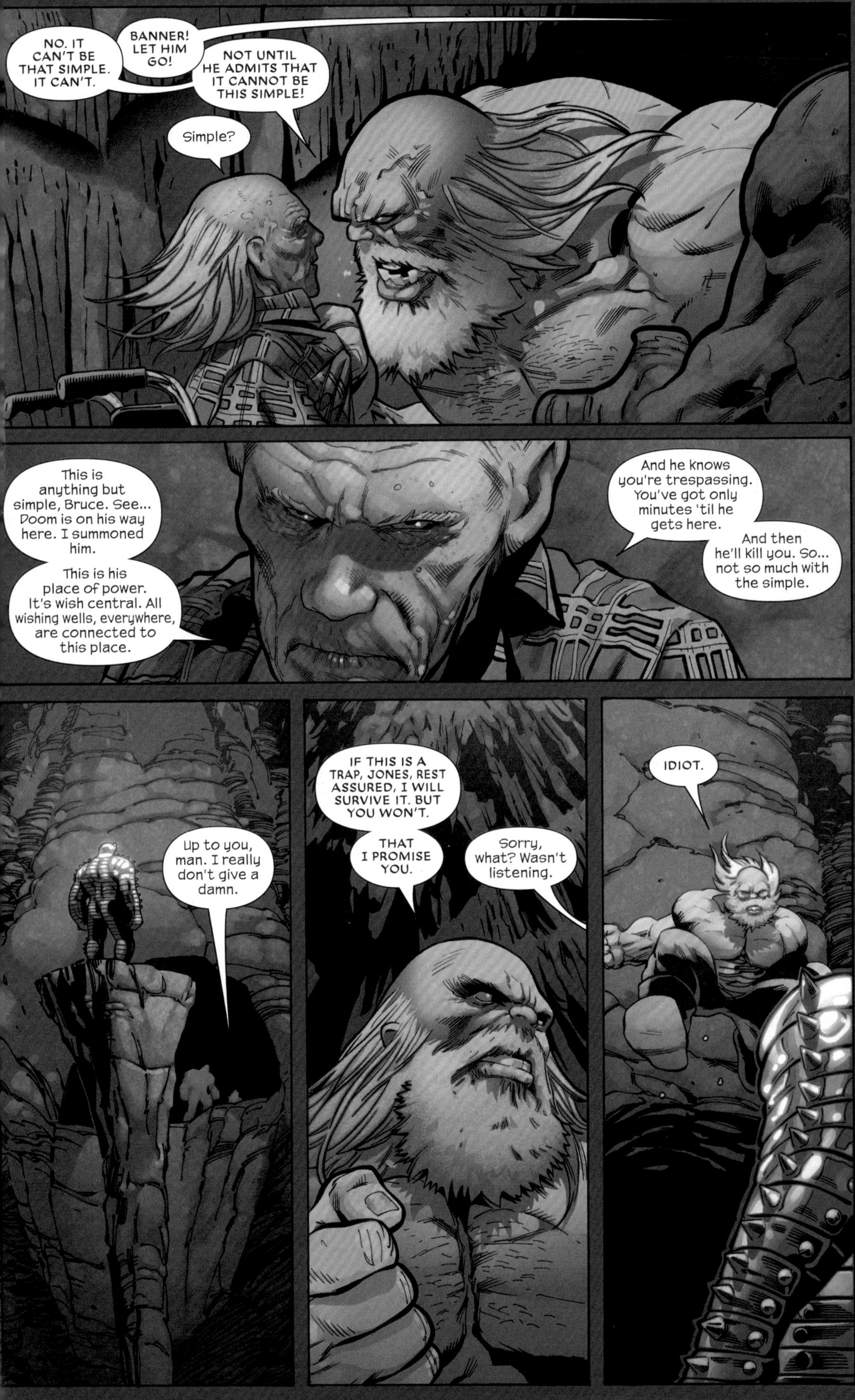
NO. IT CAN'T BE THAT SIMPLE. IT CAN'T.
BANNER! LET HIM GO!
NOT UNTIL HE ADMITS THAT IT CANNOT BE THIS SIMPLE!
Simple?
This is anything but simple, Bruce. See... Doom is on his way here. I summoned him.
This is his place of power. It's wish central. All wishing wells, everywhere, are connected to this place.
And he knows you're trespassing. You've got only minutes 'til he gets here.
And then he'll kill you. So... not so much with the simple.
Up to you, man. I really don't give a damn.
IF THIS IS A TRAP, JONES, REST ASSURED, I WILL SURVIVE IT. BUT YOU WON'T.
THAT I PROMISE YOU.
Sorry, what? Wasn't listening.
IDIOT.

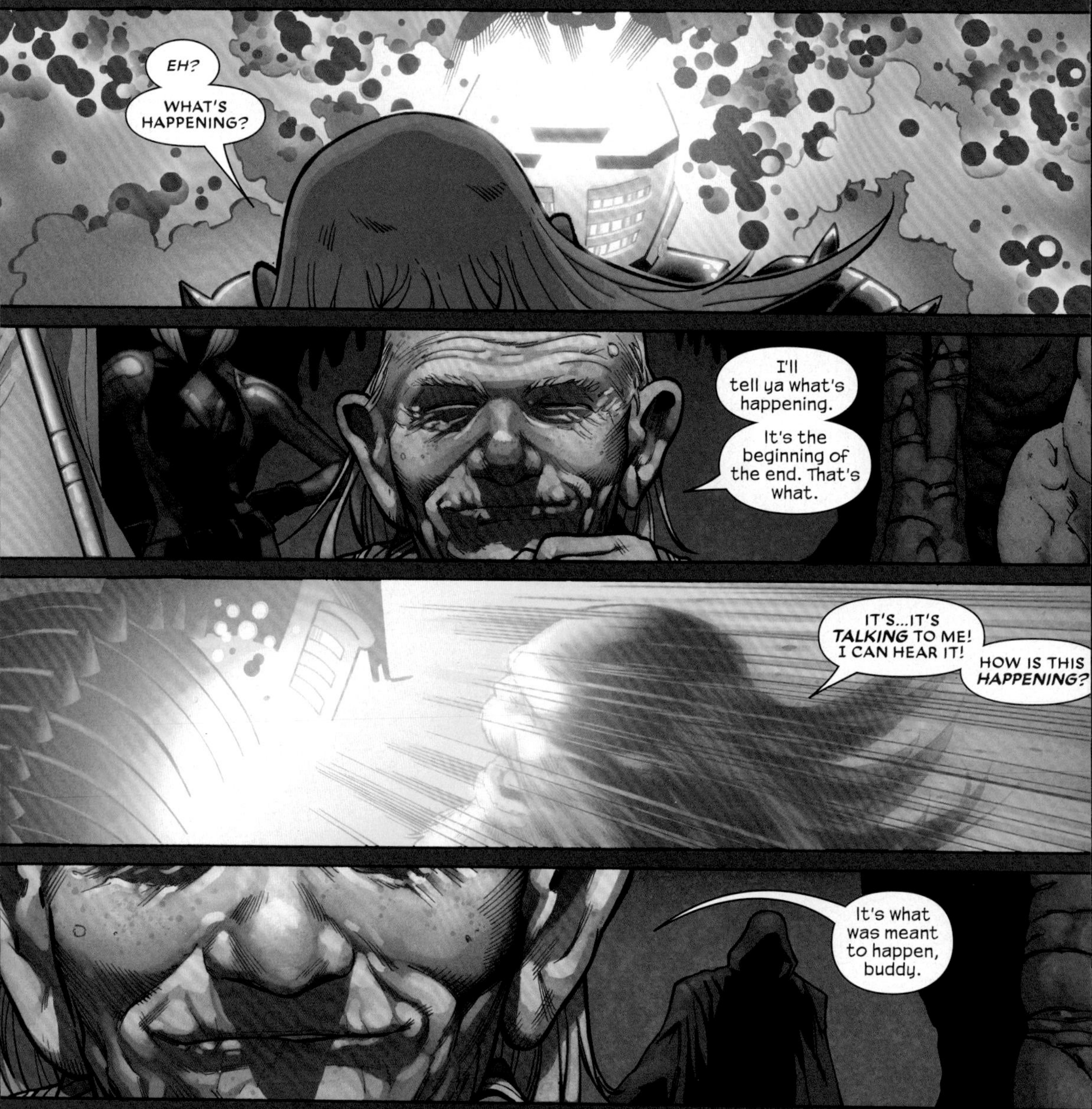
EH?
WHAT'S HAPPENING?
I'll tell ya what's happening.
It's the beginning of the end. That's what.
IT'S...IT'S TALKING TO ME! I CAN HEAR IT!
HOW IS THIS HAPPENING?
It's what was meant to happen, buddy.

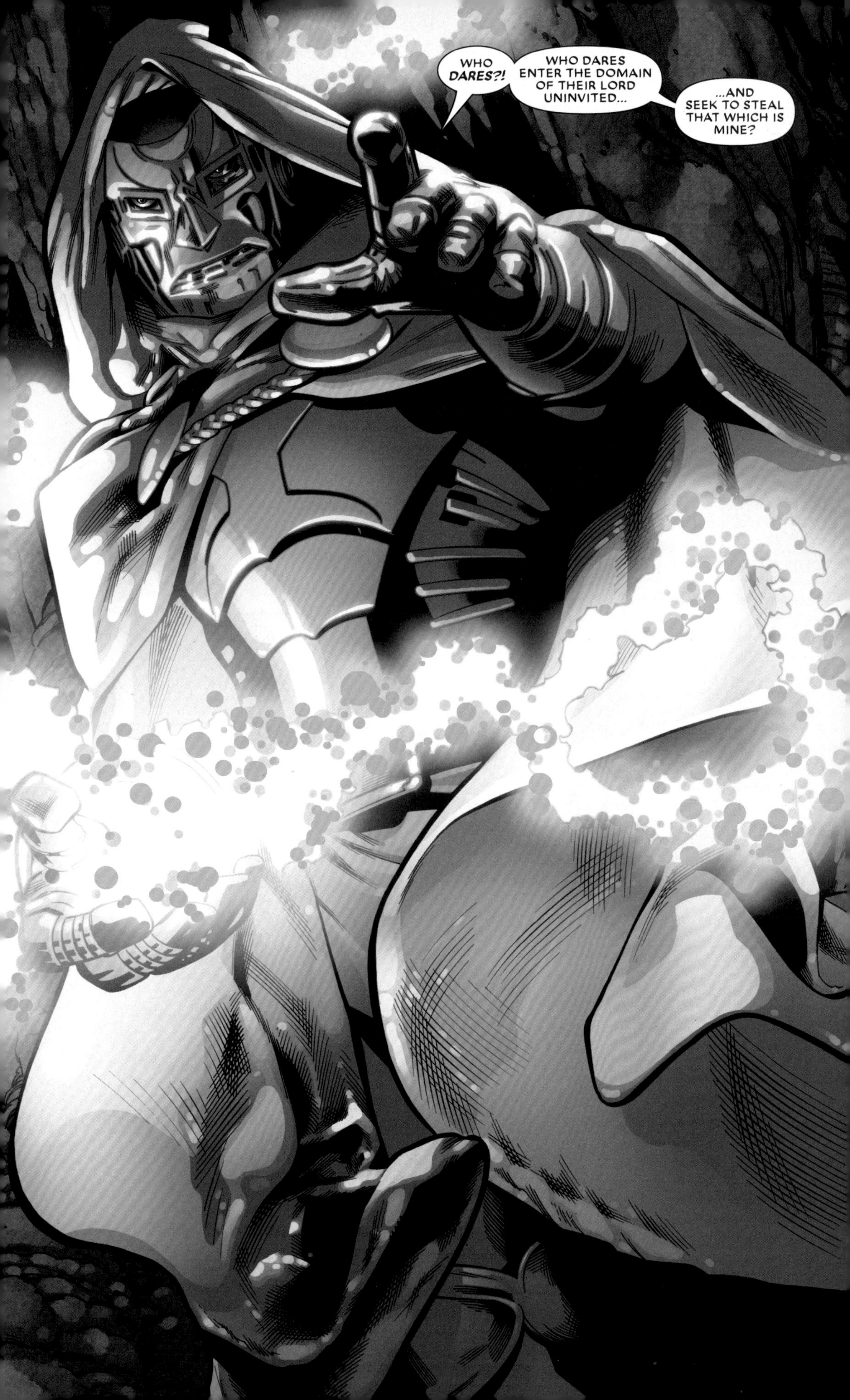
WHO DARES?!
WHO DARES ENTER THE DOMAIN OF THEIR LORD UNINVITED...
...AND SEEK TO STEAL THAT WHICH IS MINE?

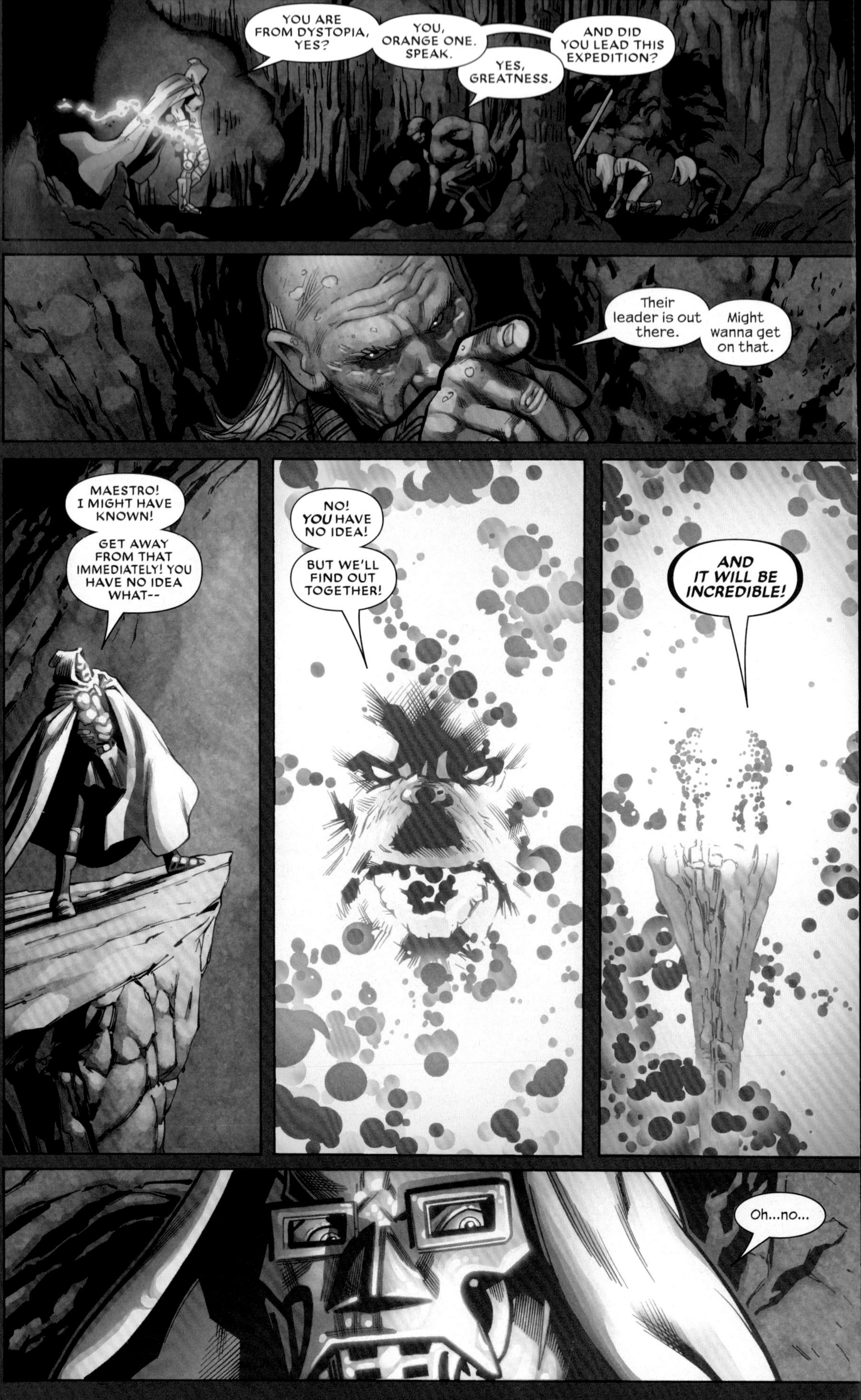
YOU ARE FROM DYSTOPIA, YES?
YOU, ORANGE ONE. SPEAK.
YES, GREATNESS.
AND DID YOU LEAD THIS EXPEDITION?
Their leader is out there.
Might wanna get on that.
MAESTRO! I MIGHT HAVE KNOWN!
GET AWAY FROM THAT IMMEDIATELY! YOU HAVE NO IDEA WHAT--
NO! YOU HAVE NO IDEA!
BUT WE'LL FIND OUT TOGETHER!
AND IT WILL BE INCREDIBLE!
Oh...no...

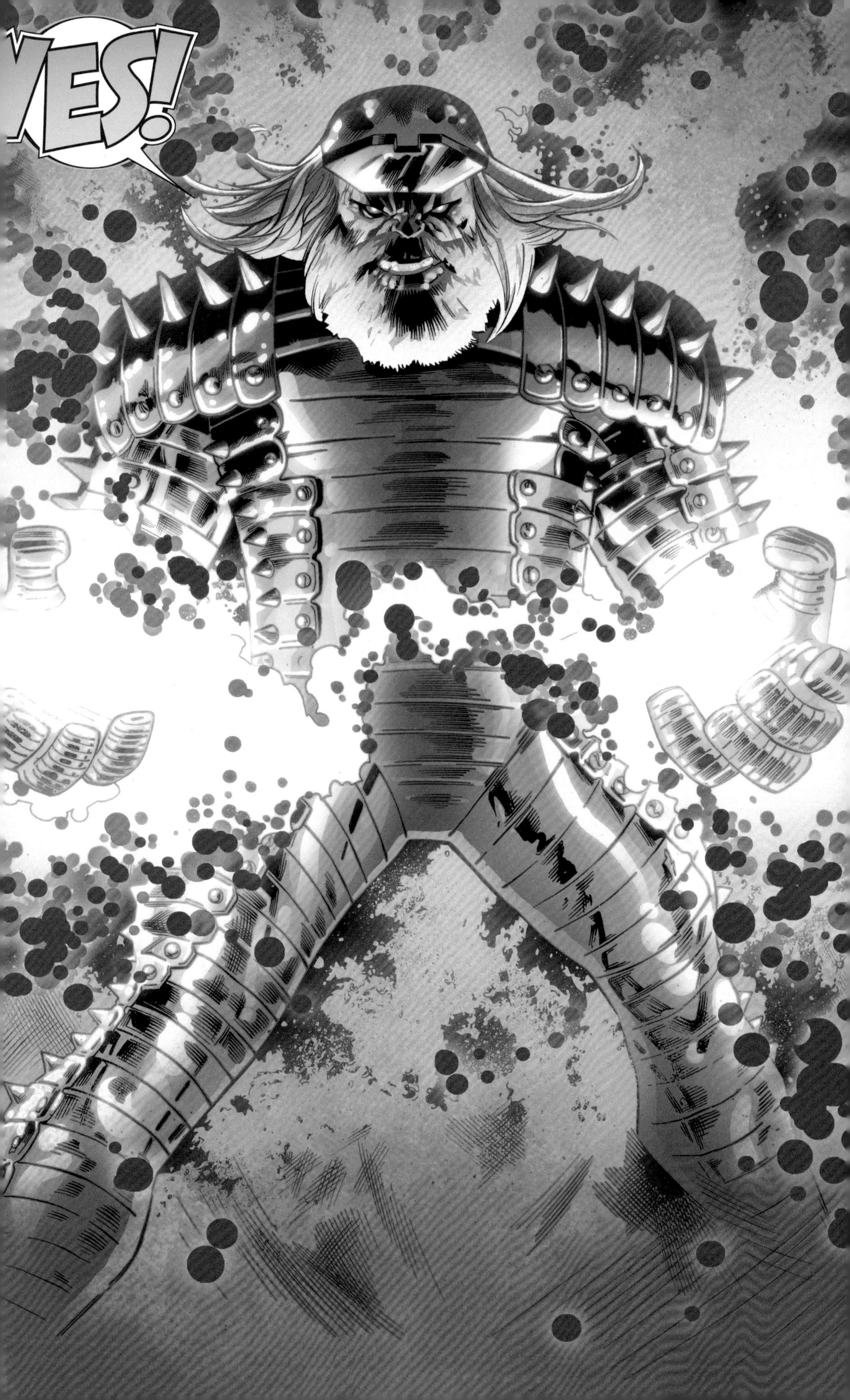
YES!

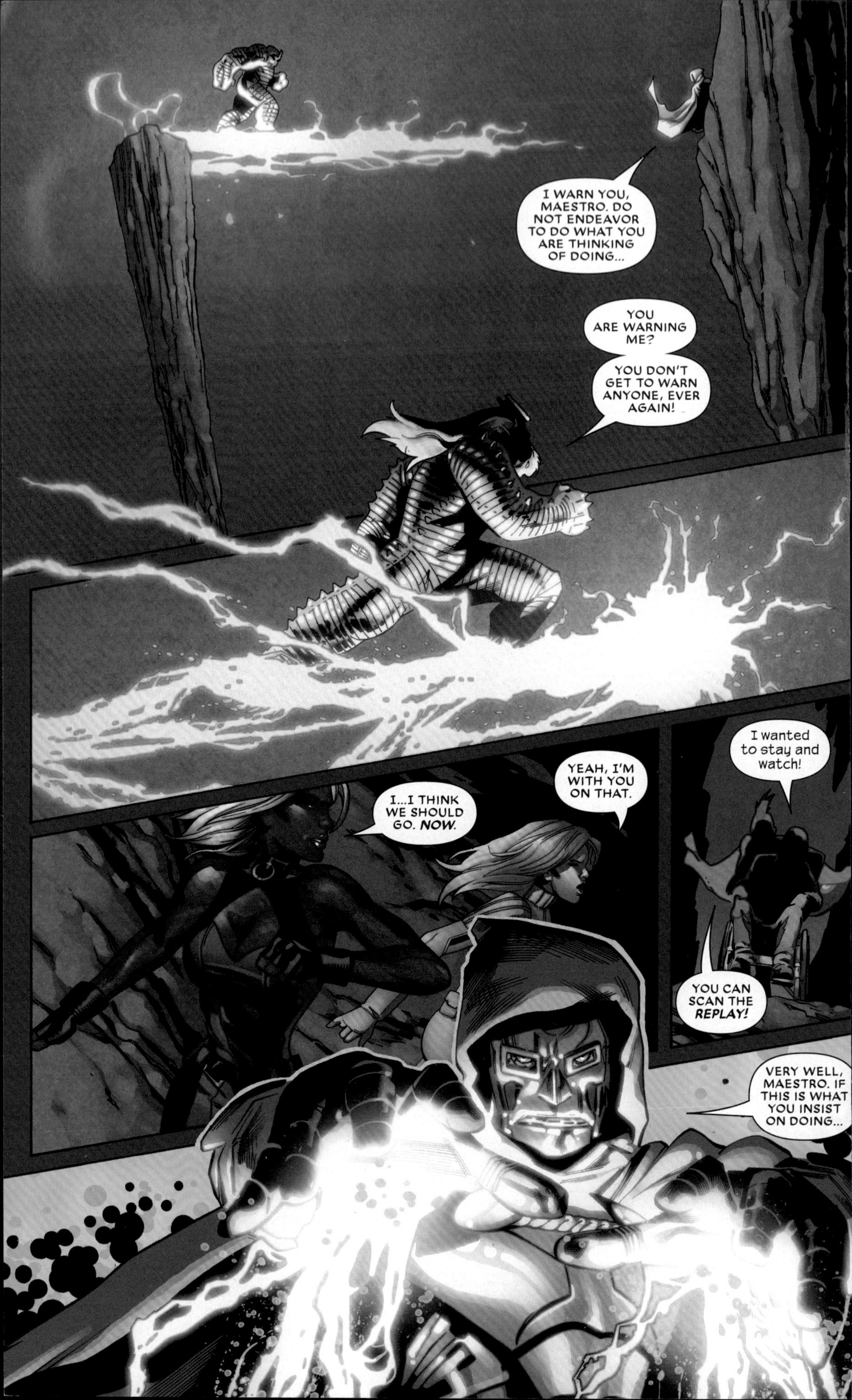
I WARN YOU, MAESTRO. DO NOT ENDEAVOR TO DO WHAT YOU ARE THINKING OF DOING...
YOU ARE WARNING ME?
YOU DON'T GET TO WARN ANYONE, EVER AGAIN!
I...I THINK WE SHOULD GO. **NOW**.
YEAH, I'M WITH YOU ON THAT.
I wanted to stay and watch!
YOU CAN SCAN THE ***REPLAY!***
VERY WELL, MAESTRO. IF THIS IS WHAT YOU INSIST ON DOING...

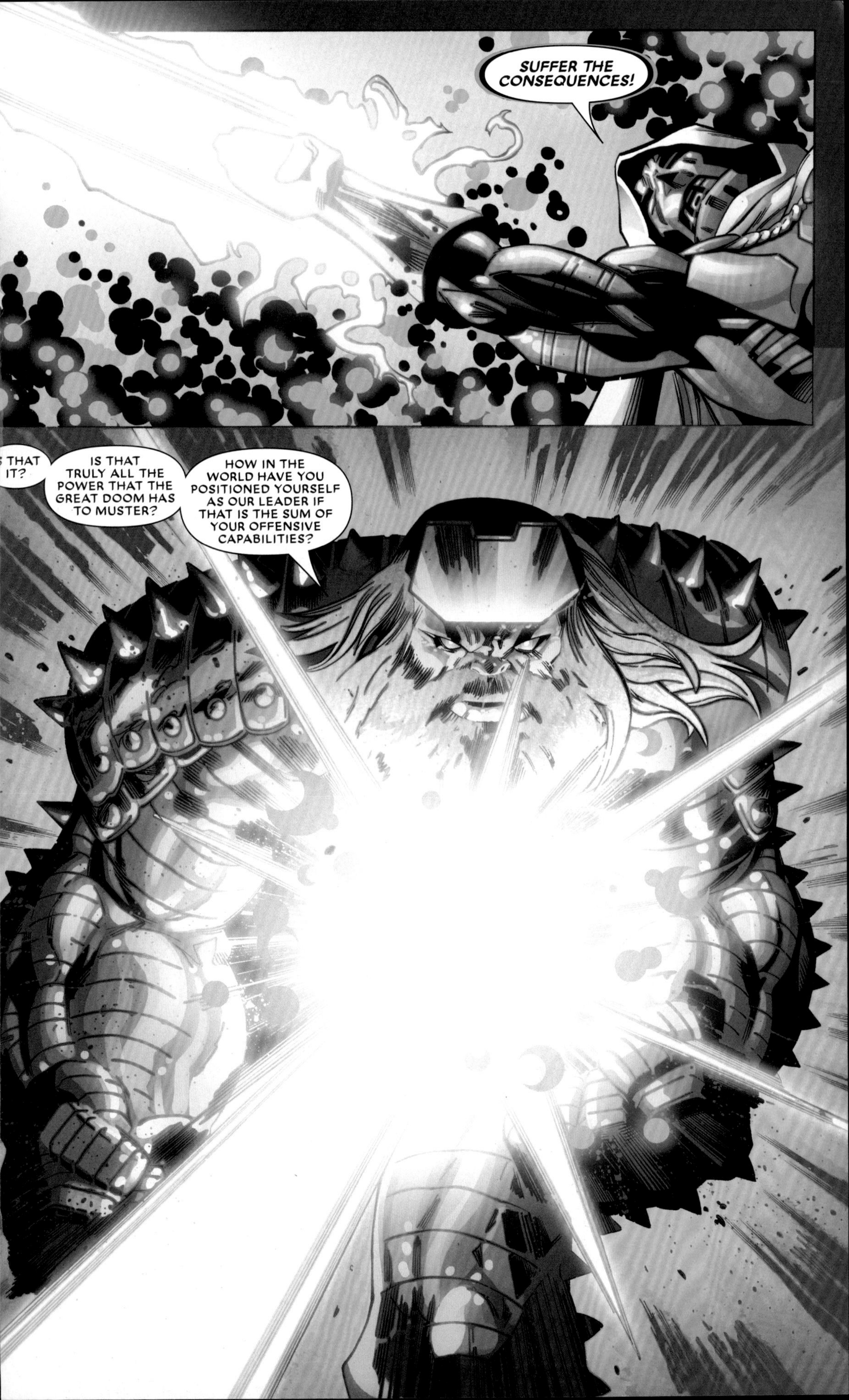

SUFFER THE CONSEQUENCES!
S THAT IT?
IS THAT TRULY ALL THE POWER THAT THE GREAT DOOM HAS TO MUSTER?
HOW IN THE WORLD HAVE YOU POSITIONED YOURSELF AS OUR LEADER IF THAT IS THE SUM OF YOUR OFFENSIVE CAPABILITIES?

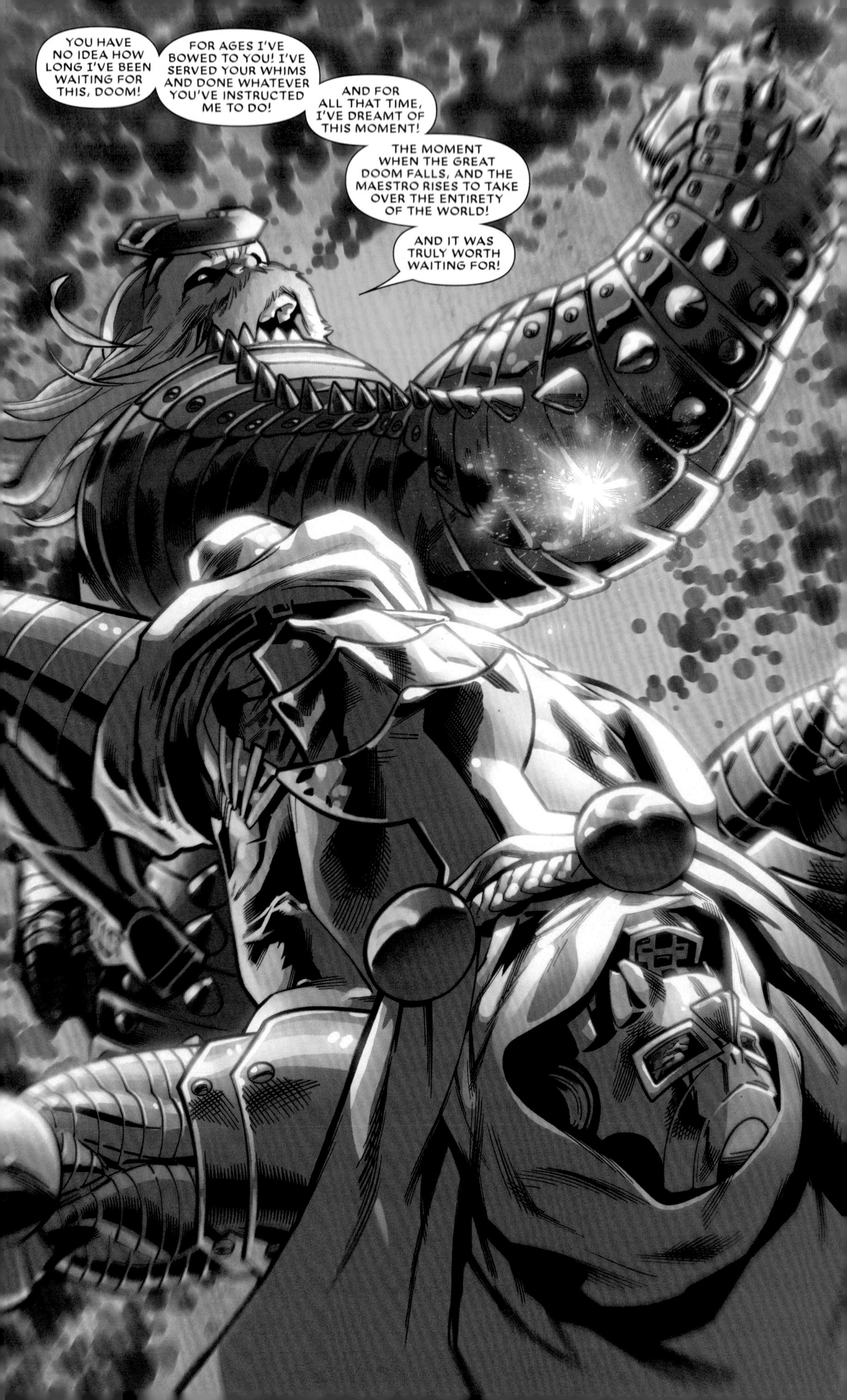
YOU HAVE NO IDEA HOW LONG I'VE BEEN WAITING FOR THIS, DOOM!
FOR AGES I'VE BOWED TO YOU! I'VE SERVED YOUR WHIMS AND DONE WHATEVER YOU'VE INSTRUCTED ME TO DO!
AND FOR ALL THAT TIME, I'VE DREAMT OF THIS MOMENT!
THE MOMENT WHEN THE GREAT DOOM FALLS, AND THE MAESTRO RISES TO TAKE OVER THE ENTIRETY OF THE WORLD!
AND IT WAS TRULY WORTH WAITING FOR!

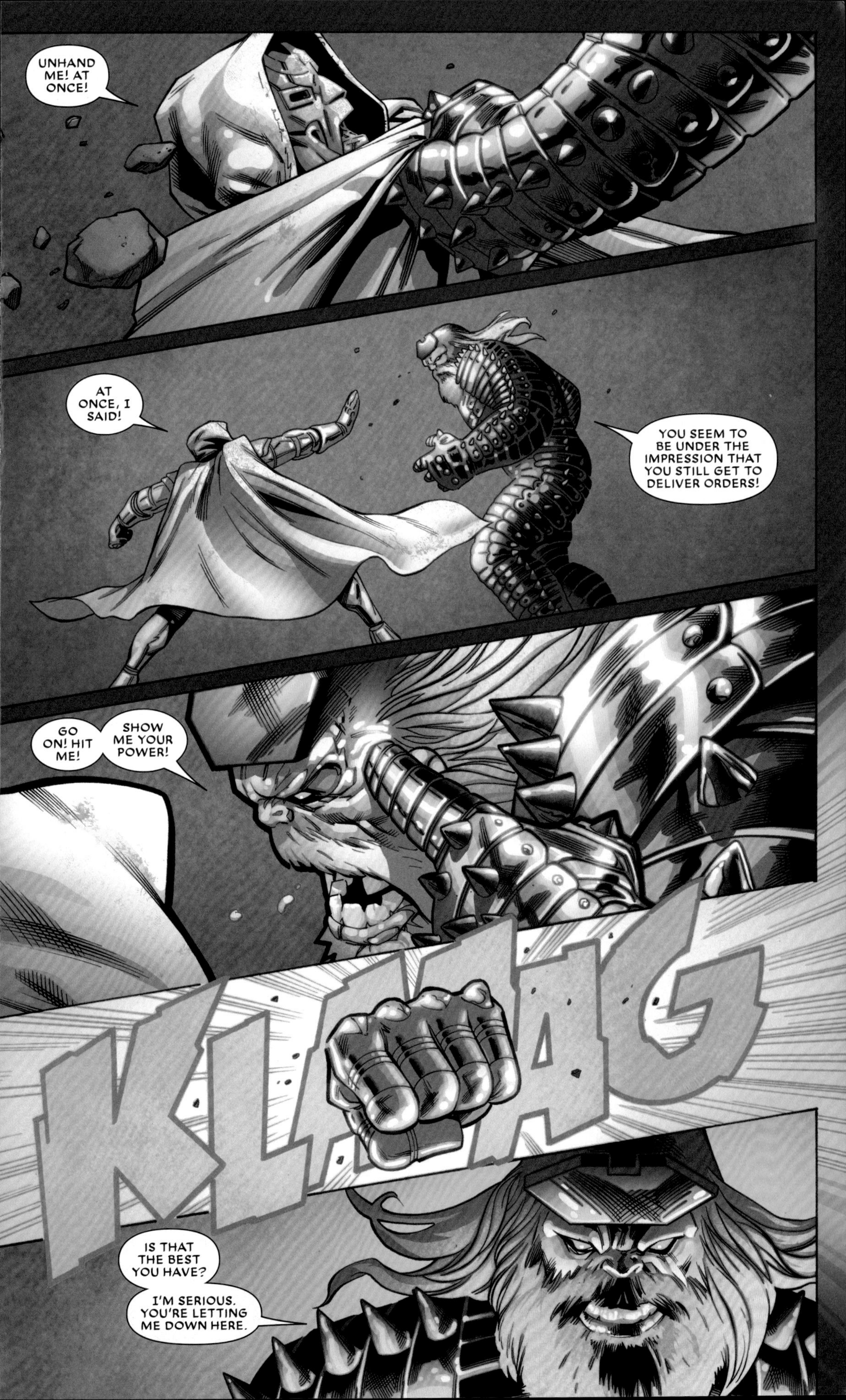
UNHAND ME! AT ONCE!
AT ONCE, I SAID!
YOU SEEM TO BE UNDER THE IMPRESSION THAT YOU STILL GET TO DELIVER ORDERS!
GO ON! HIT ME!
SHOW ME YOUR POWER!
KLANG
IS THAT THE BEST YOU HAVE?
I'M SERIOUS. YOU'RE LETTING ME DOWN HERE.

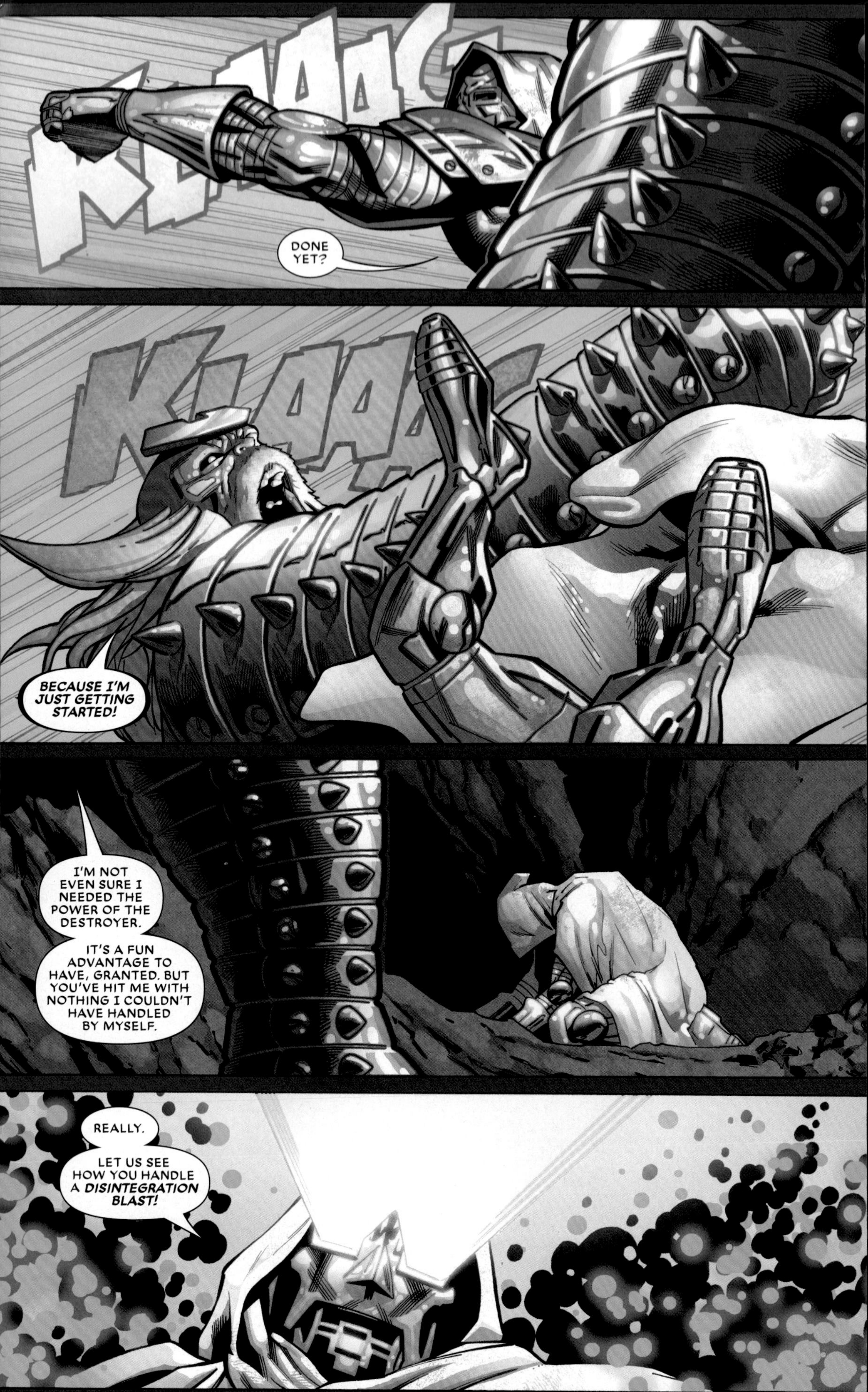
KRAAAC
DONE YET?
KRAAAC
BECAUSE I'M JUST GETTING STARTED!
I'M NOT EVEN SURE I NEEDED THE POWER OF THE DESTROYER.
IT'S A FUN ADVANTAGE TO HAVE, GRANTED. BUT YOU'VE HIT ME WITH NOTHING I COULDN'T HAVE HANDLED BY MYSELF.
REALLY.
LET US SEE HOW YOU HANDLE A DISINTEGRATION BLAST!

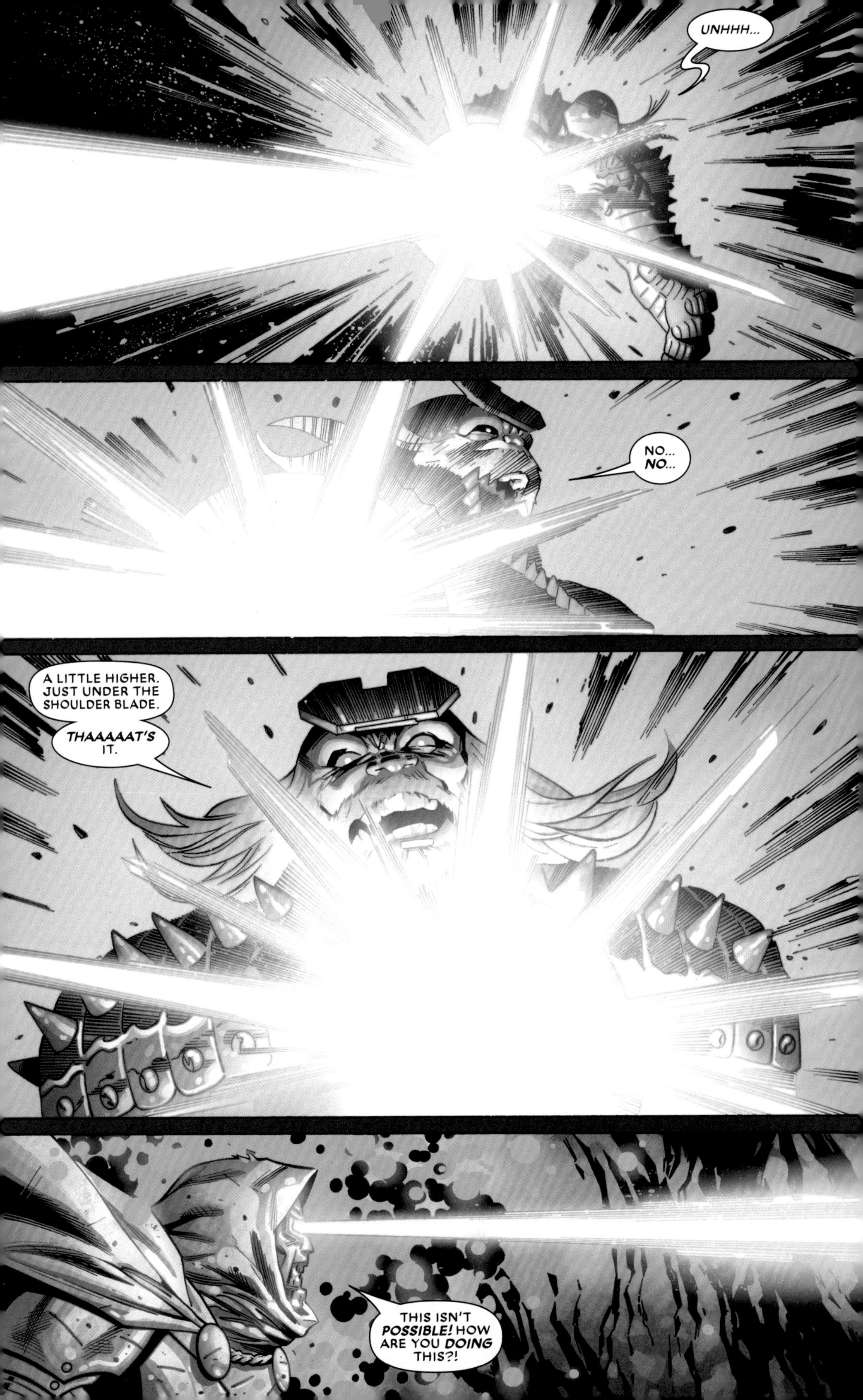
UNHHH...
NO... NO...
A LITTLE HIGHER. JUST UNDER THE SHOULDER BLADE.
THAAAAAT'S IT.
THIS ISN'T POSSIBLE! HOW ARE YOU DOING THIS?!

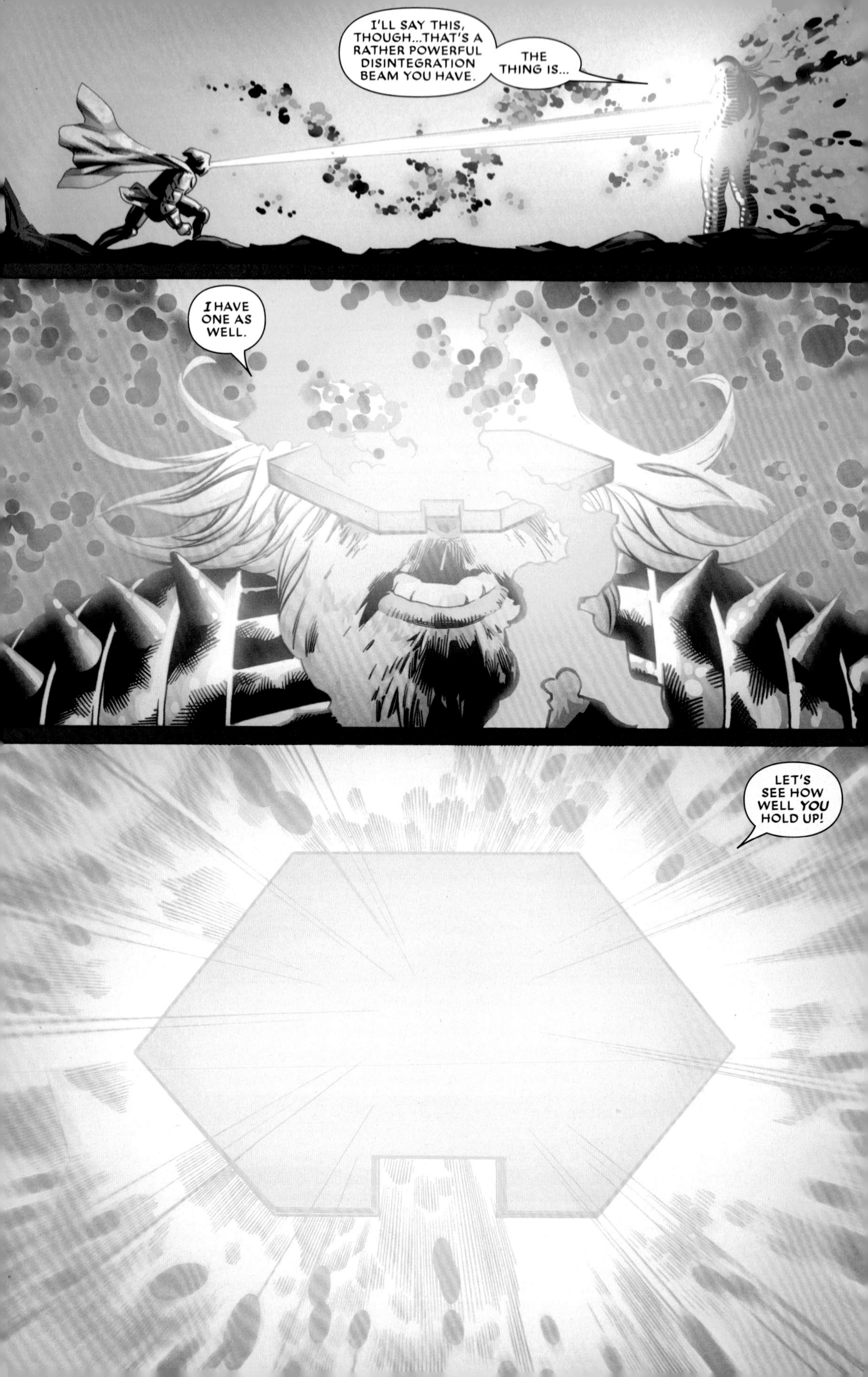
I'LL SAY THIS, THOUGH...THAT'S A RATHER POWERFUL DISINTEGRATION BEAM YOU HAVE.
THE THING IS...
I HAVE ONE AS WELL.
LET'S SEE HOW WELL YOU HOLD UP!

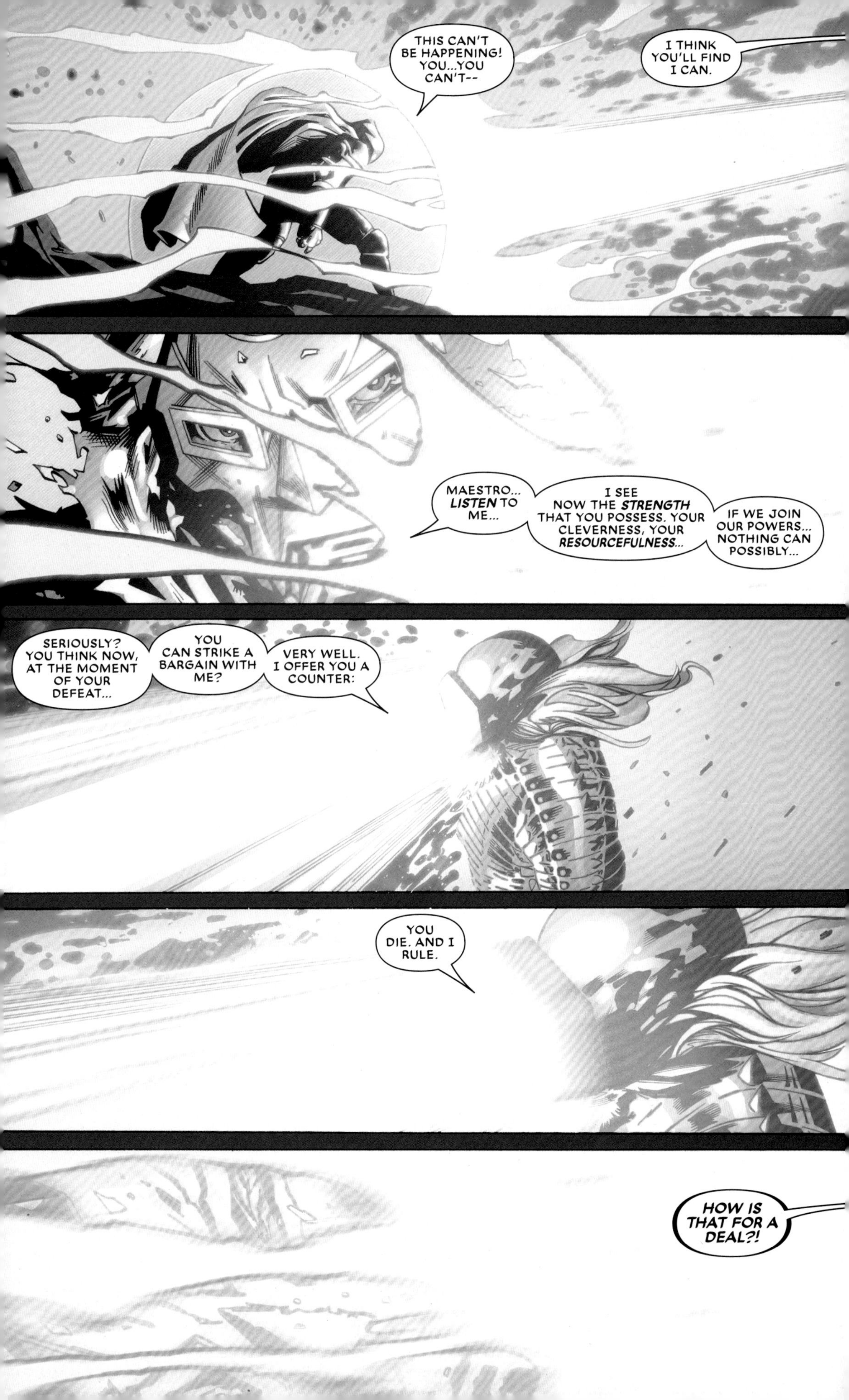
THIS CAN'T BE HAPPENING! YOU...YOU CAN'T--
I THINK YOU'LL FIND I CAN.
MAESTRO... **LISTEN** TO ME...
I SEE NOW THE **STRENGTH** THAT YOU POSSESS. YOUR CLEVERNESS, YOUR **RESOURCEFULNESS...**
IF WE JOIN OUR POWERS... NOTHING CAN POSSIBLY...
SERIOUSLY? YOU THINK NOW, AT THE MOMENT OF YOUR DEFEAT...
YOU CAN STRIKE A BARGAIN WITH ME?
VERY WELL. I OFFER YOU A COUNTER:
YOU DIE. AND I RULE.
HOW IS THAT FOR A DEAL?!

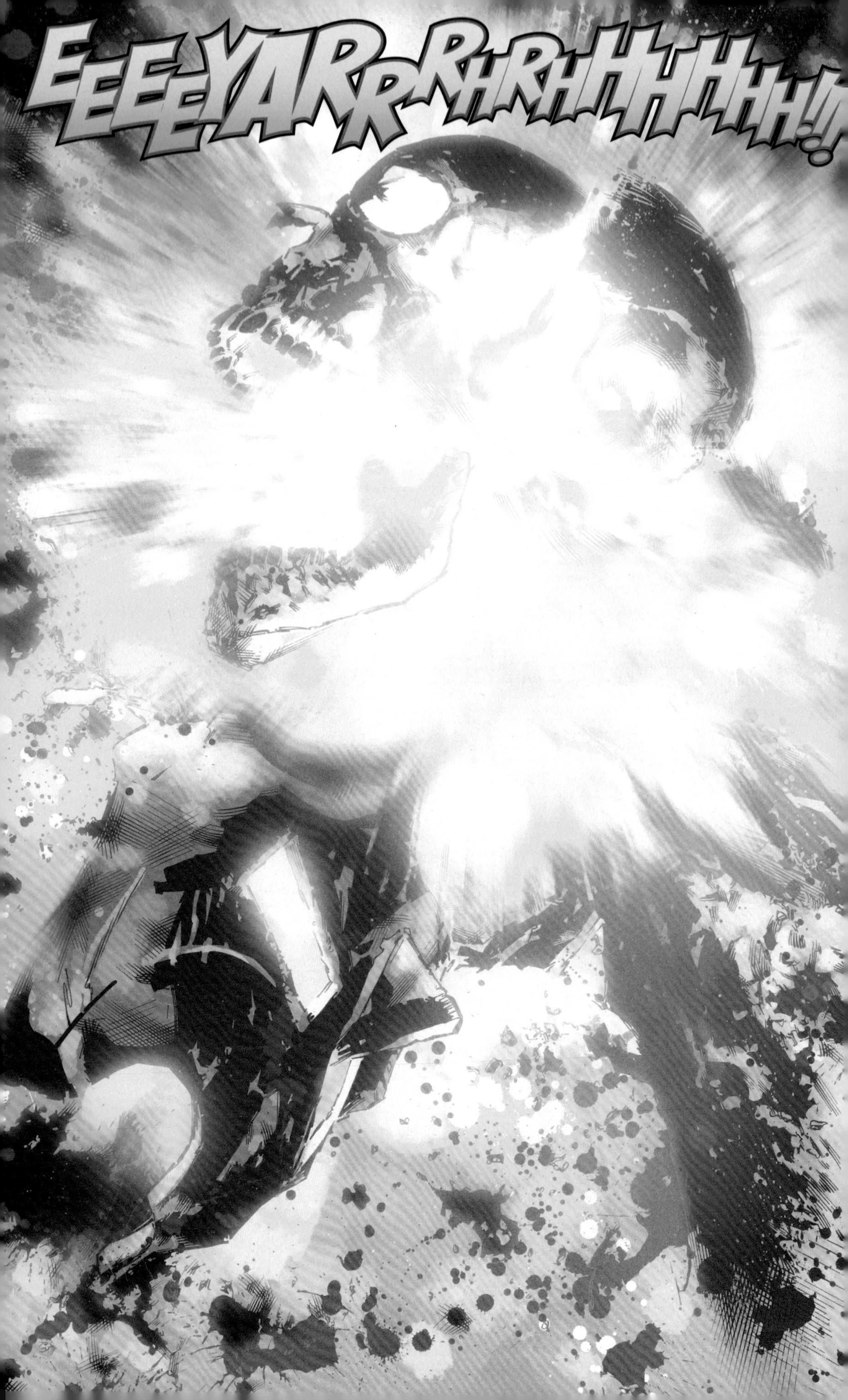
EEEE-YARRRHRHHHHHH!!

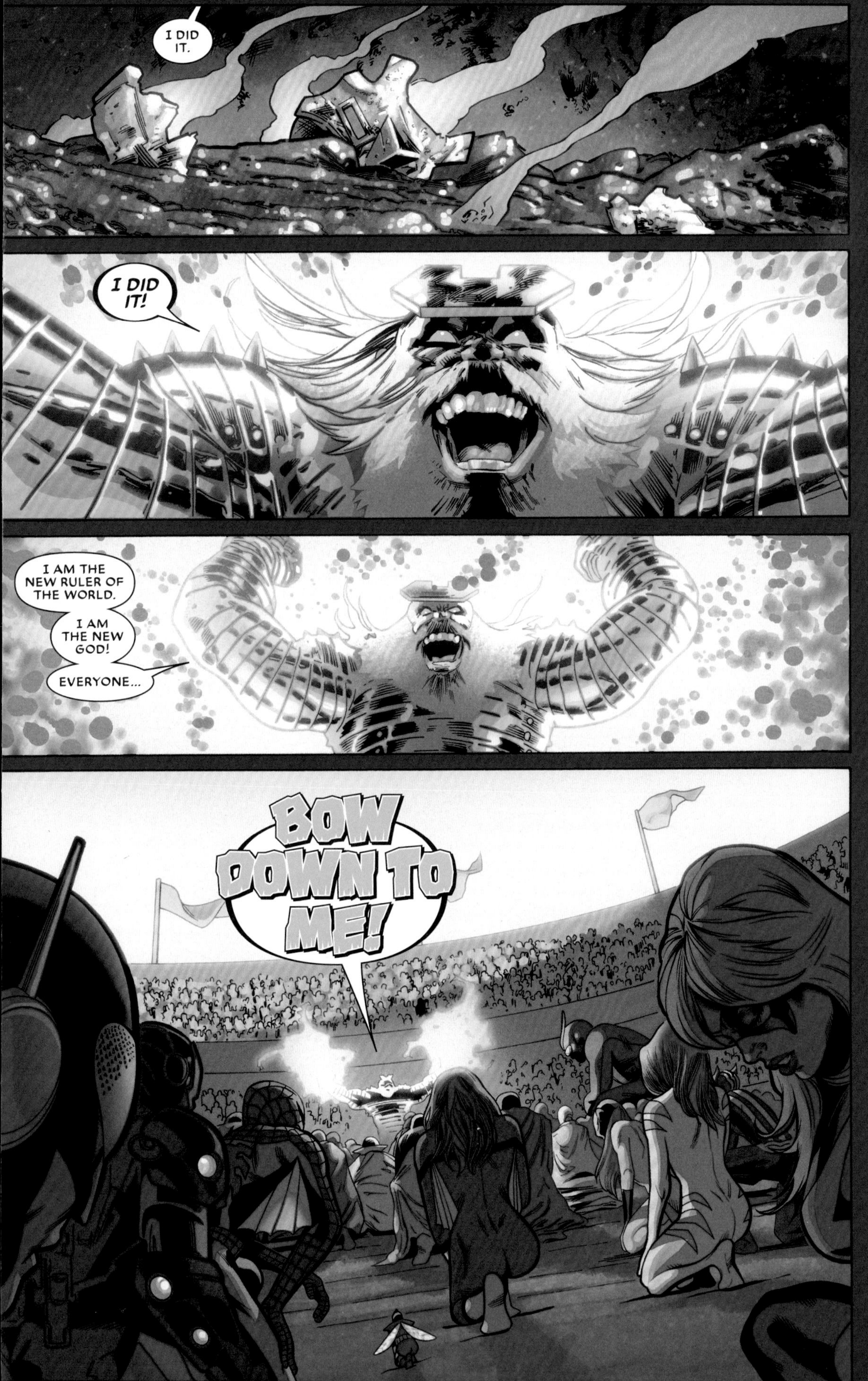

I DID IT.
I DID IT!
I AM THE NEW RULER OF THE WORLD.
I AM THE NEW GOD!
EVERYONE...
BOW DOWN TO ME!

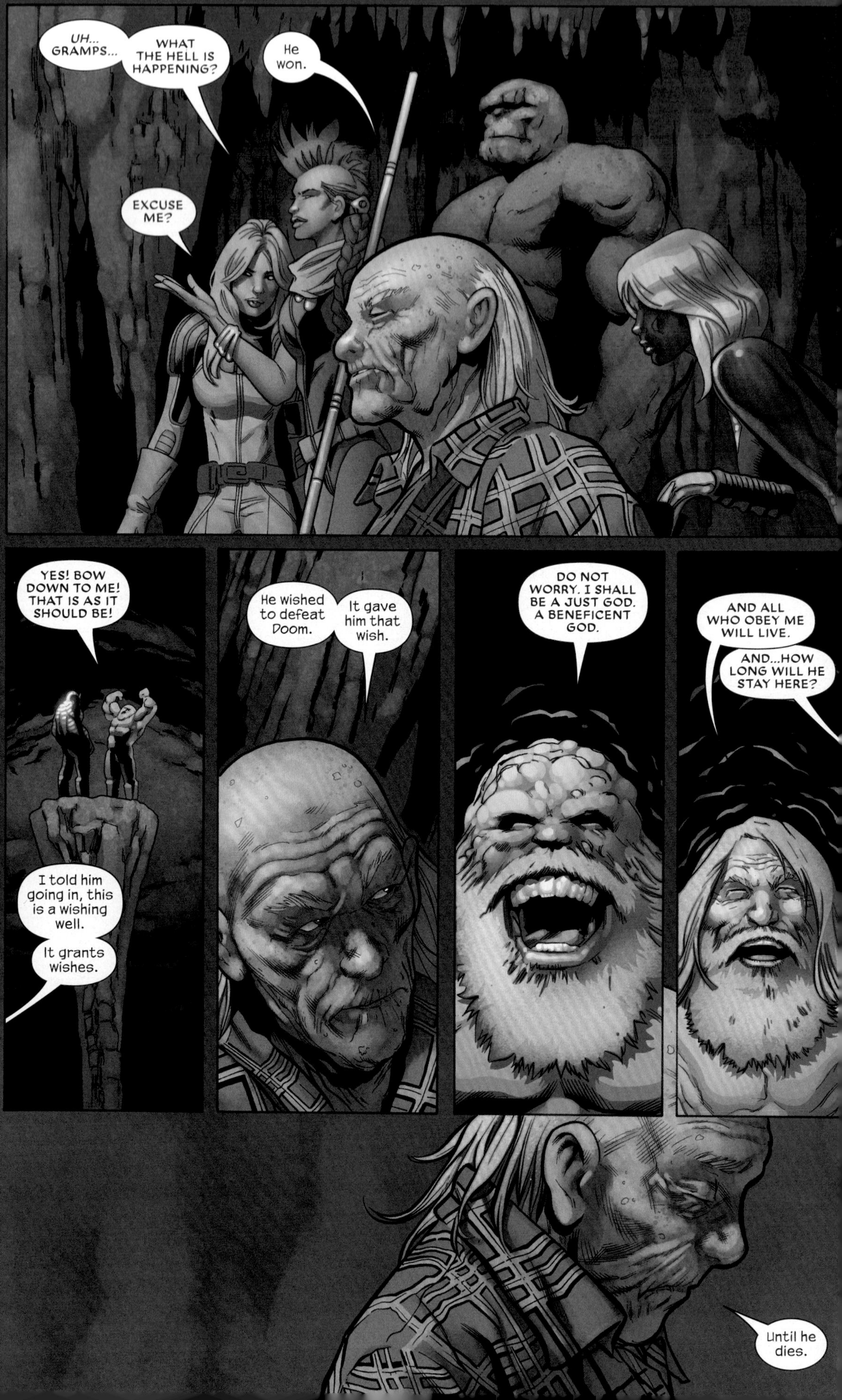

UH... GRAMPS...
WHAT THE HELL IS HAPPENING?
He won.
EXCUSE ME?
YES! BOW DOWN TO ME! THAT IS AS IT SHOULD BE!
I told him going in, this is a wishing well.
It grants wishes.
He wished to defeat Doom.
It gave him that wish.
DO NOT WORRY. I SHALL BE A JUST GOD. A BENEFICENT GOD.
AND ALL WHO OBEY ME WILL LIVE.
AND...HOW LONG WILL HE STAY HERE?
Until he dies.

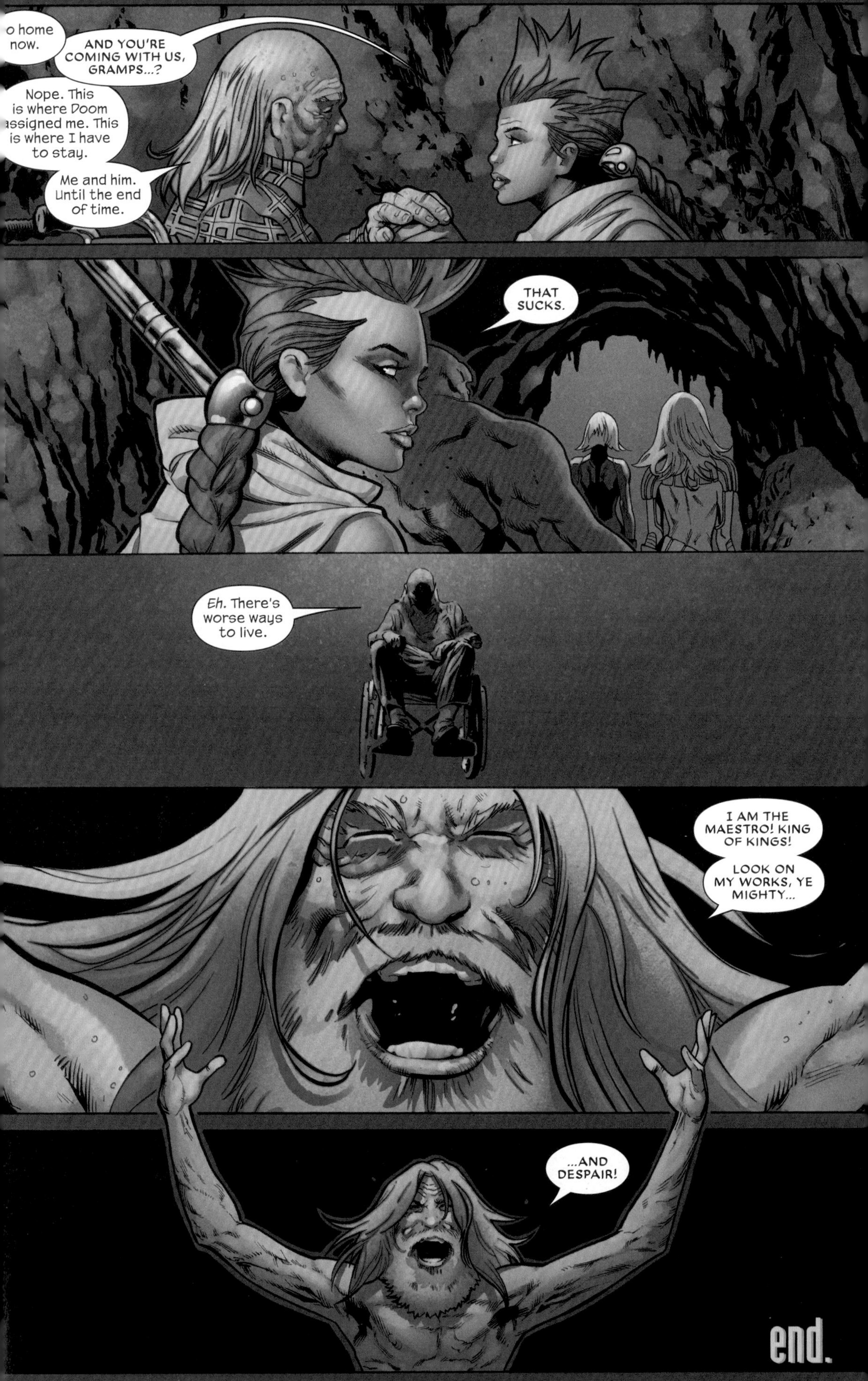
o home
now.
AND YOU'RE COMING WITH US, GRAMPS...?
Nope. This is where Doom assigned me. This is where I have to stay.
Me and him. Until the end of time.
THAT SUCKS.
Eh. There's worse ways to live.
I AM THE MAESTRO! KING OF KINGS!
LOOK ON MY WORKS, YE MIGHTY...
...AND DESPAIR!
end.

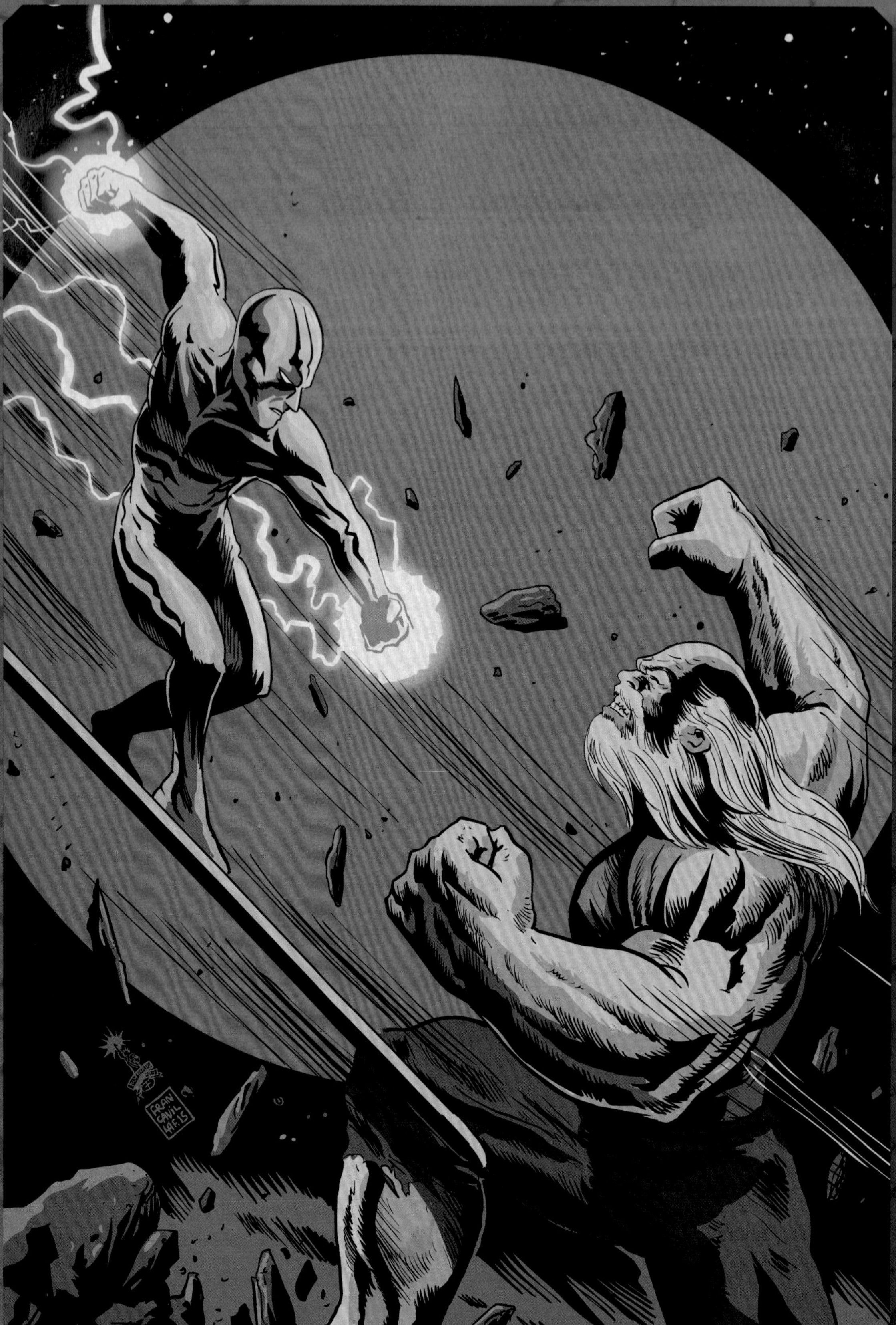

secret wars: battleworld #4

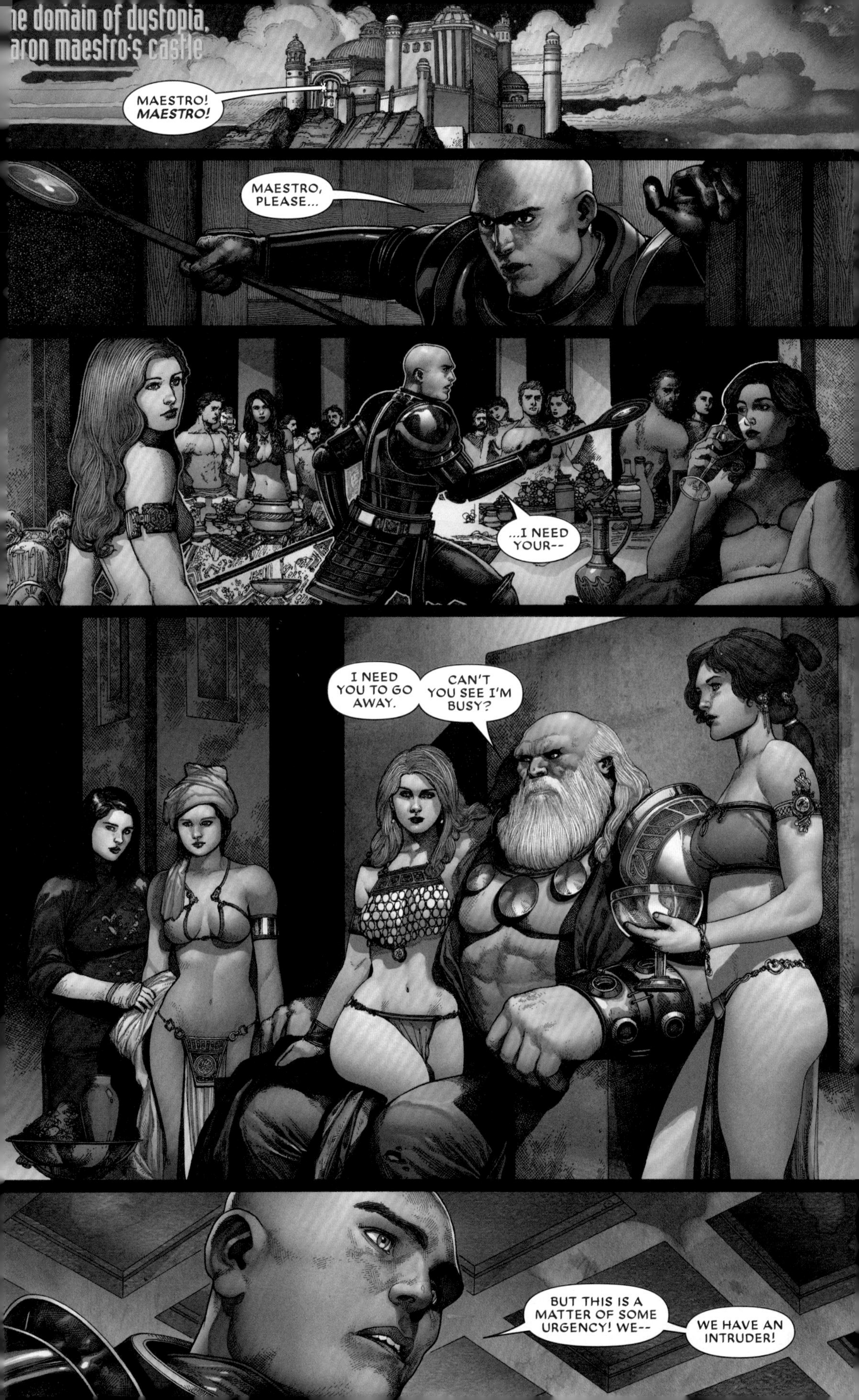

he domain of dystopia,
aron maestro's castle
MAESTRO! MAESTRO!
MAESTRO, PLEASE...
...I NEED YOUR--
I NEED YOU TO GO AWAY.
CAN'T YOU SEE I'M BUSY?
BUT THIS IS A MATTER OF SOME URGENCY! WE--
WE HAVE AN INTRUDER!

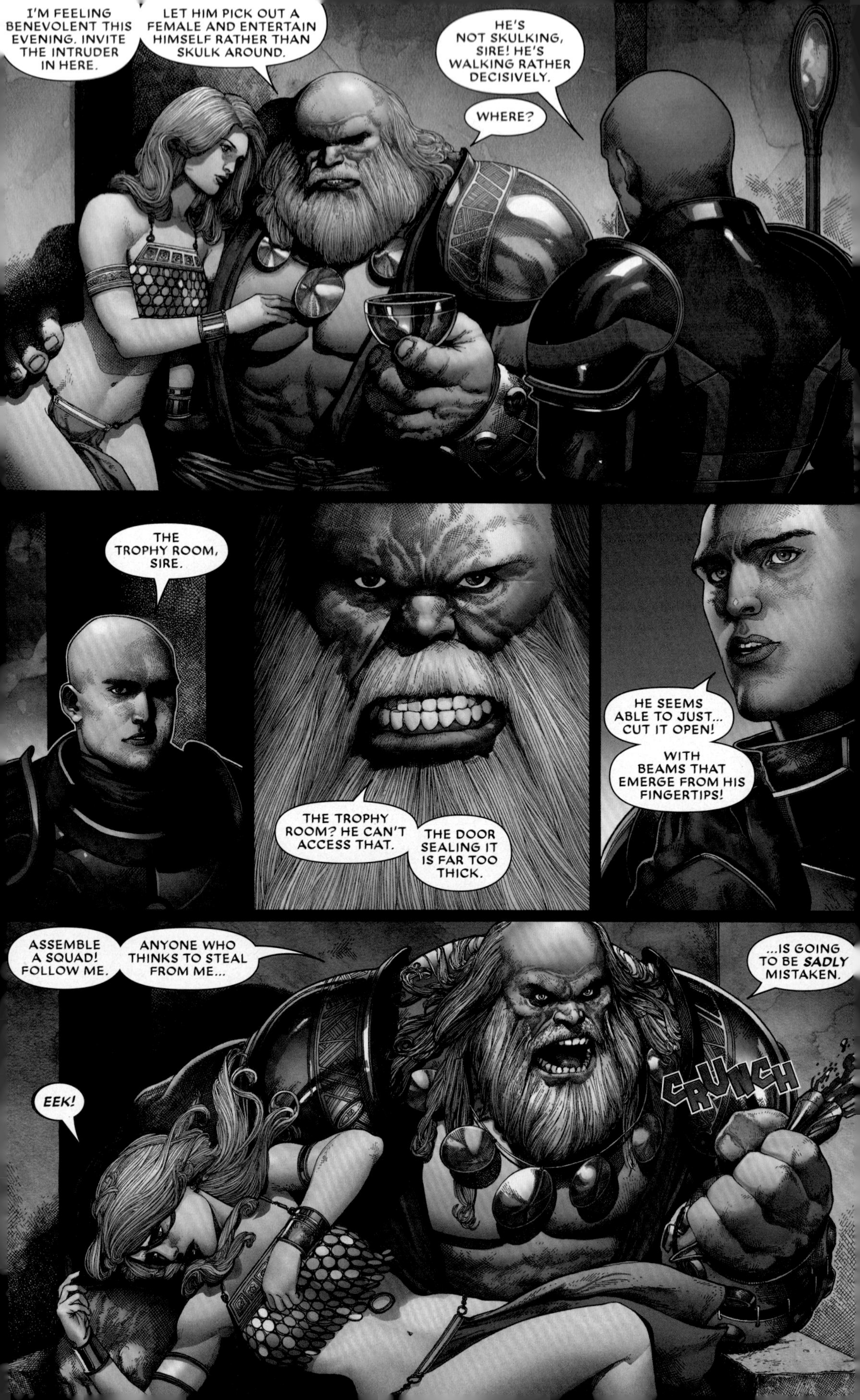
I'M FEELING BENEVOLENT THIS EVENING. INVITE THE INTRUDER IN HERE.
LET HIM PICK OUT A FEMALE AND ENTERTAIN HIMSELF RATHER THAN SKULK AROUND.
HE'S NOT SKULKING, SIRE! HE'S WALKING RATHER DECISIVELY.
WHERE?
THE TROPHY ROOM, SIRE.
THE TROPHY ROOM? HE CAN'T ACCESS THAT.
THE DOOR SEALING IT IS FAR TOO THICK.
HE SEEMS ABLE TO JUST... CUT IT OPEN!
WITH BEAMS THAT EMERGE FROM HIS FINGERTIPS!
ASSEMBLE A SQUAD! FOLLOW ME.
ANYONE WHO THINKS TO STEAL FROM ME...
...IS GOING TO BE *SADLY* MISTAKEN.
EEK!
CRUNCH

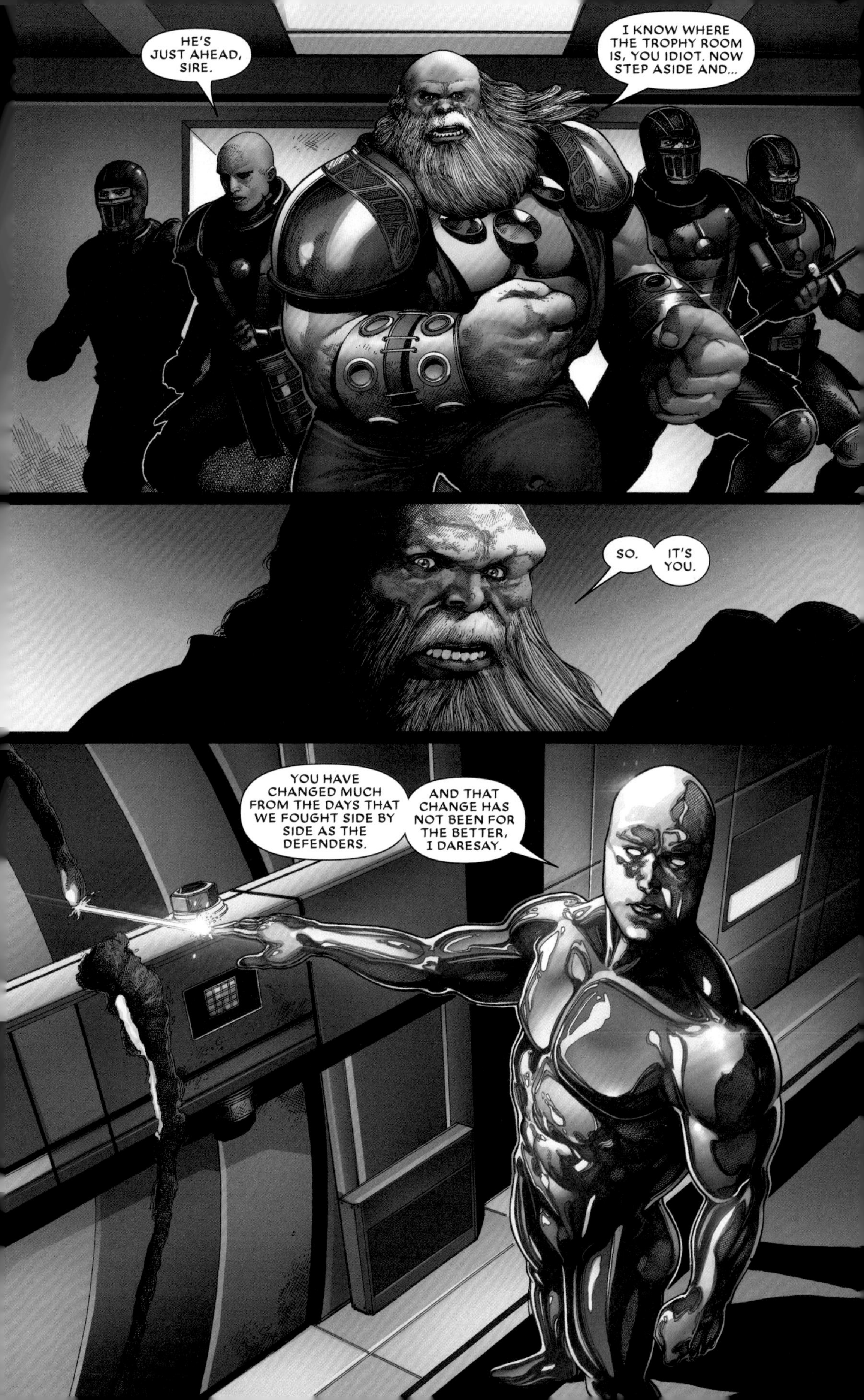
HE'S JUST AHEAD, SIRE.
I KNOW WHERE THE TROPHY ROOM IS, YOU IDIOT. NOW STEP ASIDE AND...
SO.
IT'S YOU.
YOU HAVE CHANGED MUCH FROM THE DAYS THAT WE FOUGHT SIDE BY SIDE AS THE DEFENDERS.
AND THAT CHANGE HAS NOT BEEN FOR THE BETTER, I DARESAY.

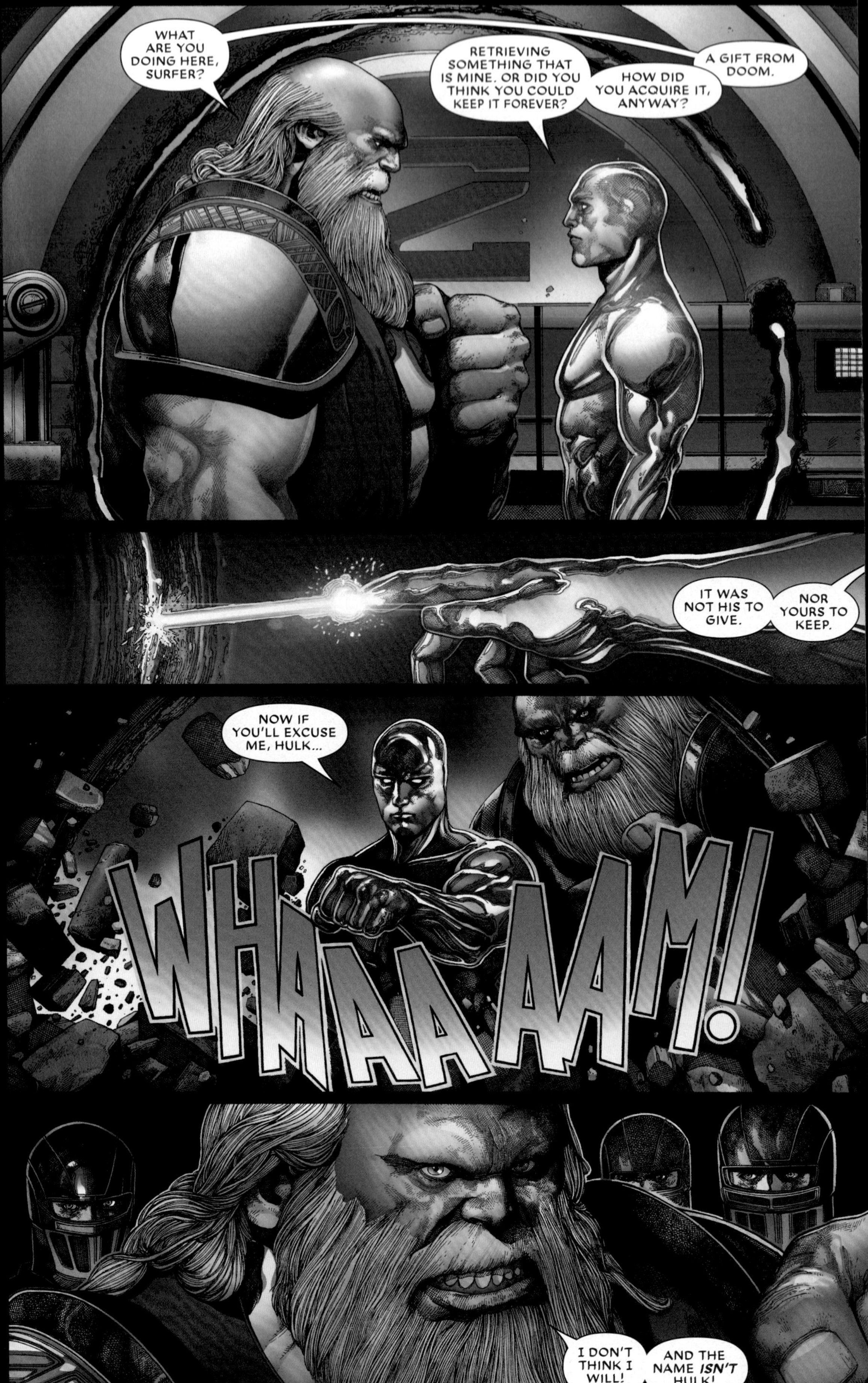
WHAT ARE YOU DOING HERE, SURFER?
RETRIEVING SOMETHING THAT IS MINE. OR DID YOU THINK YOU COULD KEEP IT FOREVER?
HOW DID YOU ACQUIRE IT, ANYWAY?
A GIFT FROM DOOM.
IT WAS NOT HIS TO GIVE.
NOR YOURS TO KEEP.
NOW IF YOU'LL EXCUSE ME, HULK...
WHAAAAM!
I DON'T THINK I WILL!
AND THE NAME *ISN'T* HULK!

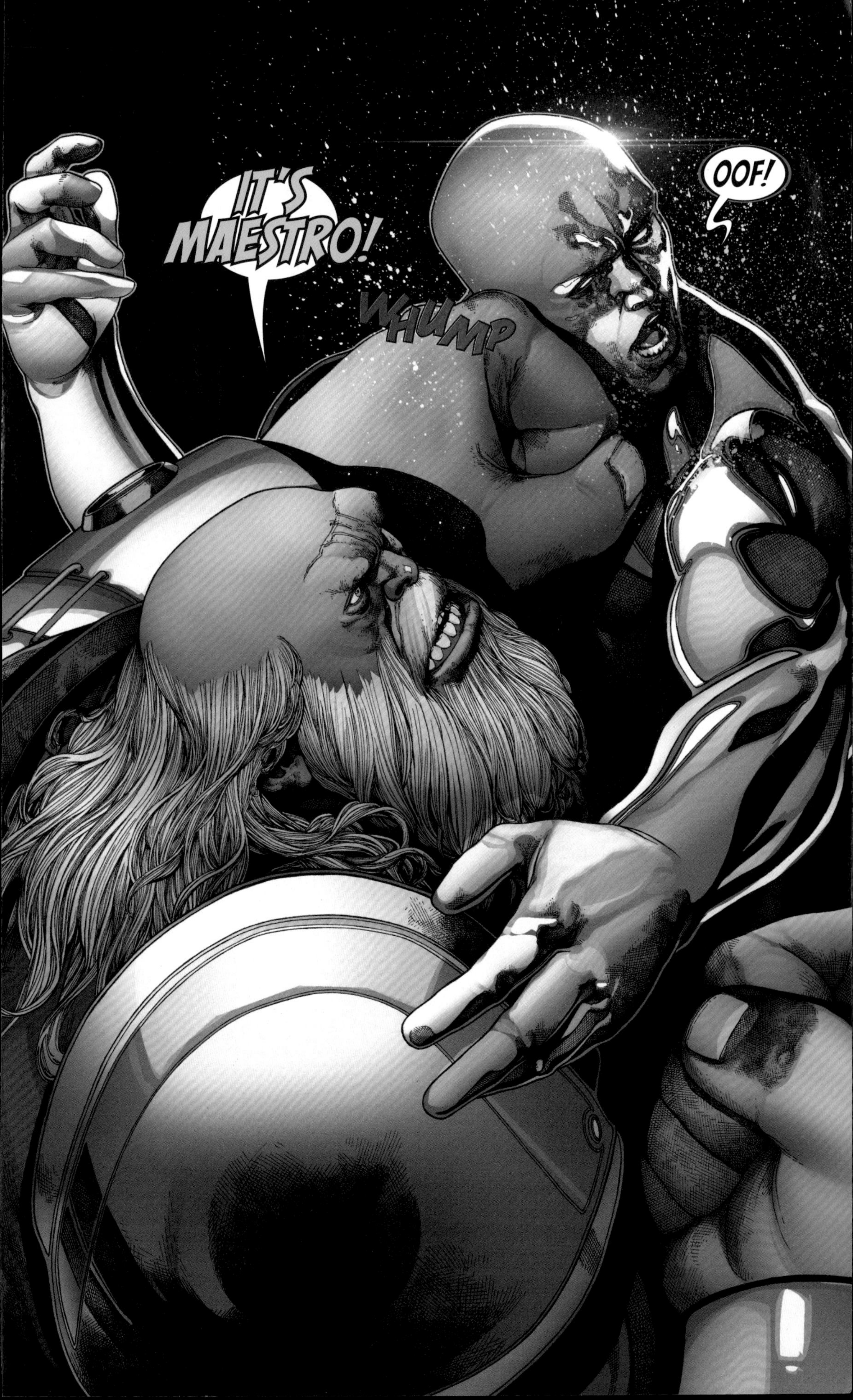
IT'S MAESTRO!
WHUMP
OOF!

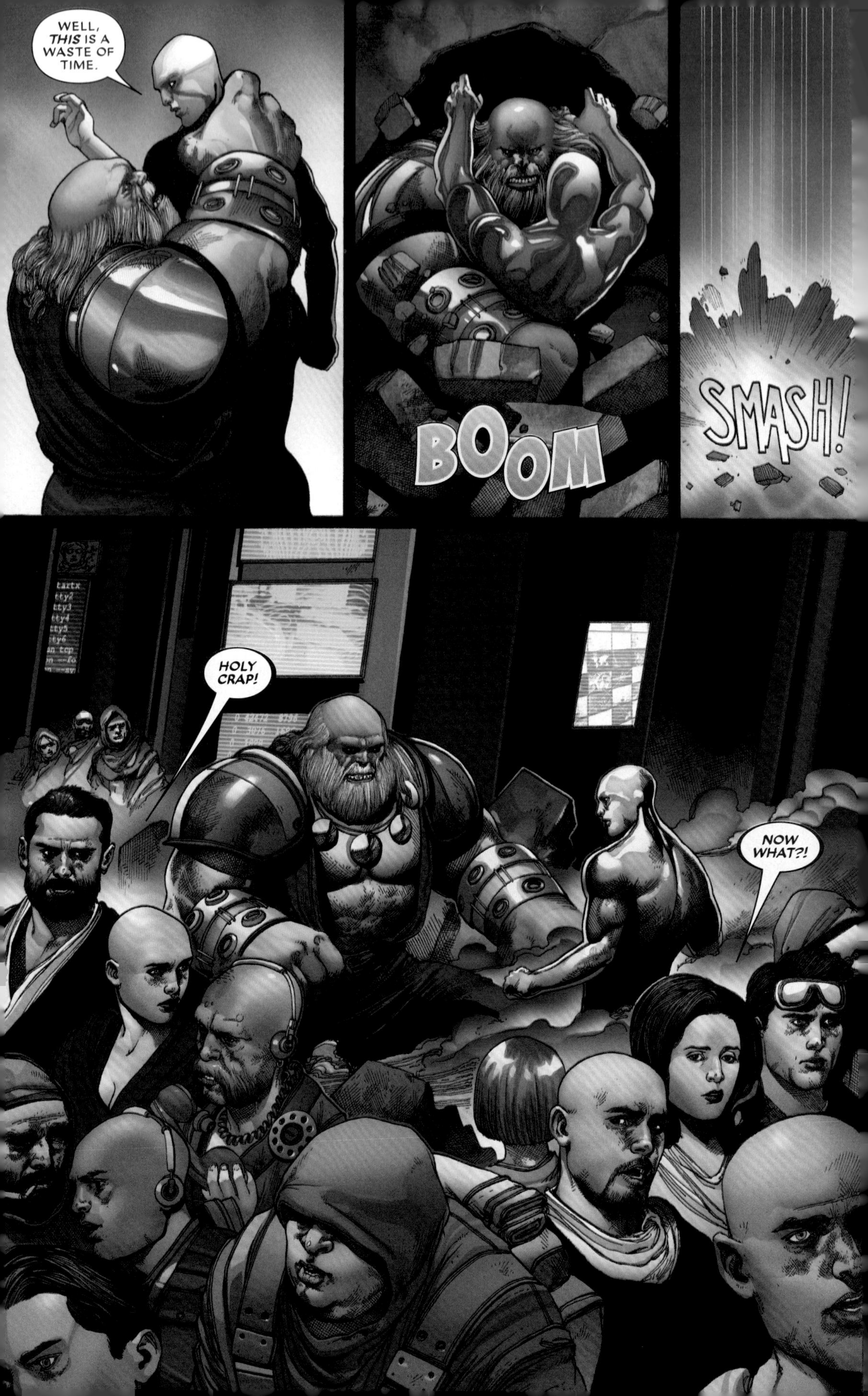

WELL, THIS IS A WASTE OF TIME.
BOOM
SMASH!
HOLY CRAP!
NOW WHAT?!

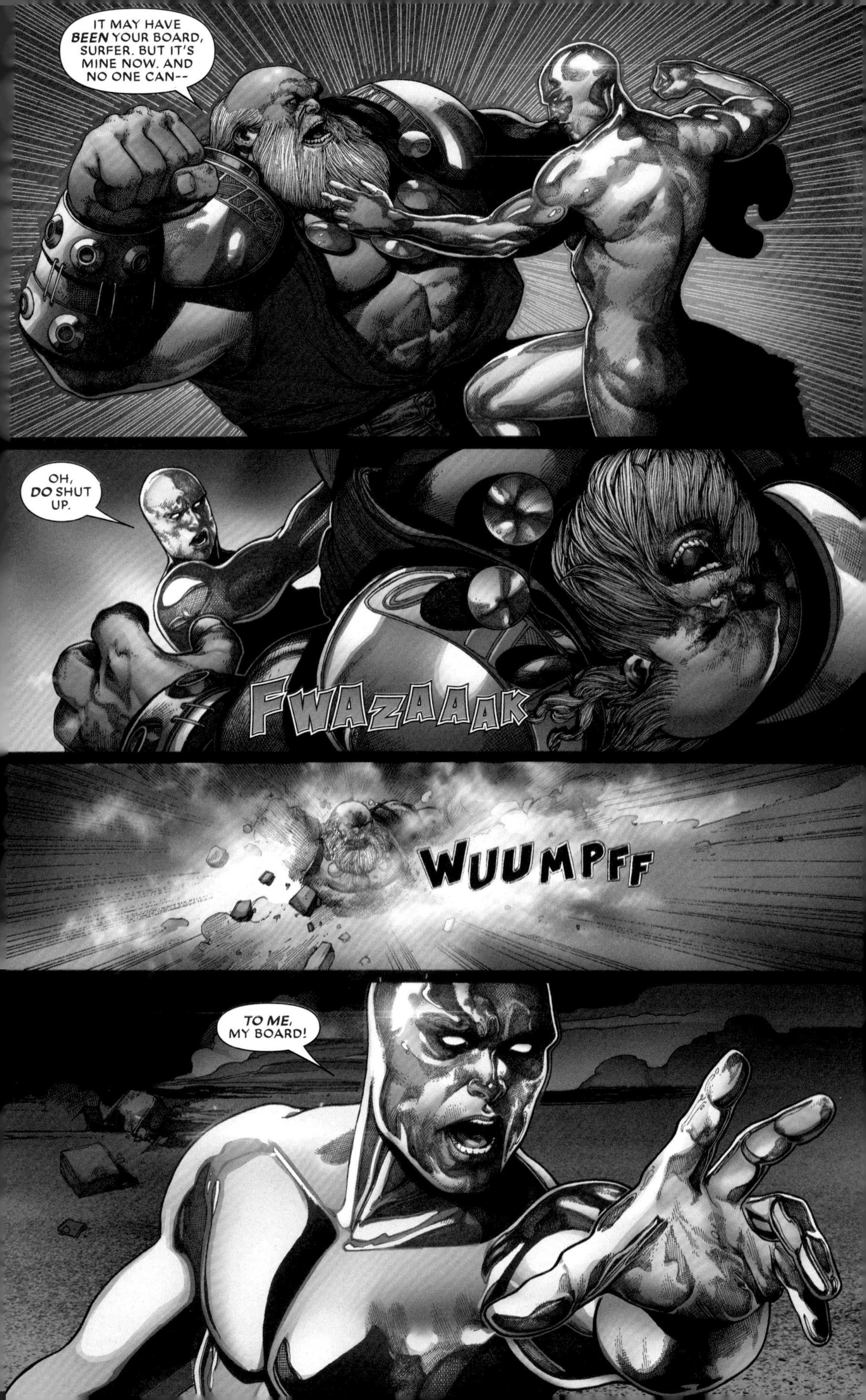
IT MAY HAVE BEEN YOUR BOARD, SURFER. BUT IT'S MINE NOW. AND NO ONE CAN--
OH, DO SHUT UP.
FWAZAAAK
WUUMPFF
TO ME, MY BOARD!

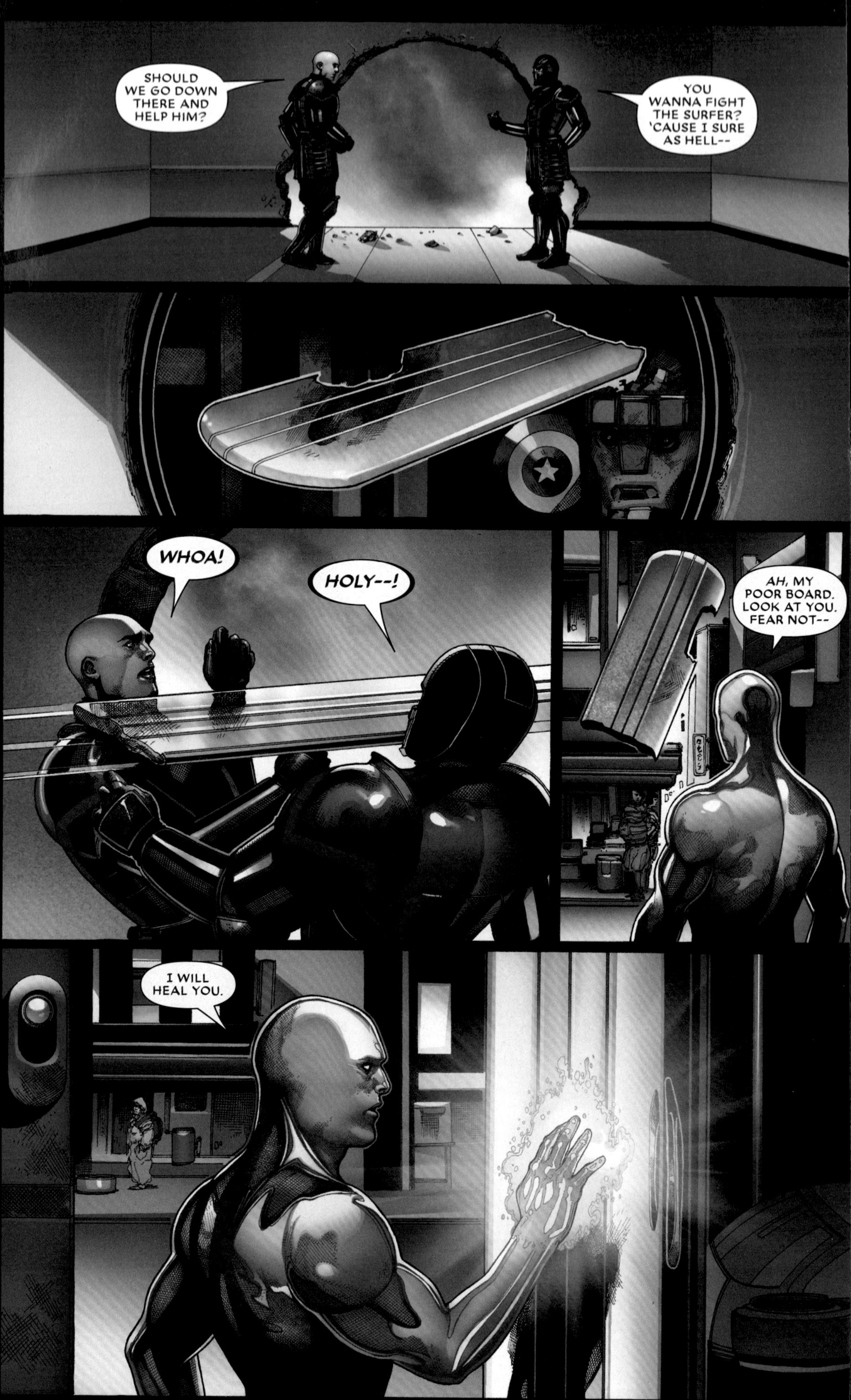
SHOULD WE GO DOWN THERE AND HELP HIM?
YOU WANNA FIGHT THE SURFER? 'CAUSE I SURE AS HELL--
WHOA!
HOLY--!
AH, MY POOR BOARD. LOOK AT YOU. FEAR NOT--
I WILL HEAL YOU.

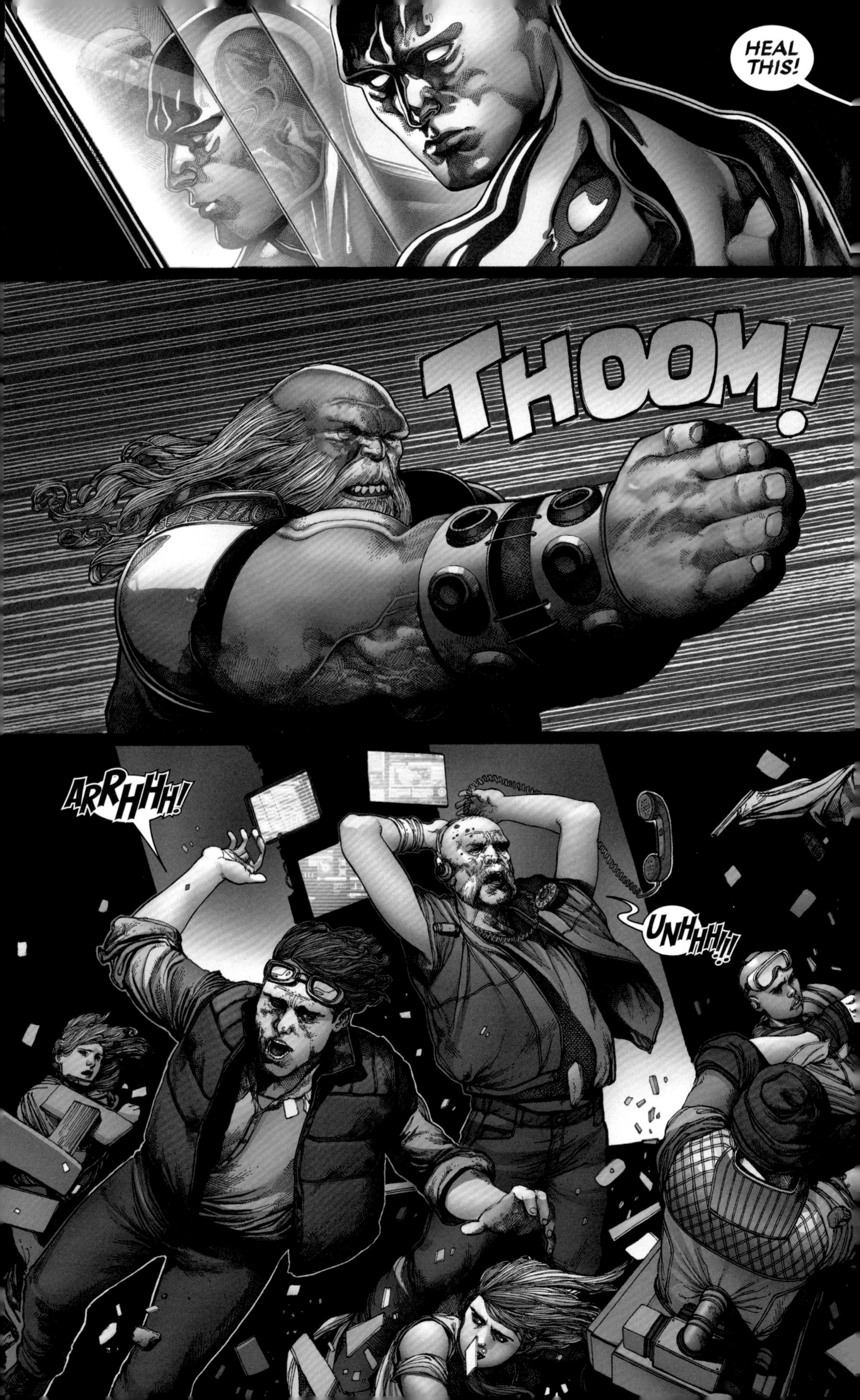

HEAL THIS!
THOOM!
ARRHHH!
UNHHH!!!

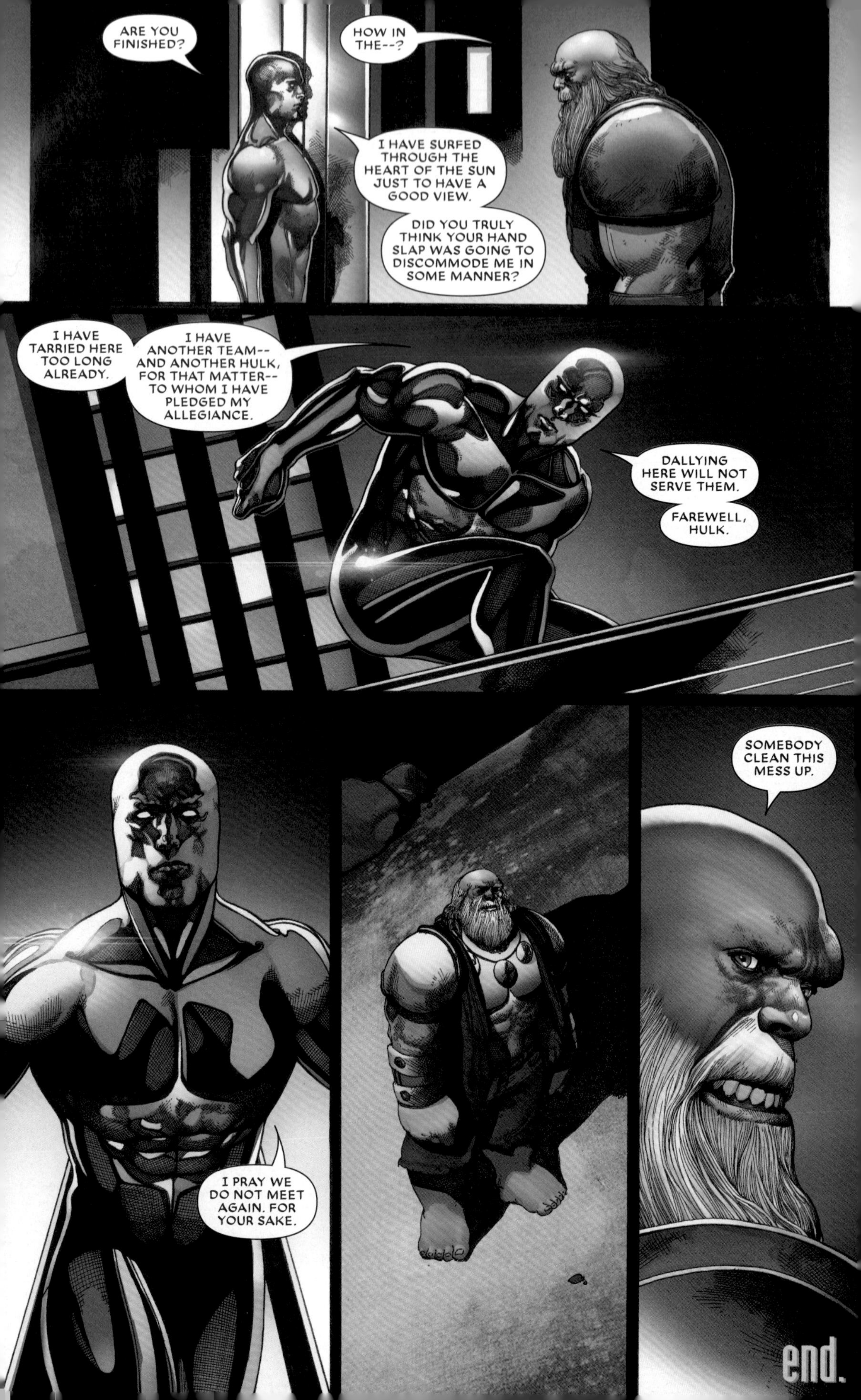
ARE YOU FINISHED?
HOW IN THE--?
I HAVE SURFED THROUGH THE HEART OF THE SUN JUST TO HAVE A GOOD VIEW.
DID YOU TRULY THINK YOUR HAND SLAP WAS GOING TO DISCOMMODE ME IN SOME MANNER?
I HAVE TARRIED HERE TOO LONG ALREADY.
I HAVE ANOTHER TEAM-- AND ANOTHER HULK, FOR THAT MATTER-- TO WHOM I HAVE PLEDGED MY ALLEGIANCE.
DALLYING HERE WILL NOT SERVE THEM.
FAREWELL, HULK.
I PRAY WE DO NOT MEET AGAIN. FOR YOUR SAKE.
SOMEBODY CLEAN THIS MESS UP.
end.

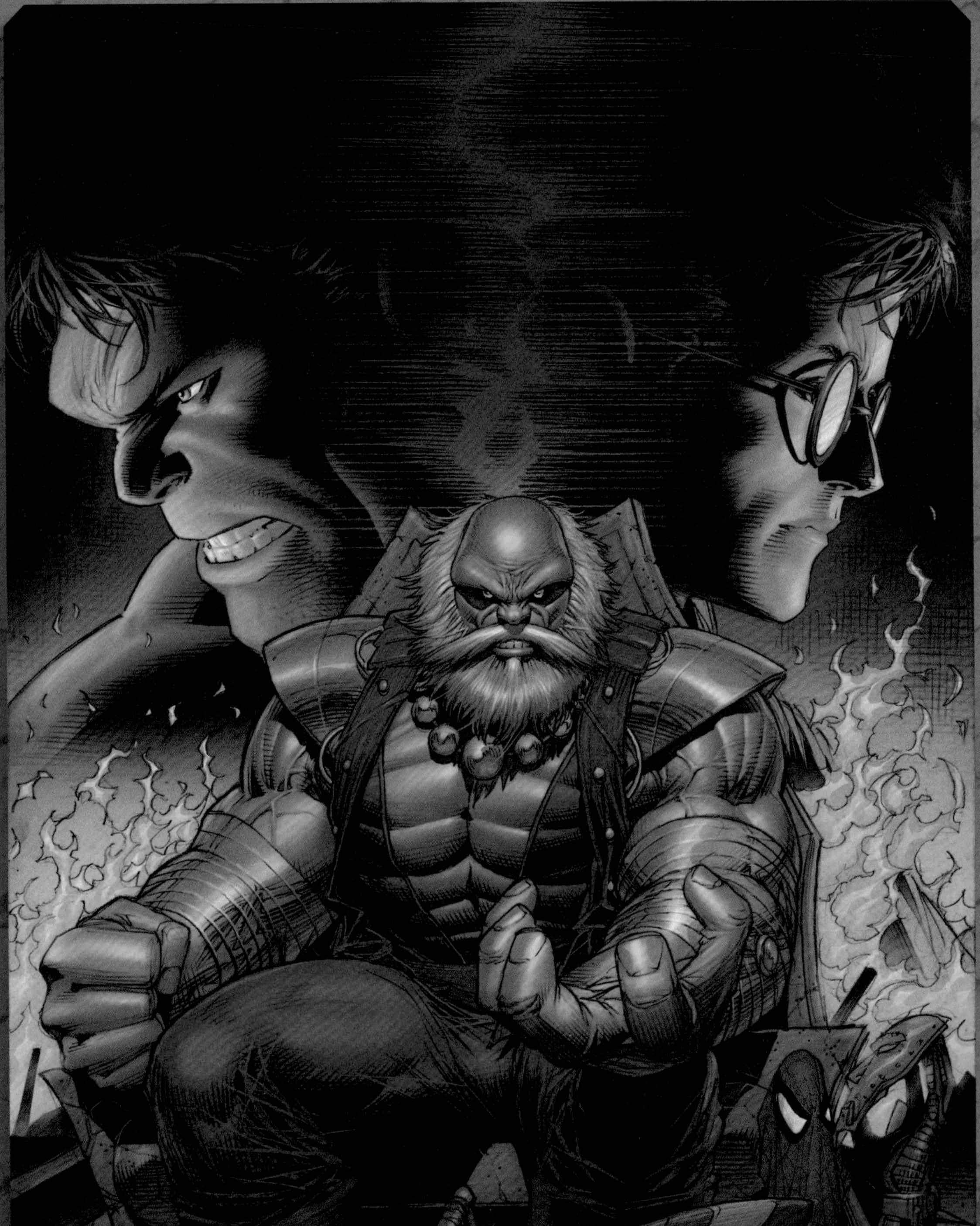

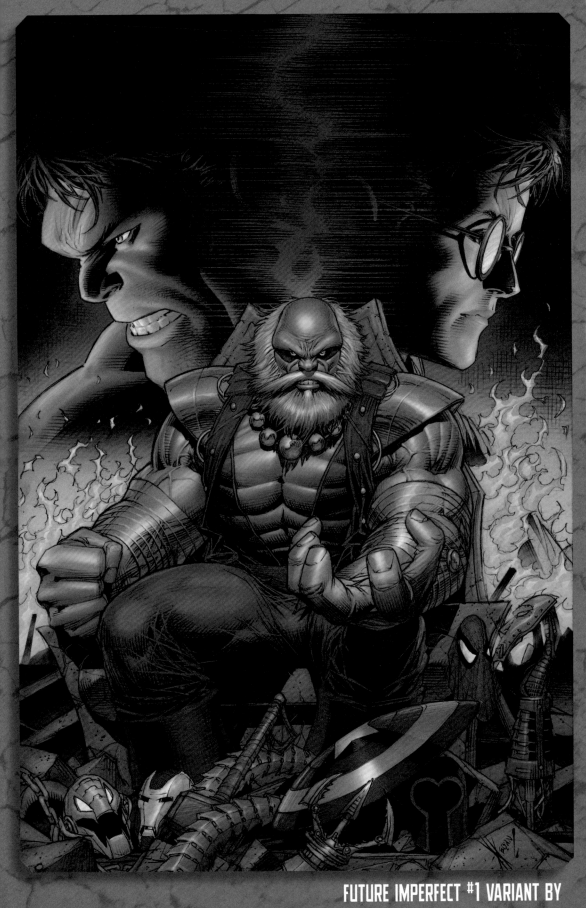

FUTURE IMPERFECT #1 VARIANT BY

dale keown & jason keith

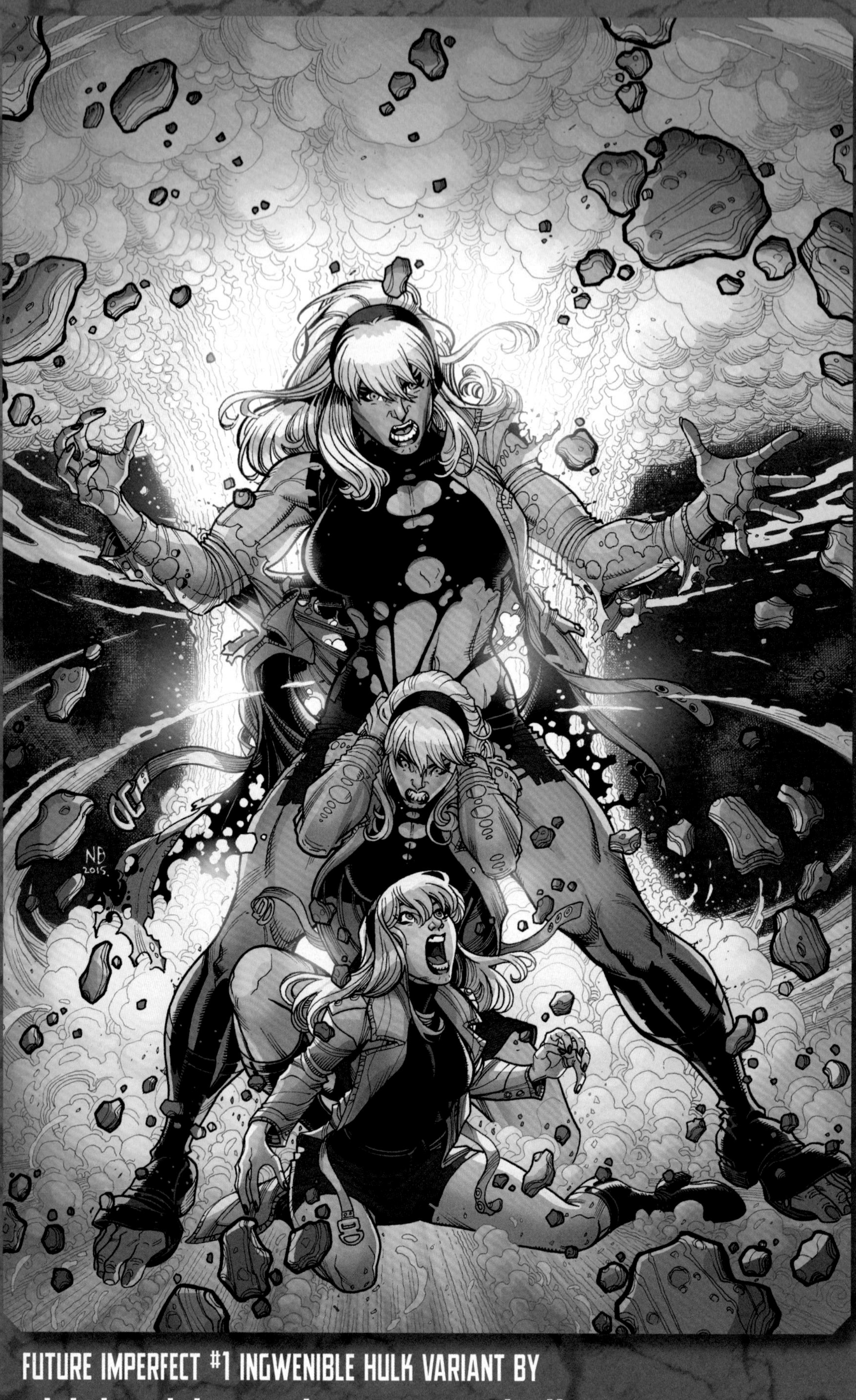

FUTURE IMPERFECT #1 INGWENIBLE HULK VARIANT BY

nick bradshaw & james campbell

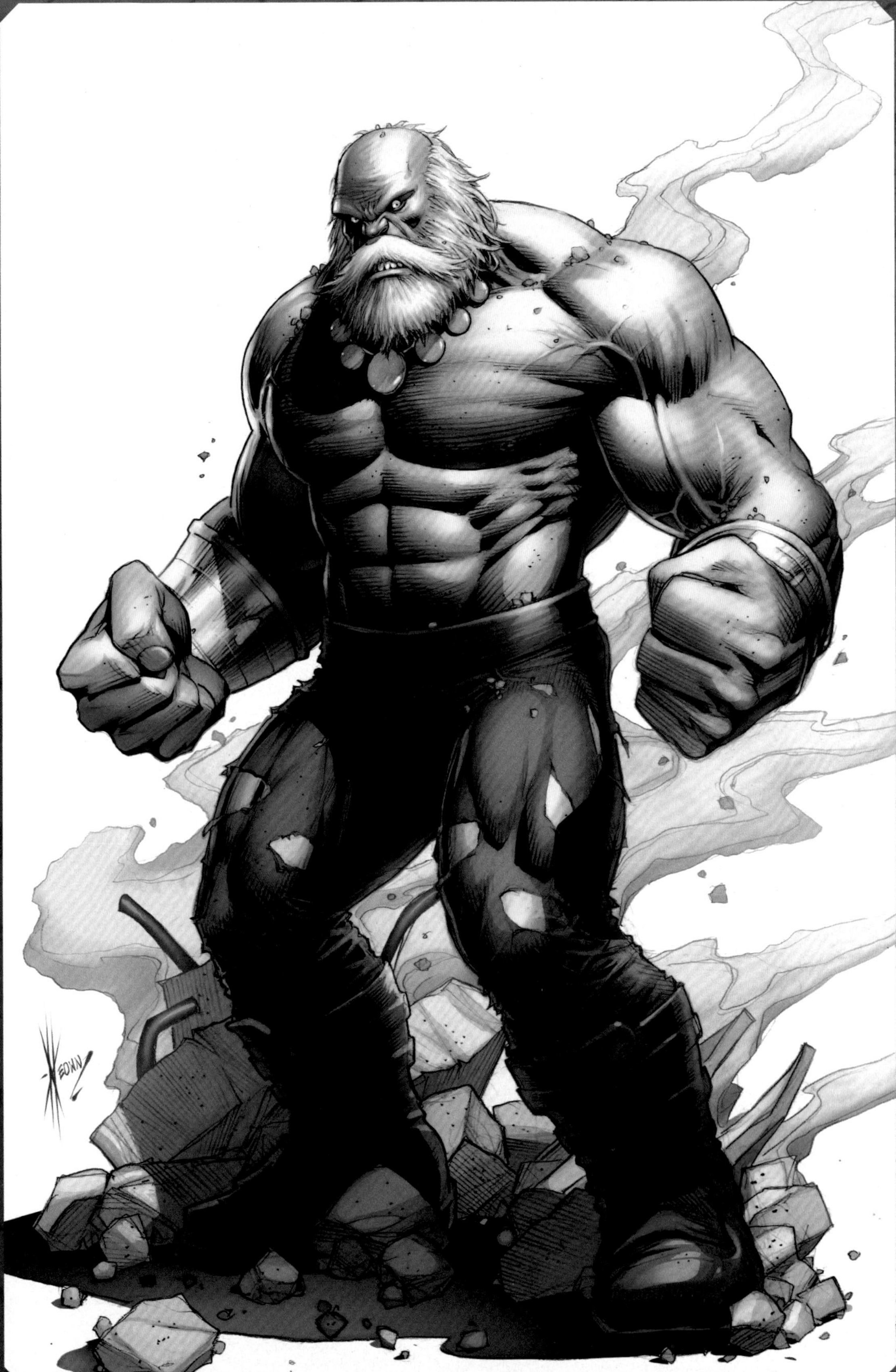
KEOWN

FUTURE IMPERFECT #1 ANT-SIZED VARIANT BY
dale keown

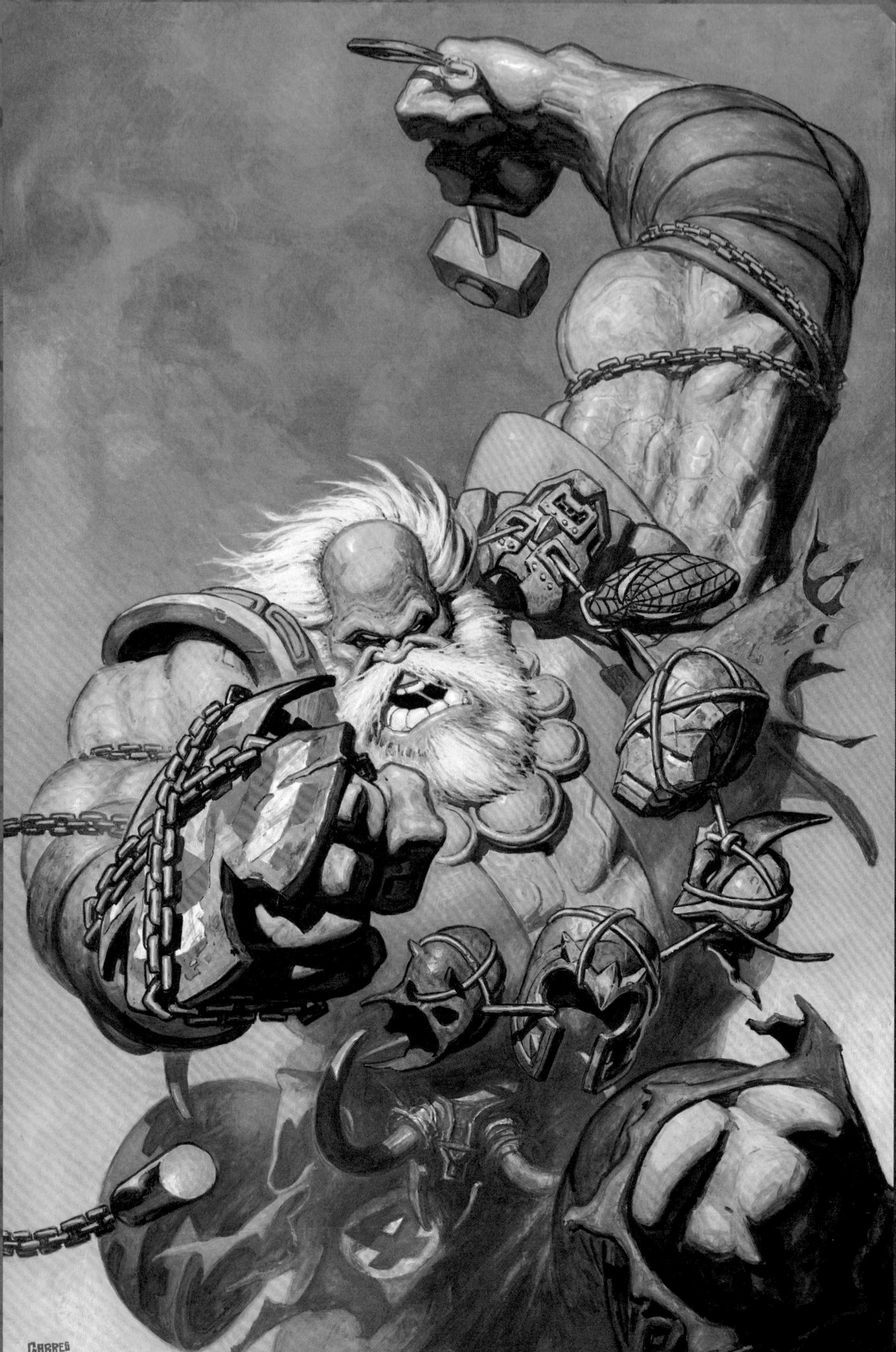
GARRES

FUTURE IMPERFECT #2 VARIANT BY

rafa garres

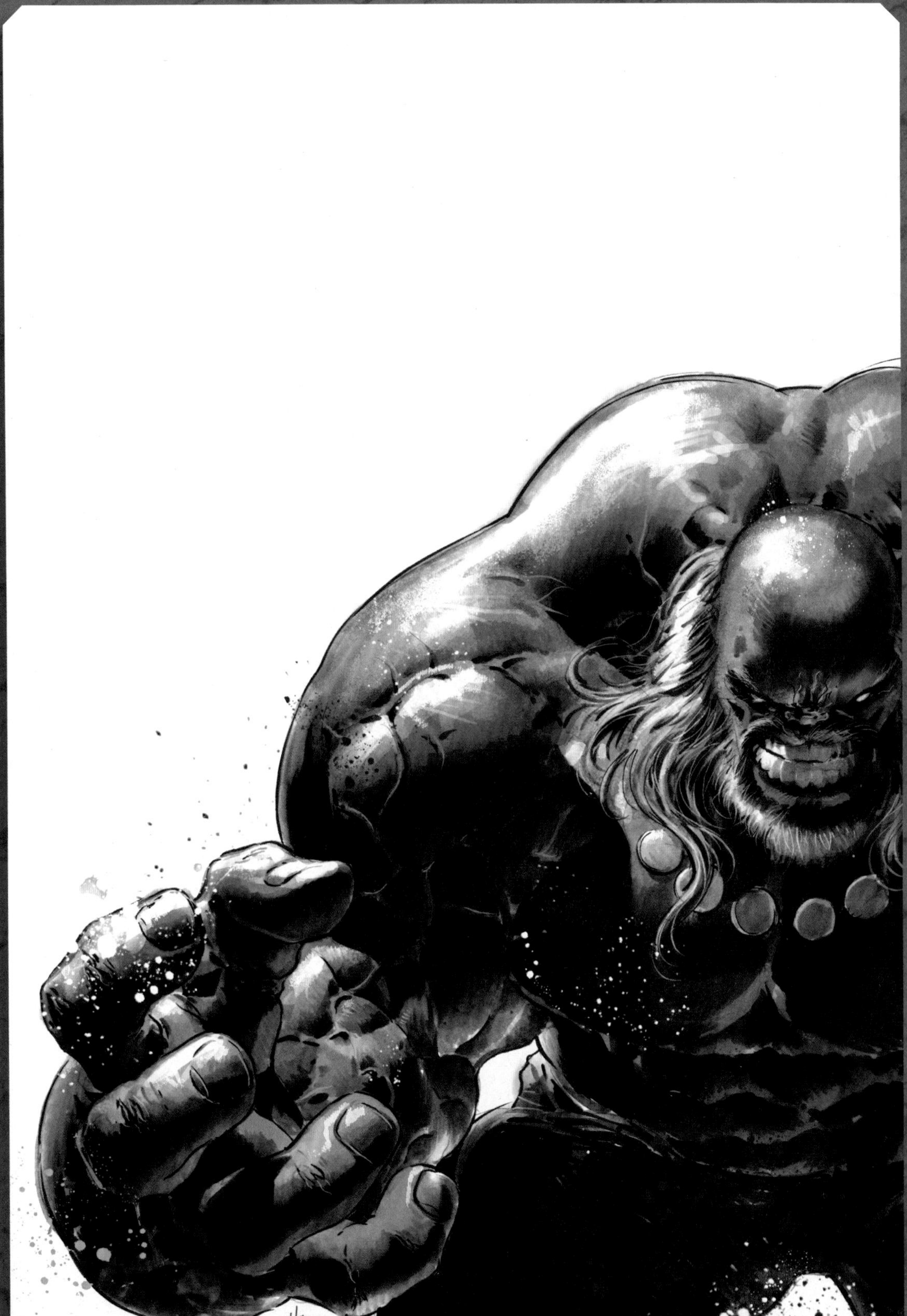

FUTURE IMPERFECT #3 VARIANT BY

mike deodato & rain beredo